CW01395434

Wolf Moon

Arifa Akbar is chief theatre critic for the *Guardian*. She has previously been literary editor at the *Independent*, as well as a news reporter and arts correspondent. Her first book, *Consumed: In Search of My Sister*, was shortlisted for the Costa Book Awards, PEN Ackerley Prize and Jhalak Prize, and it was longlisted for the Baillie Gifford Prize. *Wolf Moon* is her second book.

Wolf Moon

A Woman's Journey into the Night

Arifa Akbar

Sceptre

First published in Great Britain in 2025 by Sceptre
An imprint of Hodder & Stoughton Limited
An Hachette UK company

The authorised representative in the EEA is Hachette Ireland, 8 Castlecourt Centre,
Dublin 15, D15 XTP3, Ireland (email: info@hbgi.ie)

1

A CIP catalogue record for this title is available from the British Library

Hardback ISBN 9781399712859
ebook ISBN 9781399712866

Typeset in Sabon MT by Manipal Technologies Limited.

Printed and bound in Great Britain by Clays Ltd, Elcograf S.p.A.

Hodder & Stoughton policy is to use papers that are natural, renewable and recyclable products and made from wood grown in sustainable forests. The logging and manufacturing processes are expected to conform to the environmental regulations of the country of origin.

Hodder & Stoughton Limited
Carmelite House
50 Victoria Embankment
London EC4Y 0DZ

www.sceptrebooks.co.uk

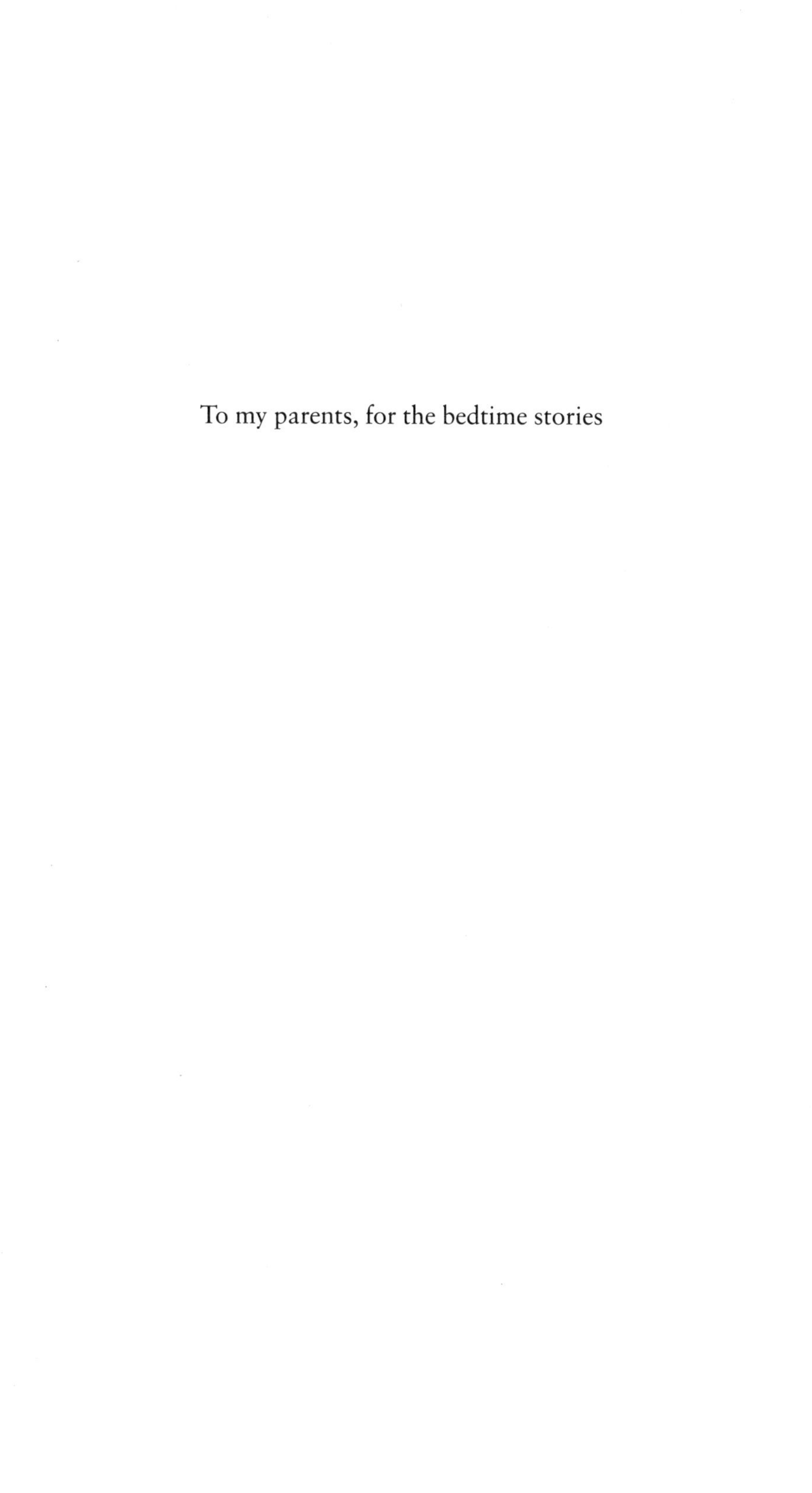

To my parents, for the bedtime stories

Contents

Prologue
Into the darkness

It is twilight and I am crunching along a dirt-track of mustard earth, waiting for night to set in. I have arrived in Sark, a three-mile landmass bobbing in the English Channel, just off the Normandy coast. It is one of the world's few 'dark sky' islands, with strict rules against outdoor electricity, so it remains free of light pollution. I am intrigued to see what unmediated darkness looks like. When the island's tall, jagged silhouette comes into view from the ferry, it looks like a serrated black knife plunged in the water.

An hour from Guernsey, it has just five hundred permanent residents and what seems like a cultivated remoteness. No motor vehicles are allowed and there is one daily shuttle to the mainland at this time of year, though even that is not guaranteed. A visitor might be stranded here for days, until high winds or a storm passes. Some resident billionaires, drawn here by the island's tax-free status, live in its outer promontories and travel by helicopter, but most get around on bicycles or tractors.

What a strange place to live, I think, as I get off the boat and onto a tractor that lugs visitors up a steep hill to the island's centre. It is a frosty Friday evening in late January and I am due back to work on Monday. I wonder, with a twinge, how I might get off the island quickly, if it came to it. Other passengers have dispersed and the path is empty. I follow my phone to the guesthouse but find myself stopping to look around in surprise. I have been prepared for the island's smallness but I am taken aback by its twee central thoroughfare: a short row of dinky stone cottages converted into supermarket, restaurant and craft shops, whose doorways are so low that you'd have to duck to enter. It looks like a throwback to a bygone Britain – a parallel 1930s universe, adrift on Channel waters. I find its olde-worlde veneer unsettling; it appears so carefully groomed. The island's economy relies on tourism and maybe this back-to-basics charm is what visitors come for. Some of the buildings I pass – the chocolate factory and the upmarket Stocks hotel – are still boarded up in wintry hibernation. A ruddy-cheeked woman appears on the track and smiles broadly as she passes. Others begin to swoosh by on bikes and greet me merrily as they go. They look like Agatha Christie characters, floating in eternal aspic.

I was due to visit the island's observatory, run from a converted shed by Reg Guille who, when I contacted him a few months ago, told me to come before the winter was over, when the planets were still visible at night. The stars, he had said, are a glory to behold. Jacqui, the manager of my guesthouse, is a plain-speaking woman who moved here from Newcastle-under-Lyme almost two decades ago, but even she waxes lyrical as she describes a sky that looks like 'diamonds studded on black velvet'.

But a few days ahead of my trip, Reg messages to say that although he caught sight of Jupiter and Venus lined up against the moon a few nights ago, the island is hopelessly overcast and my stargazing is likely to be a wash-out. I'm not too disappointed, I tell him: I'm curious to see what 'authentic' darkness looks like anyway. This is why I am coming to Sark in the first place. I have always been scared of the dark and this is an expedition into that fear.

Reg is waiting at the community hall to give me a tour around the island in lieu of studying its night sky, and points forlornly to the shed at the corner of a field that is the observatory. He is an eighty-one-year-old with a family history on Sark that dates back to 1565. There are numerous Guilles listed on the island's cenotaph, at which we stop, just in front of the cemetery.

Benign evening light hugs the path back home after Reg leaves me at a crossroad. Pretty houses with Sercquiais names have offerings of kindling at their gates, or cubby-holes with fresh eggs for sale. Reg has told me it is entirely safe for me to be out at any time of day or night. The last serious crime on Sark was the murder of one German soldier by another, in 1943, when the island came under Nazi occupation. The doors of all the homes here remain unlocked. It's comforting, but I feel the same stagey sense of a rustic façade, as if there is a hidden side to Sark behind this tourist-facing one. Or that islanders have elected to live in estrangement from the world and its modernity, in a Truman Show reality. If I walk to the island's edges, will I bang my head against plexiglass?

When I get back to the guesthouse and look out of the window of my attic room, I see the land and sky have turned black, and this darkness brings a swooping soporific effect, as chemical as a sleeping pill. It is as if the night is so potent in its ancient, diurnal effects that it penetrates the bloodstream. My circadian rhythms, implacably out of sync from years of insomnia and night work, feel instantly recalibrated. I would fall asleep straight away if I were to lean back and lie down.

Nonetheless, I push myself out at 9 p.m. and everything has changed. A smoky blackness swallows up the mustard path. There is a bite in the rain and the bullish wind seems like a living, breathing, angry entity. It yanks the guesthouse door out of my hand and slams it shut. I strain to hear others, walking or chatting, and look back at the windows of the guesthouse for signs of life, but they are dark. I am so much more confident in the city by night, where I know I am enveloped by millions of breathing bodies and beating hearts. Rural night might be statistically safer for women, but to me it feels more existential in its danger, conjuring all the things that have ever happened in it, or could happen, becoming boundless in its threat.

This island night, with its flat stretches of fields and thunderous waves, emanates abandonment. But, in the emptiness, it also takes on a sinister kind of embodiment. 'Listen, it is night moving in the streets,' wrote Dylan Thomas, in *Under Milk Wood*. It is the only thing out here now, as alive and aggressive as the wind, and I feel immeasurably grateful for the weak light leaking from the windows of some houses and for the people I imagine sitting inside them.

Jacqui has advised me not to switch my torch on straight away, so my eyes can acclimatise, but I do not feel brave enough. Occasional columns of light from other people's torches look like urgently strobing SOS signals. A few cyclists glide past, but the mood has changed and they are no longer smiling. I see what might be the kindling cubby-hole from earlier and swing my torch towards it, but it is a dagger-like rock sticking out of a gash in a stone wall and I rear back from its suggestion of violence. A tractor judders into view, lit up like a garish fairground ride, and hurtles back into the engulfing black again. There is a hallucinatory quality to the darkness, like I might have imagined it in delirium. Ahead, trees flank the path, crooked branches reaching towards each other to create a canopy of pitch black. I think of all that could lie hiding there and I decide to turn back.

It amazes me how the night has become charged with threat, even after Reg has told me it is safe to ramble on these paths. Still, he has warned that some do not feel immediately comfortable, especially women unaccustomed to walking on their own. For them, he said, it can take unlearning. I remind myself of his words but, with every step I take, my walk feels like an incursion into prohibited space. Walking alone at night has always been seen as a suspect or improper act for a woman, says Rebecca Solnit in *Wanderlust: A History of Walking*, and she talks of how an action as simple, free and seemingly democratic as this is fraught with inequality after a certain time of day.

Despite all our progress, the night outside is still a furtive space for some of us, breached at our own peril, its danger stretching across centuries and burrowing inside us. Sark might be an exception but safety, I realise, is not only a fact but a feeling. I have carried my fear onto the ferry and into this three-mile sanctuary, from other dimly lit streets. I am breathless by the time I get back to the guesthouse. It seems like I have ploughed deep into Sark's night but I realise, sheepishly, that I have only walked a few hundred metres.

The following day, when I am telling Jacqui of my wobbly exploration over breakfast, and of how silly I had felt scrambling back into the house, she sits down beside me and says she felt exactly the same when she arrived from the Midlands. 'We're taught to keep ourselves safe,' she says, and she talks of the historic darkness, freighted with warnings for women. It took her two years to unlearn her fear and feel comfortable in Sark's night.

What does it mean to be a woman in the night beyond this safe darkness, back on the mainland?, I wonder. To work in it, as I do, to walk in it, or to party through it – it carries excitements too, of course, not only dangers. And it was at night, on Charles Dickens's nineteenth-century insomniac walks, that the Victorian paupers, prostitutes, criminals, Bedlamites and spectres stepped into his path, to reveal a community on the other side of day. Those were the night's citizens then. Who wanders in it now, which women?

I am settling into bed the following night when I hear the sound of boots climbing the stairs. They thump closer, and stand silent on the landing until I hear the jangle of keys. Jacqui told me there was another – male – guest at the house tonight, but it takes me a moment to remember. I should feel reassured by the company but the permanently unlocked door downstairs, the proximity of the heavy-footed stranger next door, unsettles me. I strain to hear him moving in his room but all returns to stillness after he goes in. There is only the continuous crash of the wind outside. I put off sleep for a while, but when I am relaxed enough to finally switch off the light, I feel the darkness surging towards me, heavy as a blanket, and smothering.

This dark seems full of unknown and dangerous quantities, too; maybe more so than that outside. Why? I snap the light back on and plug in a night-light I have brought from home. The room glows yellow. I make sure, at home, that I am never in complete darkness. There is always a curtain slightly open, a night-light on. Electric light is everywhere in London, pouring in through the windows, and it is a feature of city living that I love. I grew up in a first-generation British Pakistani family, hearing supernatural tales of shape-shifting djinns and bloody-thirsty daayans emerging out of the dark, and these have left me with an unresolved, child-like, superstitious fear.

Across the room now, my dress rests on the back of a chair, and I think I see the slightest twitch of its hem, blown by a draught or a cold channel of air. I get out of bed and peer at the sky outside. There are no stars, just a sliver of a new moon. A professor, explaining the effects of the lunar cycle on human physiology to me a few days ago, spoke of how sleep, and women's sleep in particular, was found to be affected by the full moon for reasons that remain unknown and under-researched. A 2015 clinical trial at the Surrey Sleep Research Centre, by Professor Derk-Jan Dijk, involving 91 men and 114 women sleeping in a windowless laboratory, found that 'the phases of the moon may modulate subjective sleep quality' and that in the women, the amount of deep sleep and REM (or dream sleep) was reduced close to full moon nights, while in men, REM increased around this time. It sounded like the stuff of gothic fiction – conjuring mental images of possessed women and yowling werewolves – yet I recognised something in it. I have felt an unaccountable drop in mood, hormonal in its switch, on full moon nights. This morsel of science worms its way back into my mind, its mystery as yet unlocked. Just because something is inexplicable does not make it irrational or fantastical, I think, but I am unsure of where that leaves me in this room's unnerving dark.

I should have carried on walking tonight, underneath the cat's cradle of bare branches, into the corridor of pitch black. I should switch the light off now and prove to myself that there is nothing to be afraid of. I pull the night-light out of its plug and the dark uncoils in an instant. I stare hard into the black swarm, at where the dressing table stands, the shape of the window, the spot where my dress lies on the chair, and wonder for a moment if it is still swaying, if one of its airy arms has been raised in animation. How ridiculous, I think. But if there really is nothing to fear, why do I feel so viscerally afraid as the dark levitates towards me, everything and nothing thrumming inside it?

Part 1

Night shift

Chapter 1
Zero hour

I am cycling home from the West End after a trip to the theatre. It is 11 p.m. and my review of the play I have just seen is due to be sent off first thing tomorrow morning. I am hurtling along The Strand, keen to get home to record my thoughts while I feel their clarity. The street still throngs with traffic, tourists, straggling commuters, the hungry-eyed homeless. This urban night looks like a dimly lit version of the day, as absently lost in itself, the theatres still blazing with life; here the Aldwych twinkles flirtatiously as I glide past, the Novello beside it wreathed in dressing-room light bulbs, and then the Lyceum's billboards smiling into view. Their lights beckon an audience that has long since gone home for the night. Some boutiques along this central drag flash and glow with screen advertisements on repeating loops. It is hyper-capitalism at its most surreal – all this promise of conspicuous consumption with no one to consume it.

A battalion of night-workers zigzags around me on the road: men in hi-vis jackets in their beeping dumper trucks, security guards, street diggers, rubbish collectors, some wearing face-nets as they clean or dig, like nocturnal beekeepers. There is an army of cyclists too, carrying brick-like bags on their backs and looking like giant, branded beetles: Deliveroo, UberEats, Gopuff, Just Eat. The zero-hours workforce has punched in, attentive to the value of every minute. There is a tunnel-vision efficiency to the speed of their journeys, just as there is to mine. It seems as if everyone is, simultaneously, in a rush to enter into the labour of the night and trying to run away from it.

Some are fresh-faced, others look as if they have already worked a day shift. The roads are filled with them; the night-time economy report of 2022, published by the Office for National Statistics (ONS), listed 8.7 million people working nocturnally in the UK. Of those, 4.9 million were male, and 3.9 million female, a ratio which slightly closes the gender gap compared with previous years. 'More machine hours' is how one aspirational government pamphlet justified the expansion of America's night-time economy in 1942, and we still seem to be striving towards this relentless goal, one of non-stop, teeth-grinding productivity. But this crew of gig workers around me are surely the casualties of late capitalism rather than its beneficiaries. The day has been extended into the night to squeeze as much commerce from them as possible, at the lowest cost.

As a theatre critic, I cannot count myself among them. I skate along the fringes of darkness, bleary-eyed some days, but I am not forced to be up all night. I am nothing like the overworked and under-paid street workers I cycle past, nor the crews of nurses, doctors, carers, cab drivers, packers at fulfilment centres for online deliveries, supermarket shelf stackers, all of whom might be lucky to snatch an hour or two of sleep a night, if that.

While I was growing up in the 1980s, my father worked one of these night jobs, as a British Rail guard. Train guards were paid more for night work, as opposed to day work, so in times when my parents found it hard to pay the bills, he would take on a block of overnight shifts. My older sister, younger brother and I would tiptoe around the flat while he slept, my mother ushering us downstairs in the mornings and ordering us to turn the volume of the TV so low that we'd strain to hear it. He would emerge, groggy and remote, by the afternoon, and not quite return to his usual gregarious self until he was back on days.

When he retired, he felt lost without a routine, or without *work*, so he tried his hand at several odd jobs and in 2002, at the age of seventy-one, he got work as a security guard on a rotation of day and night shifts at the Courtauld Gallery in central London. I have cycled past the building countless times on my way back from the theatre. It sits within the stately splendour of Somerset House, a dramatic architectural complex with cobbles and a grand quadrangle on the north side of Waterloo Bridge. My father would leave home after dinner for a 7 p.m. start, working until 7 a.m. the following day. Security staff worked in pairs and took a circling night patrol around the gallery's three floors.

I remember him telling us, more than once, that there was a basement room which some men were afraid to enter because they felt an oppressive presence there, which seemed to amuse and frighten him – and us – in equal measure. I both believed him and didn't. We had grown up listening to his stories about dark forces unleashed in the night, gleefully told to scare us, but even then I saw he was also scaring himself. Some of the tales were those his older sisters had told him as a child, growing up in Shimla, in pre-Partition India – a baroque mix of gothic South Asian folklore and Islamic supernatural belief, of djinns capable of immense violence, of daayans with feet on backwards, disembowelling their victims with their bare hands. His sisters made sport out of terrorising him with these stories, he said. But maybe their menace chimed with the greater political disturbance and threat rising around his home, which culminated in an explosion of violence in 1947, when his family was forced to leave Shimla for Pakistan following Partition. My father's distrust of the dark remained well into adulthood and was openly acknowledged in the family. My mother, who had no such fear, would laugh at how cowering he became even climbing the small flight of stairs in our family flat without a light on.

In his retirement, the effect of overnight work at the Courtauld was very different from the woozy detachment of his British Rail night shifts. Perhaps it was his age, but he seemed physically changed by it, his skin growing sallower by the day, as if he were jaundiced, his thinking confused. He was always on the brink of an unarticulated panic, it seemed. Yet strangely, the Courtauld invigorated his imagination. He talked about the work animatedly, the other guards, the gallery ghost, and he seemed to get a kick out of being in this empty, unpeopled space, among its priceless artworks at night.

In all the years of passing the gallery, I have been inside once or twice, and then only when a friend has roped me into seeing an exhibition in its upstairs space, but I have never wandered beyond those few upper rooms. Perhaps I have deliberately avoided the building. My father was hospitalised soon after this work, in 2003, at the age of seventy-three, when he was diagnosed with frontal-lobe dementia. The illness was, in all likelihood, taking grip when he was at the Courtauld – he began to have erratic mood swings and become anxious about things he couldn't name. I have even wondered if the story about the gallery spectre was real, or a manifestation of the dread brought on, and keenly felt, from his emerging, as yet unknown illness.

It is almost closing time when I step inside the gallery, twenty years after my father's night shifts. It is a frosty February, minutes before sunset, and darkness is beginning to cling at the windows. The man in the ticket office is testy, reminding me that the building is only open for another fifty minutes. A stone staircase with a bright blue balustrade runs up its spine. It is long and narrow, like the stairs to my attic flat, which leave me puffing for breath as I climb. How many times did my father have to go up this staircase on his night-time patrols?

I decide to get the lift to the top of the building. I need to be brisk if I want to cover all three floors of the gallery before it closes. I start scouring the space, not sure what I am looking for. Am I searching for clues to my father's illness, his excitement in being here, or both? Rooms in the cramped left wing are designed like those in an old, aristocratic townhouse with a huddle of tasteful rugs, fireplaces and walls painted in an urbane Farrow & Ball palette of powder blues and olive greens, while the opposite wing, which houses early Impressionist works, is white, airy, modern.

A last trickle of visitors are making their way around and I walk among them, taking in the paintings at speed until I begin to recognise the images and slow down in spite of myself. They are familiar because they are so iconic: Van Gogh's self-portrait in which he wears a bandage around his head, after famously slicing off part of his ear. Manet's Gallic barmaid staring out from the canvas of *A Bar at the Folies-Bergère*, an enticing embodiment of the night's revels with her porcelain beauty and copper fringe, the champagne bottles lined up around her. A tender explosion of pink flora that I recognise as another Impressionist masterpiece – Claude Monet's *Vase of Flowers* – the flower heads so alive they seem to bounce in the spring breeze. A Modigliani nude. A Rodin bronze. Gauguin's *The Haystacks*. Such gems and blockbusters. I have seen all these images in art history books but here they are, in my father's past, in every one of his night shifts – his familiars.

I stop at a serene image of a man in a green meadow. It is *Spring, Chatou* by Renoir. It seems as if the lone figure in the field might be out for a walk, but he could just as well be lost in the bewildering long grass around him. He is too distant for us to see his face but he looks vulnerable in his solitude. My eyes well, and I am shocked by the sadness I feel. In the early days of my father's dementia, I would be caught suddenly breathless with the realisation that he was here, alive, in front of me, yet inaccessible, somewhere else altogether, lost to me. He is this man, frozen in his lonely green field, someone I can only glance at from the outside now. I carry on, slower, and I am struck by the number of night scenes I pass: a painting by Cézanne of two men in hats playing cards over a cloth-covered table, which is full of good-natured evening ambience. In a room downstairs, a moonlit landscape by Rubens, which was created in the last year of his life when he was painting for pleasure rather than profit. And below that, in the first-floor collection of medieval works, Saint Francis of Assisi, talking to the birds on a decorative tree, surrounded by winking stars and azure sky. I think of my father stopping in front of each painting, taking them in. He loved birdwatching, playing cards, nature, beauty. It has been years since he has been able to talk to me properly about these things, but all his passions are collected here, as uncanny reminders. How could I have forgotten them?

I find it soothing that he was surrounded by this night-time beauty – canvases filled with all the things he loved. I begin to feel not only as if I am retreading my father's footsteps but that he is walking with me. The floorboards creak in some rooms and I imagine his pace mellowing over the course of the night, becoming softer and quieter in the small hours. He spent most of his early years walking for pleasure in Shimla and carried on walking in London, taking us, as children, for trips out to the city's parks that lasted most of the day; the pace of these walks was always unrushed, allowing time to dawdle, observe, take everything in. I imagine the same slow, sure, curious footfalls of his night circuits here.

I take the stairs back to the second floor, and look out of the window at the courtyard of Somerset House, which is now submerged in black. I enter the central, ornate room, filled with large-scale work by Rubens; the canvases featuring a dramatic swirl of ancient figures, some naked or dead, others watching the clouds part to reveal a party of terrifying cherubs, all the more striking for the darkness outside, it seems. The gallery is almost empty now but still there is the sense that I am not entirely alone, with all this noisy visual melodrama around me. I imagine my father held by their stories criss-crossing each other in the silence of the night. I stray across to other rooms and the walls glitter with more iconic images: Lucas Cranach the Elder's *Adam and Eve* glints nakedly from one corner, Cain slays Abel on top of a fireplace, Botticelli's monumental *The Trinity With Saints*, featuring Mary Magdalen and John the Baptist, takes up an entire wall. I want to study the detail in each artwork but I feel an urgency to glimpse all the work my father would have walked past, so I push on to the medieval and renaissance collections on the floor below.

Thirteenth-century panels and altarpieces gleam bright, as if trying to light up the night outside with their gold embossed brilliance. They don't look ancient at all; buffed to a sheen, but eternally new. In the gallery's emptiness, I see more and more security guards, all of them male. Many look like they are of South Asian heritage. I think about stopping to tell them my father once worked here, and giving them his name. I resist because they look far too young to have worked with him, but they smile back at me, as if in thoughtful recognition of something.

After surveying all the floors, I go down to the crypt, to look for the basement room that so scared the guards on my father's watch. There is a shop, full of bright, elegant bric-à-brac, but no other room open to the public. I wander around the corridors, sniffing out signs of a ghostly presence, although again, I have no idea what to look for because the details of what exactly scared my father are gone, and it all looks eminently ordinary. I am reluctant to leave even so, although it is minutes to closing time, so I head up to the top floor again, to walk around the gallery one final time. When I reach the top of the stairs and enter the main exhibition space, I see that the security guards have congregated here and I feel their agitation, the longer I linger. They want the last visitor out so they can end their working day. I find it a wrench. I would like to stay, walking the floors, passing these canvases over and over, all night long if I could, until the first signs of day, just as my father would have done.

Maybe the ghost I came looking for is that of my 'well' father. This job was the last time he was – or at least seemed to be – entirely himself. And as romantic as he made the work sound, it would surely have felt gruelling for a man his age to be up and walking all night long. He became gradually more ill after retiring from British Rail, easily agitated and restless. Professor Dijk, from the Surrey Sleep Research Centre, has investigated links between disrupted sleep and dementia. Broken sleep is prevalent in people with Alzheimer's or mild cognitive impairment; and my father would undoubtedly have been living with the latter by this time. Sleep disturbance can also be an early sign of dementia, showing up before other symptoms. Professor Dijk's 2022 study suggests that people with mild dementia may function better in the daytime if they have continuous rather than interrupted sleep, and while his findings imply that it is the illness that triggers disordered sleep, a lack of continuous sleep might worsen the effects of dementia. I wonder if my father's night shifts hastened the onset of his illness, with the massive effort of staying awake nocturnally for twelve hours at a time. Would he have suffered such a sudden and dramatic descent into dementia if he hadn't been walking up and down this gallery's floors? He became sicker and more scared of the world while working here, speaking of the misfortunes that he was so sure were coming his way but could never name when I asked him to, until the night, the darkness, finally came for him, and swallowed him up.

Beyond Somerset House, past the Aldwych, is Theatreland. I have not considered how close my father's work then was to mine now. It is a stone's throw, separated by two decades. Both close, and far away. For most of my life, I have worked in the day, but I have always had a fraught relationship with sleep, although, strangely, that corrected itself when I was in my forties. It must have occurred gradually because, by the time I had noticed, it had already happened. The better I slept, the less nervous I became about sleeping. My mind had learned how to switch off, without a conscious striving for it. Sometimes I couldn't even remember falling asleep because it happened so quickly. It seemed miraculous, but also puzzling. Just like the insomnia, this easy sleep seemed like something that happened to me, involuntarily, over and above my own effort or will.

I began my job as a theatre critic in my late forties and the work didn't disrupt my newfound equilibrium at first. There was such a buzz to the opening night of a show, when the press is invited to review it. I'd get back home charged with adrenaline, ideas fizzing, sleep irrelevant. As time wore on, I began losing track of the day, dislocated from the cycles of morning, noon and night. In his book *The Nocturnal Brain*, Dr Guy Leschziner writes of environmental cues that nudge our circadian rhythms forward or back, and enable our internal clocks to remain synchronised with the outside world. These include light, temperature, physical activity, noise and food. Those cues, for me, became unmoored. I ate dinner at 5 p.m., or midnight. I left the house for the first time after 6 p.m., my skin soaking up darkness instead of sunlight. I no longer felt the rhythms of a day's passing. Day and night felt like the same blurred continuum. The headiness of the job butted up against all the old, returning apprehensions around sleep. This, once again, became the big battle that I fought each night.

I felt a certain solitude creeping in too, despite the buzz of the job, and how communal the theatre experience felt in the auditorium. There was an element of waiting for night to fall so my day could begin, passing the world on its way home as I was leaving mine. Then, returning to my flat to see the closed eyes of the neighbourhood's windows and tuning into the enviable silence of other people's sleep around me. The night and its infernal sleeplessness had claimed me again.

First the insomnia came back, then a leaden sleepiness I had never known before. I collapsed into bed, too exhausted for insomnia, until my alarm wrenched me not out of sleep but a different unconscious state, it seemed, deeper and blanker. Sometimes, I would consider not getting up that morning, that day, that week. It was a delicious thought, to sleep on indefinitely in a luxurious eternal night. When I spent a few consecutive evenings in, it felt like peculiar relief. I remembered what it was to be on this side of the day, how long the night was, what it meant to feel refreshed in the morning.

And yet, there was a part of me that bridled against these early nights too, so bland in their moderation. Maybe the night had not, in fact, claimed me but I had returned willingly to its addictive excesses. To be up at night meant more day, *more life*, as it had meant to my father, perhaps, before his crash into illness. Was that a fair comparison to make? Some experts in the field speak of a sleep personality, which moderates how much we need, individually, and which is shaped by social factors – whether we grew up in the countryside or the city, in a culture accustomed to siestas or late-night dining, and so on. But like our conscious 'day' personality, our unconscious sleeping personality has an element of genetic influence too.

I consider this notion. My father had always been a skittish sleeper, easily woken, even before the night work. Is my insomnia a learned pattern, or is it an inheritance? And if the latter, might I have found the perfect work for my sleep personality? I didn't plan for a job that required me to be up at night, but it seems right for someone who has always been unable – unwilling? – to sleep regular hours, and has sought ways to push the day to its furthest extremity. Isn't there an inevitability about it? Did I, in fact, choose it? And – it feels puzzling to even ask the question – could there be a connection between my father's night and mine? When I had spoken to Professor Dijk of my under-sleeping, I'd told him that I no longer feel tired in the day, after four or five hours of sleep, sometimes. He responded with a scientist's ambivalence. 'Many people probably don't realise how tired they are. You can get used to being sleepy and not experience it as such.' Had my father felt this conflation after his shifts at the Courtauld, and would I, like him, eventually crash?

CHAPTER 2
Stars at night

I am in a darkened auditorium, concentrating on keeping my eyes open and my head upright. Not because the show is dragging, but because I have been watching Nat Randall and Anna Breckon's experimental play *The Second Woman*, performed by the actor Ruth Wilson at the Young Vic theatre in London, for the past twenty-three hours. The theatrical marathon began yesterday at 5 p.m. and is due to finish at exactly that time today. There is one more hour before I can go home, to bed.

The play is based on a single scene from John Cassavetes' 1977 film, *Opening Night*, a strange and magnetic backstage drama about actors rehearsing a play, starring Gena Rowlands as Myrtle, a Broadway star going through a midlife crisis. The single scene that plays out before me now is of Myrtle meeting her on-stage lover and having an awkward dance, before breaking up with him, repeated over and over. Wilson performs it with a hundred different partners with whom she has never rehearsed. It is intense and surreal and weirdly mesmerising.

I didn't have to be here for the full twenty-four hours, but I was drawn to the extremity of the endeavour. It is perverse, given that sleep is so difficult to achieve, even on a usual night. Then again, I have had many training hours of unwanted, gritty-eyed wakefulness, and perhaps this is an experiment into what might happen if I carry on resisting sleep. I am surprised I have made it this far, but I am also disturbed that a night has vanished before my eyes, swallowed up by tinny bright wakefulness. Some hours have stood excruciatingly still, others accelerating. My body aches, my temperature soaring and plunging, in flushes. Embarrassingly, I have had to ask ushers to help me back to my seat from the theatre's toilets because I have forgotten the way.

Ruth Wilson has spoken of her preparations for her own, high-pressured wakefulness, and all she will do in its lead-up. I have followed her pointer about limiting coffee intake so the caffeine will have greater effect when you really need it to. But I have made mistakes too, getting up early, which means I must stay awake for thirty-six hours in order to make it to the end of the show, and going to the gym for a rigorous workout beforehand, as if limbering up for a physical endurance challenge – a triathlon or cross-Channel swim – which has left me physically tired.

I feel as if I am entering into the unknown when I walk into the auditorium. Will it be like a day of abstaining from food? Will my body weaken? Might I faint? I catch my reflection and I look drained, as if exhausted merely by the thought of being awake for so long. I have packed for a long-haul flight, with snacks, a toothbrush, and a travel pillow for when I expect the room to empty, and I find myself already scouring for a row of empty seats on which to spread across later.

The revolving door of actors performing opposite Wilson mostly play lovers, some domineering, others pliant, some spurned, others doing the rejecting. There are high-wattage celebrities among them – Ben Whishaw, Idris Elba, Andrew Scott, Toby Jones. Several men come with elaborate back stories that cast Wilson as their mother or an older lover. There are a few women, including Anna Richardson, who turns the drama into a story about betraying sisters, which I want to keep watching. The knowledge that there have been no rehearsals brings an extra frisson of nervous energy, and I wonder how far the actors will go to try and catch Wilson out.

After the first two hours, she has grown bolder and it is her who seems like the more dangerous party. She introduces deadly silences, glaring at the most overbearing men. A hug becomes an act of violence, the dance between the couple a wrestling match. A few men lunge in for a kiss and she parries their attack with exaggerated contortions. Others build emotional intensity so that when Wilson dismisses them, it feels like a small tragedy. The crowd flows in and out through the night, the post-pub groups growing louder, beer bottles or wine glasses in hand, responding to each scenario with gasps, claps, boos, as if seeing the endlessly repeating scene for the first time. I feel buoyed by this warmth and energy.

Eight hours in, the auditorium is thinning out, and I relax, preparing to sneakily spread out on the seats and sleep. I have already heard how some have been dozing on the higher tiers of the auditorium earlier in the evening. But then, a spurt of newcomers arrive and fit themselves snugly around me. They'll go soon, I think, happy to wait. A few more hours in and the theatre is so full that people are standing at the back, as if at a gig. Many of those who sat around me a few hours ago are gone, newcomers in their place. I have lost all sense of how long they have been there. The seats are swiftly filled, with ushers leading people in and the crowd along the back wall eagerly eyeing the auditorium for an empty seat. I am packed in, squashed by the heat of bodies. I listen to the chatter and realise there is a queue forming outside, around the building. Some theatregoers have apparently been waiting for up to six hours. I am shocked, then discomforted. When will the crowd go and let me catch the few hours of forbidden sleep I've planned for?

We have been told, before coming in, that audience members are not allowed to doze in the seats at any point, and we can only be away from them for ten minutes at any one time. I have taken off my shoes and my head is resting on my travel pillow but I am nervous about closing my eyes because ushers are walking through the theatre, policing our levels of wakefulness. I feel prickles of desperation at 3 a.m. and hit my first wall, breathless at the sea of hours before me. I remember the advice of a journalist colleague who sat through a 24-hour show in New York some years ago; he'd said I should focus solely on my experience, in *this* moment, rather than a calculation of how many hours I had sat through, how many there were to go. It sounded like a strategy for endurance athletes, to enable them to resist the soul-crushing power of future projection. It is all and only about the present moment, I remind myself now, as my colleague, Alex, has said.

I try to pin myself to 'now' and the panic ebbs. But by 5 a.m., it returns, like a hammer blow, and I stagger to the foyer for recovery, only to find the queue of people waiting to get in so big that it has folded itself inside the theatre, like a coiled snake. I am choked by wakefulness and rush back in. Ruth Wilson's performance has become cruder, more physical on stage, as if the lack of sleep has made her manic. She lollops in the men's arms, her movements charged with ferocity. She tears off their jackets, garrottes them with their ties or drops her full weight onto them until they are forced to drag her around for their dance. It becomes a comic, grotesque parody of a couple's romantic goodbye.

Waves of people enter boisterously with cups of coffee. I smell the outdoor freshness on them, and I yearn for it, but a grim determination has set in. I stagger to the foyer and order two cups of black coffee. The caffeine works its way into my nervous system, and my mood lifts. I watch Wilson repeating her scene and I am fascinated again. I marvel at her energy. It seems so inconceivable.

A few hours on from my bleakest moment, I feel bullet-proof, only to crash again a few hours later. It goes on like this until the end, the fatigue coming in sudden, engulfing waves. Sleep has become so seductive it sweeps over me every time I blink. In the final hours, I start counting down the time, ticking off the minutes, even though Alex has told me not to. I am doing so not with an eagerness for the performance to end now but with a feeling that verges on regret that it will. It is the opposite of hitting a wall: an opening, and a floating. I could stay here, in this twilight state of sleepy wakefulness, entranced by the headiness in the auditorium, the gripping repetition on the stage, forever.

And then it is over. Ruth Wilson has made it. I have too. The light is so sharp outside it hurts my eyes. I feel like I am made of wool as I walk to the tube station. I am relieved it is a windless day so I will not blow away. I sit on the train and it feels like I am falling, even though I am upright in my seat. I am in bed minutes after entering my flat and wake up to my alarm, sixteen hours later, shattered.

I realise that I can stay awake for longer than I have imagined; that the sky will not fall down or the body collapse. 'Not sleeping' need not be feared and loathed. But I'm not sure it's a step towards self-knowledge or overcoming the fear of insomnia, either. The most unexpected thing is that the tiredness will not go away. At first I am interested in it – the slowed-down brain, the mixed-up words and lack of balance in my yoga class, the gasping when I climb a flight of stairs, the dizziness. It is an unfamiliar fatigue that no amount of sleep can lift and it lasts weeks that extend into a month, then two, maybe more – enough to make me wonder if those twenty-four hours have left a permanent scar, even though I have read about people going without sleep, in much more extreme circumstances, for far longer.

Pioneers of sleep science have been known to keep themselves awake for days at a time to seek out their groundbreaking discoveries on REM sleep and the effects of insomnia. In his book, *Mapping the Darkness*, Kenneth Miller describes how the scientist Nathaniel Kleitman conducted work on human sleep deprivation in 1925, at the University of Chicago, by 'subjecting himself and several graduate students to bouts of experimental insomnia lasting up to 155 hours'. It is reassuring, in the light of my comparatively smaller experience, but it still makes me flinch to read it.

After the first twenty-four hours, Kleitman's team found it necessary to have some form of continuous speech or action to stop them from dozing off. I understand now why I might have had more difficulty staving off sleep than Wilson – she was almost constantly on the move, while I was passive. Still, I feel astonished that thirty-six hours awake can have such a profound effect on my body and mind. I carry on forgetting words, and panting up stairs. The fatigue lifts imperceptibly until one bright morning, I feel refreshed, fully awake again. I might have inherited my sleep personality from my father in his ability to push sleep away, and blur the boundaries of the diurnal cycle, but my experience of surfing the night is not a forewarning of illness. It is a reminder of the body's remarkable gift for renewal.

****

Most night-workers do not get the luxury of such renewal, of course. The theatre industry is part of the night economy, albeit at the starrier end of it, and the work done in theatres, behind the scenes, is gruelling as well as glamorous. If I am up half the night, the cast and creatives of a show are more so, often sleeping in their dressing rooms in makeshift beds in between and around their performances. Statistically, the arts, entertainment and recreation industry has the second biggest proportion of night-workers in the UK, according to ONS's 2022 night-time economy report, and stage actors usually keep far later and more irregular hours than those working on screen.

A year after my overnight experience at the Young Vic, a musical adaptation of Cassavetes' film *Opening Night* opens in London. It is an unusually experimental production for the West End, conceived by the Belgian director Ivo van Hove, with songs by the Canadian-American musician Rufus Wainwright, and starring Sheridan Smith as the troubled midlife actress, Myrtle. I ask the production company if I can go backstage at the Gielgud Theatre for their opening night, which kicks off a little earlier than most evening shows, at 7 p.m., and follow them well after the show is over, so that I can see how actors' worlds come alive after dark. To my surprise, they say 'yes'.

As a critic, I rarely meet those on the 'other side' in this way. The production company, Wessex Grove – founded by Benjamin Lowy and Emily Vaughan-Barratt – are at the innovative end of theatre production; their shows feature big names but take more creative risks than typical West End and Broadway fare. I am surprised to find the team so young. Ben is a sweetly hipsterish New Yorker, Emily has a down-to-earth English glamour, and the company's general manager, Tom Powis, seems quietly canny. I'm told they are among a dynamic new generation of producers rising from among the ranks of the older, stuffier establishment, and the team in their Soho office certainly has the cool millennial slickness of a TV or film production company.

Ben is working on the complexity of the seating plan when I arrive. There is a razzle of famous names on the whiteboard; theatre royalty in one corner, celebrities in another. The placing, they tell me, is a sensitive matter, the central flank a golden position, rather like the front row of London Fashion Week or the power-and-wealth tiers of an ancient Greek amphitheatre. A big Hollywood agent is coming and he will get prime seating in the stalls, Ben says, along with the investors.

It is still light outside when we arrive at the Gielgud, and I feel the thrill of entering through the stage door. I have not seen the narrow, messy intestines of this theatre's backstage area before. It is a warren of faded corridors and narrow staircases that seem to rise, perpetually, into the back of the gods. Cassavetes' original film shows all the off-stage mechanics of a production: Myrtle smoking in her dressing room, her costume changes, the sound of stage cues, the curtain rising and falling as actors enter and exit, and it feels like I am travelling through that world now.

The director's room has two beds, for him and the set designer, Jan Versweyveld, who is also his partner. They have requested this, I'm told, and over the course of my guided tour, I see that most dressing rooms have rag-tag sleeping areas, either a sofa used as an improvised bed or duvets under a dressing table. A few actors linger outside their dressing rooms on the upper floors, handing out gifts to each other, and showing no signs of nerves when I pass them, although they are due on stage in a few hours. We travel through the Gielgud's entrails and at last make it out onto the stage. It is like an untidy living room with its mess of props and a hoover plugged into the mains. An empty auditorium is splayed before it in gilt and red velvet. I look out at the rows of seats, feeling as if I am looking at the ghost of my 'night' self, sitting invisibly in the stalls, and I feel the weight of the not-yet-present audience bearing down with their expectations and their judgements on this side of the proscenium arch. But I also feel the airy unpredictability of the empty room, the sense that any kind of magic might be conjured in it once its seats are filled and the curtain is raised.

There is a sub-stage department under the ground floor – a theatrical dungeon filled with high-tech sound and automation equipment. Above us is the fly crew, who manually raise or lower rigging and hoist the curtains. Directly at the back of the stage, there is a glass cubicle where the deputy stage manager sits to oversee 'The Book'. It is on a stand, like a composer's sheet music, and it is the bible for the show, denoting every move the cast makes, every note they sing, every last instruction and checklist. The Book must remain in the theatre at all times, apparently, so that even if the stage manager is suddenly incapacitated, the show can still go on. Sarah Alford-Smith, who spent decades as a stage manager before becoming a production coordinator, tells me how it feels to sit in this glass box as the show begins. 'There's a perfect moment when you are just waiting. It's like being at the very top of a rollercoaster, that pause, and then everything starts and you fall forward.'

By 6 p.m., the entire company has converged on the stage; I watch the cast limber up, alongside the producers, and they begin with what looks like a scrappy aerobics routine to music. Rehearsals of the 'fight' scenes in the play follow, which is part of general theatre protocol, and I see Sheridan Smith wrestling a lampshade, which she will later do in the show. There are other rituals: more exchanging of gifts; teary words between actors and chanting in a circle of linked arms before the cast disappear into their dressing rooms.

After this, a hushed silence. From Sarah's walkie-talkie I hear the radioed message that everyone is now seated and I feel the moment at the top of the rollercoaster that she spoke about, before the hurtle of sound, lights, action, as the curtain comes up. It is a thrilling blast of energy and action: the opening strains of the orchestra, an actor bursting into song, exchanges between characters I have heard before, spoken as if they are not lines at all but life taking place. Things fall seamlessly into place after this initial bang, and the production whirrs calmly into motion, like a noiseless, well-oiled engine.

There are no 'wings' in this show, only two glass doors that lead onto the stage. I see actors poised behind them, waiting for their cue. What is striking is the quietness and the unfussy precision of it all. No one looks nervous. The drift of actors on and off stage seems so strangely ordinary too, as if there is no divide between the people they are here, in backstage darkness, and those they will become in the next few seconds, beneath the spotlights and caught up in the drama of their roles. At what point do they become the character they are playing? I wonder, searching for a glimpse of that switch, but the actors' faces remain inscrutable. Peeping from behind these glass doors feels like being on the other side of a TV set, or even inside it, with a fuzzy quality to the sound and the peculiar feeling that whatever is going on in front of the audience is not all there is to it. Backstage is humming and clicking with its own drama.

When the curtain comes down, I creep behind the glass doors to see the final bows. They seem full of restive energy. The cast runs downstage, almost sprinting, as if burning off excess adrenaline. I look beyond them to see movement within the auditorium. The crowd is getting to its feet and the sight of the audience, rising tier by tier like a slow-breaking wave, makes me feel like I am simultaneously over here and over there. I see myself in the auditorium again, clapping this time and feeling the swooning collective high of a stirring show.

The opening-night party, afterwards, starts after 10 p.m. and is for six hundred guests at a high-end hotel, across a warren of blood-red rooms. The venue has the opulence of a Fellini film-set, the central chandelier blazing like an open, cut-glass fireplace. A photographer has been flown in from New York. Everyone I have seen earlier that day, backstage, is now immaculately groomed. The maze of rooms includes a bowling alley, a karaoke space, an ice-cream cart, a 'grazing table' of food, and several bars. There are circles within circles of access into VIP alcoves and backstage areas here too, cordoned off by bouncers. The party revs up quickly, each room thick with bodies by 11 p.m., the replenishing of food and drink endless, its volume and spirit lifting with every passing hour. I am curious about who sits in the inner sanctum and I try to peer into the most cloistered rooms, but I cannot see into these well-guarded spaces. Jay Gatsby himself might be sitting, elusive, in an antechamber, in retreat from the party's high jinks.

There is a subtle shift in mood among the production team at midnight when Emily, Ben and Tom untangle themselves from the throng to gather in the 'war room', or so it is called on

Broadway, to go over the newspaper reviews that have just gone live online. About twenty minutes later, I see them coming back out into the party. Their faces are changed, uncertainty drained away. Emily tells me all is well. Ben goes back to milling with the crowd, wearing a smile. I pick up unspoken disturbance all the same: the show has divided the critics, receiving both effusive praise and savage maulings. It will go on to close before its full run as a result, but no one knows that just now.

I think of the backstage beds, the surging adrenaline of the evening, the enormity of the effort. It feels, in this moment, like passing or failing a test, and even though I am usually on the other side of this, part of its critical adjudication, I feel shaken for them. A young associate director, so animated a few hours ago, looks like he is overcome with exhaustion, so tired that he might cry. There are large brown insomniac bruises under his eyes. I bump into him again at 1.30 a.m. when he has perked up and is sipping from a bottle of beer. He tells me he is finally able to relax. It takes time for adrenaline to leave the body, he says, and after this party is over, he will go home to read half a book. Only then will he attempt to sleep. Most of the actors remain impervious to whatever has happened in the war room. They are burning off steam, in party mode. They are still in full throttle when I leave at 2 a.m., the bowling alley bustling, the karaoke area busting its sounds, spirits so high they are close to wild. For them, the opening-night party is only just beginning.

****

I first saw Maria Martins on the steps of the Gielgud Theatre. I met her at the start of the evening, when guests were still coming in for the premiere of *Opening Night*. It was raining outside and I was standing at the theatre's threshold so I wouldn't get wet while watching the red carpet parade, with its sleekly dressed stars and its shoal of paparazzi. Maria was one of two security staff stationed on either side of the door, and I didn't immediately clock her gender because she was wearing a unisex uniform of shirt and trousers. She looked tough, no-nonsense, and when she turned to speak to me, I thought for a moment that she was scolding me for standing in the wrong place, but I realised she was making a wry joke about the soggy red carpet.

She had worked at night-time venues for fifteen years, from gay clubs like Heaven in Soho and East Bloc in Old Street to upscale restaurants and cocktail bars across town, she told me. She'd been with the Delfont Mackintosh Theatres group for the past two years. The company runs eight theatres in the city, and Maria is sent to different parts of London for her shifts every week. She is of Portuguese origin but grew up in Zimbabwe, in extreme poverty, emigrating to Britain in 1992, in hope of a better life, and she speaks of looking after a disabled sister.

She was quickly warm, and open, when we spoke. I was surprised when she told me she was almost sixty-one years old. She had the confident physicality of a much younger person. Most days, she worked from 5 p.m. until 11 p.m., and these hours were tame compared to the double shifts she had been working before the pandemic – as a waitress from 9 a.m. until 5 p.m. and then, at the weekends, as a doorwoman, from 10 p.m. until 5 a.m. She had needed the two jobs because she wasn't earning enough money with just one: 'I wanted to lift myself up,' she explained. I kept my tone neutral in reply but I was horrified by the relentless hours, both appalled and impressed by her stoicism and understatement.

The night shifts paid little more than the waitressing, and left her with only a few hours to sleep between the end of one shift and the beginning of another. Eventually, it took its toll. 'There was a lot of pain, a lot of sickness. It was affecting my heart.

I went to the doctor and she said it was my lifestyle – that people who do night shifts die ten years earlier. The body is not made to work sixteen hours without rest.' It is different now, even with the evening shifts at the theatre, she said. She gets to bed before midnight and usually sleeps until 6 a.m. 'I now believe sleep during this time is sacred.'

Thank god, I thought, but statistically, it is female night-workers who seem to be at greater risk of harm to their health. Some studies point to greater cognitive side effects of nocturnal shift work on women than men. There are no categorical reasons for this disparity, though metabolism, hormones and the menstrual cycle play a part. It is disturbing information, especially given that more women in the UK started working at night, full-time, in the decade between 2012 and 2022, even as the number of men in these jobs fell, according to the ONS's 2022 report.

I asked Maria what door work was like, if she had ever seen violence, whether she had felt afraid of rowdy or drunken punters. Most people out at night are nice, she'd said, and when they aren't, she knows what to do to stop things from escalating. She spoke with ebullience about her job and talked with pride of earning enough to care for her sister. I was in awe of her fortitude, but it also seemed like a graphic example of the silent disparities in night work: a woman guarding the door, a few feet away from those inside the club or party or show, yet a world apart. How did Maria remain invisible to me?

After meeting her on that opening night, I began to see her on other trips to the West End, standing at the same spot by the door, checking people's bags, sometimes mine, as I go in. The truth is, she has always been standing there. One evening I see her outside the stage door, after a show has finished, as I am unlocking my bike. She is managing a flock of fans who are waiting for a celebrity to leave the theatre and I almost don't recognise her because she has the physical authority of a bouncer, her feet planted firmly, her body braced, ready to contain the rearing crowd. When I next speak to her a few weeks after we first meet, she is preparing to start her shift at the theatre that is showing Lin-Manuel Miranda's sell-out musical, *Hamilton.* Oh, I say, excitedly, that's a good one. She smiles back politely, waiting for the next question, and so I ask her if she ever gets to see the productions inside? Surely, I think, it must be one of the perks of her job. 'No,' she says, stubbing out her cigarette and chuckling at my naivety. 'I'm not there to watch the shows. I'm there to watch over people like you.'

Chapter 3
Invisibles

For a while, I go looking for other invisible women like Maria and this takes me back to my father – to the home he lives in, and his night. When he was first diagnosed with dementia, I was told its average life expectancy could stretch to twelve years, though that figure may have shifted since then. I remember calculating the age at which he was statistically due to die. But twenty years later, into his nineties, he has far surpassed that marker. In the early years, he was shuttled from one nursing home to another because there were so few care centres trained to deal with his relatively rare strain of frontal-lobe dementia. But he settled, and has been in his nursing home, on a flower lined residential street near my flat, for well over a decade.

In all the time he has lived there, I have been inside the home only a handful of times during the night, and it feels very different in its pace from the constant movement of the day, when meals are being either being served or taken away, visitors signing in, carers – overwhelmingly female – bustling in and out of the sitting room. There is less reason to visit after seven or eight o'clock in the evening, when I know my father will be in bed, possibly with the light off in his room, and just the flash of Indian song or dance from his cable TV.

There are times when I am summoned there, in an emergency, if he is showing worrying signs or has refused to eat during the day, and the nurse in charge that night is thinking of sending him to hospital. When I have visited on those occasions, there is a changed rhythm to the home, with an unfamiliar team of carers and a different intensity to their routines. They walk past briskly, busy with medication rounds, and are all unrecognisable to me. The residents are mostly in bed and there is a prevailing sense of sleep in the corridor that leads to my father's room. I have imagined the home to shut down eventually, after I leave it, and collectively go to sleep, including the nurses and carers, at some point.

My father has seemed different in my evening visits too, much less tightly wound than he is in his wheelchair, by day, when he sometimes looks through me or shouts. There are times when he holds on to my hand tightly, as if he fears being sucked under by quicksand, and tells me the sky is spinning, that he isn't safe and that I have to save him. Then the rare, precious times when he is, miraculously, his old self, mellow, making jokes, remembering everything – the address of our family home, the car he drove, what I do for a living, a friend from his childhood; these are only glimmers, lasting a few hours at most, but it feels momentous, like slipping through a portal, back to my other father who emerges from 2003 to meet me in these moments.

In the evenings, he is more like this relaxed old self. He seems to remember me better, and is ready to be sociable. But I have heard that he can be the opposite of this amicable father when I am not there. The carers will speak of a 'difficult' previous night when I visit the next morning to find him especially severe or black in his mood, closing his eyes disdainfully or turning away in disgust when I ask him how he is. These are the nights when he has been volubly agitated, shouting for hours. I only ever know this in the aftermath; I have never been there to hear it myself. I go in one morning and a carer tells me he was screaming for me the previous night, and I feel a sharp sense of having let him down by not going to his bedside when he called for me.

My father's distress is part of a phenomenon called 'sundowning', when those with dementia become agitated at sunset or begin to hallucinate as the light leaks out of the day. It is a time-specific discombobulation, but I wonder if it is perhaps an existential anxiety too, at heading into the metaphorical night, when all daytime distraction from the illness is removed, the primal, untethering horrors of dementia now filling that space. I imagine the fearful prospect of heading into a never-ending night, from which there may be no waking, looming like a sinister shadow in the dark.

Until now, I haven't given much thought as to who looks after my father on these bad nights, but I begin asking his day carers if they have worked night shifts. They have all done so at one time or another, sometimes juggling day and night shifts simultaneously on a weekly rota, and they have shocking stories to tell, relayed matter-of-factly. One speaks of being enlisted for seven consecutive night shifts in a previous home, along with his usual day hours, because of the acute staff shortage during the pandemic. He worked around the clock that week, sleeping in snatched hours, on a chair. It is an extreme example, but this practice of double shifting is not an aberration for people in the care industry, with over 40 per cent working at night, according to the ONS, some alongside day jobs and childcare.

It is a parallel universe for those who inhabit it, says Amanda Scott, the CEO of Forest Healthcare, which runs my father's home. She was a nurse before entering into leadership, decades ago, and still vividly recalls the strange sense of alternate reality. She started out as a trainee nurse in Leicester in the 1980s, and did nights in a rehab unit for the physically disabled. 'You felt like you'd left a population of people, detached from the world you knew, and entered into another universe. You'd be walking through a darkened hospital, unrecognisable from the day, and see faces that you'd never seen in daytime.'

There were times when she accompanied patients transferring to hospitals with more beds or greater expertise in what was classed as a 'blue light transfer'. This meant travelling long distances in an ambulance, kneeling beside her patient, and returning home the following morning. The image of a figure kneeling, as if in supplication, beside an ailing body, against a backdrop of timeless darkness, seems ancient, biblical. The experience, with its solitude and unspoken trauma, left her at a certain remove from the day-world, she reflects. 'I'd get home and my husband would say, "How was your night?" I couldn't explain I'd been to another city, swinging around in an ambulance with a patient. In his world, I'd just been to work.'

Others speak similarly of entering into a surreal space, intensely charged but invisible to most. Felicity Bano is a junior doctor who regularly works ten-hour night shifts in an A&E department. Three doctors work across eight wards which contain six hundred patients, the maths alone of which sounds like a terrifying responsibility, and she talks about the high-speed drama of her night – time moves quickly, there is no slackening of pace, and the brain must stay constantly alert, making decisions and carrying out vital tasks. Every action requires mammoth concentration and effort. 'The first few hours are fine, but between three to five in the morning, the body and brain don't work the way they normally would. So I double-check every medication and dose. When someone's heart stops, our bleep goes off and several of us will do "resus". If that happens at 3 a.m. or 4 a.m., you can see people's brains are functioning differently . . . when we're working out a dose, there are four of us trying to do basic arithmetic, which would normally take seconds for any one of us.'

Amanda Scott also tells me about the distortions of time in intensive care, where she worked after her training. This work doesn't have a clear day and night distinction, she explains; while those in a regular ward are stabilised enough to sleep through the night, sicker people can fall seriously ill at any time, so night feels like a continuation of the day; there is no organic quietening down. In her windowless hospital A&E unit Felicity feels detached from the markers of ordinary time, too: outside it could be 3 a.m. or 3 p.m.

Felicity's descriptions are more troubling though, containing an underlying sense of negative transformation. After a batch of night shifts, her self-perception has skewed. When she looks in the mirror, she sees her face has physically aged. She has got lost while cycling home after work, she says, and it reminds me of the journey back to the tube station after my twenty-four hours of wakefulness at the Young Vic. Even the simple act of walking required an effort, an active remembering of how to do it.

****

A few weeks after speaking to Felicity and Amanda, I am making my way to a care home on the commuter belt fringes of Hertfordshire. I am observing a night shift there, but its manager has asked me to drop in beforehand so I can see the home in the daytime first. When I arrive, it has a bright, bustling energy which I recognise from visits to my father's nursing home. There are forty-one residents here, with conditions ranging from Parkinson's disease to dementia, some mobile, others receiving end-of-life care. Many sit in the living room and turn their heads to smile as I enter.

The room is emptying out when I return for the night shift. I have been told to come in for 7 p.m., so I can observe the official transition between day and night teams. The home is tucked within a matrix of quiet residential streets and there is already a sleepy quality to the evening as I weave my way there, although it is not yet dusk: windows glow with light indoors, while out here there is just birdsong and bare streets. A handover meeting is taking place when I get there, which involves a brief inventory of every resident's state of health: whose blood pressure needs checking, who didn't eat, who was especially agitated or gregarious. Once the information has been logged, the night routine commences with a swift, peaceable efficiency: residents are helped to their beds to be washed and changed by carers, medication is handed out by two duty nurses. There are no emergencies tonight and the hours towards midnight tick over steadily, the team moving from one task to the next, as if working through a well-rehearsed tick-list. This has its own flatlined intensity. There is an hourly circulation of the rooms to make sure the residents are breathing, that they have their alarms near them if they need to call for help, that drinking water is within reach, that those at risk of falling aren't attempting to get out of bed unaided. Around 11 p.m., carers begin cleaning – wiping down chairs, hoovering, putting on the laundry.

The team is made up of five carers, along with the nurses, most of them female, which is consistent with national trends: almost 80 per cent of the care industry is female in England. And while all night-shifters are more likely to be low earning – according to the ONS report, 15 per cent of night-time employees were in low-paid roles in 2022 compared to 10.5 per cent overall – women working nocturnally are likely to be even more so, with over 16 per cent of female night-workers classed as low earners compared to 13 per cent male counterparts.

Nocturnal shift work is indisputably bad for both sexes, its effects associated with everything from cardiovascular disease to obesity, Alzheimer's, depression, hormonal disorders and more. The World Health Organization includes Circadian disruption in its list of probable carcinogens, and Dr Leschziner suggests that 'by regular exposure to light at night [which suppresses the production of melatonin and its possible anti-cancerous effects], perhaps we are lessening our resistance to cancer.' Dementia was the leading cause of death for females in the UK in 2022, a condition that has been linked to a lack of sleep, alongside illnesses like diabetes and heart disease, and there is some evidence of greater cognitive side-effects of nocturnal shift work on women, but no categorical reasons for this disparity. Metabolism, hormones and upsets to the menstrual cycle play a part, with findings of longer and more painful periods for women who work night-shifts.

Lost sleep cannot simply be made up in hours, either. The *time* of sleep influences its quality and structure, Kenneth Miller writes in *Mapping the Darkness*, citing a NASA-commissioned study that reversed the hours of waking and sleeping for its control group, to find that the body's rhythms spontaneously drift towards 'chaos' under these conditions; internal clocks become confused and the secretion of important nightly hormones is scrambled, with cortisol – which manages stress and sleep – falling out of sync, and all the usual stages of sleep disrupted.

There is no official sleep allocation for staff in a care home. Carers get a one-hour break across a twelve-hour shift, which is divided into four parts here. Again and again, I am told that women prefer night shifts to working in the day, but it is clear that childcare necessitates this preference; for carers at least it is the only way they can earn and look after young families, assuming there is someone at home to look after their children while they sleep. Before studying medicine, Felicity Bano worked as a one-to-one care assistant to earn extra cash. It was at a mental health hospital and it consisted of observing a single high-risk patient across a shift as they slept, logging their condition every fifteen minutes. She was employed on a zero-hours contract, and paid £7 per hour. For her, it supplemented student life. 'The big difference between me and the others there was that it was something I chose to do, whenever it suited me. But there were people with three children who didn't have that choice.'

Joanne Campbell, the deputy manager at this care home, worked a long stretch as an NHS nurse, as part of a night team, when her two daughters were young. After a twelve-hour shift, she would scramble home to take them to school. Before their return, she would squeeze in about five hours of sleep. Her body never acclimatised to this upside-down day, as the science attests, and she constantly felt below par: 'You're fighting against your biological clock all the time, you think you'll get used to it, but you don't.' Elaine is one of the nurses working tonight and she has a similar story – she works at night so she can be with her three small children by day. She'll work this way until they're old enough to take themselves to and from school, she says. She is harried yet remains vivacious. She can't afford to be tired, she tells me, pushing her trolley into the lift for her medication round on the first floor.

The night's other nurse, Elena, is doing the same round on the ground floor and I follow her as she makes her stops along the corridor with her trolley. She is in her thirties, originally from Romania, with a young daughter. When she has had a particularly difficult night, she tells me, she goes for a run around the park before going home, so she can ready herself for the next part of her day as a mum. She has an easy rapport with the residents and tells me snippets about whoever we meet: a hundred-year-old who wears Chanel dresses; a former music teacher with two harps in his room; two Turkish Cypriot sisters who tell stories about each other; and Italian residents whose rooms are across the corridor from each other. When one begins speaking Italian to herself, the other hears her and replies from his room, which has the delightful ring of a bed-bound romance to me. The residents ask Elena for things along her route, and she responds, before carrying on with her round. One of the sisters wants cream rubbed on her legs. A man asks for a banana. Several want to chat. It is patient, painstaking work that requires a practical sort of kindness, and some decoding because words do not always come out clearly formed. 'You've brought me my drugs!' says a sprightly man, who, Elena tells me, used to be a photographer. He is sitting in an armchair with a laptop, and he thanks Elena when he first sees her. She bought him a birthday card last year for his ninetieth birthday, she explains afterwards. 'He thanks me for it every time he sees me.'

I meet the full cohort of carers at 2 a.m., when they have their nightly meeting. Figures from the ONS show that the night-time economy relies heavily on people born outside the UK, with 69 per cent of such night-workers making up the 24-hour health and personal services industries. Tonight's team corresponds with that figure; only Elaine is white British. The others are from Ghana, South Africa, Greece, Eastern Europe, including the two men who are working tonight.

Cosmas, of South African origin, has been at the home for several years. He speaks about the residents with such affection and intimacy that I realise he has built close bonds with them during the night, in hours which are sometimes fraught with agonised wakefulness for those who live here. Charles is the other male carer, and he juggles his own childcare duties with the job; he meets his wife at a halfway point from their home in the mornings so she can get to work on time, while he takes their four children to school and picks them up again before leaving for the next night shift. Some of the team say they are used to the lack of sleep, while it's clear that others function alongside the tiredness. 'I'm struggling,' Charles admits, his eyes swollen red and his desperation visceral. The beauty of our biological clock is that it can be shifted back, I have read. We all have the capability to reset it; we simply turn out the lights earlier and our body tunes back into the environmental cues. But how many can afford to do this? Certainly not Charles. Both he and Cosmas have bus rides to and from work that take well over an hour, and I think of the strangers I have seen dozing on the train in the mornings. They may not be people who have stayed up too late the previous night, as I have assumed, but those who have been working, and not slept at all.

In an experiment, the nineteenth-century Russian physician and biochemist Maria Mikhaĭlovna Manàsseina found, after keeping ten puppies awake for more than a week, that sleep deprivation could be deadlier than starvation. Where other tests had proved the puppies could survive without food for twenty or twenty-five days, they were 'irreparably lost' after four to five days without sleep. Later experiments on humans found that deprivation of this kind led to visual hallucinations, reduced physical strength and slower reaction times. The lack of sleep involved in night work might not be as extreme as these experiments, but all the research points to a serious grinding away of good health and wellbeing.

****

The night world feels painfully hidden, its realities cloaked in invisibility for those who live here. On the medication rounds, I see the vulnerability of the residents more starkly. Some are volatile, others acquiescent. Many look so fragile. Almost everyone is in bed and some people talk with their eyes closed, as if in a dream. Some look desperately pale or sallow, with bird-like limbs. A few swallow their tablets with aching slowness, and the action is alarming in its laboriousness, as if the tablets are too bulky for their delicate throats. Most have several tablets to take. I see pictures of families on walls, birthday cards, black and white images of who the residents were as children, on their wedding days, as proud, bright-eyed mothers or fathers. They are undimmed reflections of former selves, in the world, 'out there'. One sweetly smiling woman has a notebook on her bedside table that lists days of the week, with occasional names in the next column. I imagine this is her roster of visitors, and it is desolate in its sparseness.

The night at this home is neither quiet nor passive. What is striking is how busy it is. So much happens beyond sleep. The steady rhythm of tasks for the carers starts up again after the 2 a.m. meeting, but now there are more skirmishes. Some residents become disorientated, thinking it to be morning, and they struggle to get up to begin their day. A woman is still watching

TV at 3 a.m. Another wakes up at 4 a.m. and attempts to walk across her room, trailing her catheter, to eat a packet of muffins. Another sings. I wonder if this is a pre-dawn equivalent to sun-downing: an anxiety over the end of the night's repose, and the prospect of the upcoming confusions of another day. Someone shouts, a long, plangent holler, beyond words, which wakes up the others. I think of my father, the people around him. I realise now what it means when I'm told he has had a difficult night. So much packed away in that little sentence.

But I also see why he might shout. Maybe I would too. The night acquires another meaning in this setting: I know insomnia, and disturbed sleep patterns, are a common feature of dementia. Night wakefulness has a way of making emotions more acute but I feel the undertow of something else here too: a contest for survival. I sense that night-time battle against mortality even amid the beeping sensors, alarms and vigilance of the carers.

There is a curious intimacy to a space in which someone has recently died, hospital nurses have told me, and so some abide by certain rituals in the aftermath of a death, such as the opening of windows in a room where someone has just passed away. My father's home, like a hospital, is a place where many live, but where many die too, and the space accommodates that natural inevitability. The communal rooms here look larger and emptier in the night, more haunting, with their vacant chairs and tables. I mention the hospital rituals at the 2 a.m. meeting and Charles nods, speaking of the Ghanaian tradition of keeping doorways clear, as a symbolic gesture to allow a path out of a building, and the world, for the spirits of the newly departed. Another carer swears she hears music from an upstairs common room, when there is no piano, and several concur that they do not like entering that room at night, alone. There is something unnameable and oppressive in it, they say, and each has their own theory on what that might be. Cosmas shrugs and says he can't take any of these stories seriously.

Maybe we are doing nothing more than amusing – or distracting – ourselves, I think. There is pleasure to be found in being scared, and scaring others. I know that from the thrilling terror of my old bedtime ghost stories.

Morning takes forever to arrive, but when it does, the pace accelerates; carers start washing and dressing the early-rising residents from 5.30 a.m., who begin drifting down to the living room soon afterwards, taking their seats for breakfast, some bright, others bleary and seemingly surprised to be here. They have made it to another day. The morning is calmer than the night has been. More residents join the early starters, and all sit quietly, as if exhausted by the commotion of the previous hours. Clean, sleepy, expectant, grumpy, smiling. This is how I variously find my father when I visit.

Birdsong follows me back to the train station and it sounds like the chorus of the previous evening, leaving me feeling as if no time has passed between now and then, that the night shift happened in another realm, like Amanda Scott had said. It *is* a parallel universe. I am glad to leave the shift behind, but the upside-down lives of the carers niggle at me: Charles, whose life has turned sleep into an unattainable luxury. Elena, running laps of the park to shake off the stress of a hard shift. Elaine, going home to cook breakfast for three children while I flop into bed. I feel an urgency to get myself home, but I become confused when I get in, and experience my craving for sleep as hunger, so I make myself a meal before brushing my teeth and drawing the curtains. At long last, I think, and it does feel like a luxury, hard earned. But as I fold myself into bed, I feel the familiar twitch of a lively tiredness and I know that any attempt at sleep is instantly, irrevocably useless. The minute I close my eyes my mind is both exhausted and as awake as the new day.

Part 2

Lights out

Chapter 4
To sleep

I can't remember when I first stopped sleeping soundly. Maybe as a child, in the bedroom I initially shared with Tariq. I would wait for his breathing to quieten, then strain to listen beyond our room in the hope of being the last one awake, and I would feel myself expanding into the liberating space and solitude. By my early twenties, that childhood game of holding on to wakefulness while others slept began playing out against my will. Sound seemed to be the trigger. It was as if the silence I had tuned into as a child was now a requirement for sleep. Any sound was noise: the burr of the TV from next door, the ticking of a clock in another room, the buzz of midnight conversations carried up through cavities in the walls. When one layer of sound reduced its volume, another rose from beneath it, each intrusive and underscored by my unending thoughts. Noise blaring from without and within, until I felt too tired to sleep, like the weary alertness after my night shift at the care home in Hertfordshire.

The artist Louise Bourgeois suffered a bad bout of insomnia in the 1990s, during which she created a series of drawings. Among them I find an image that features musical notes in red ink, zigzagging across a sheet of paper. They look like the jagged score of an ECG graph which has recorded an alarmingly arrhythmic heartbeat. It sums up the torment of my insomnia: there is a raised heartbeat in every sound.

I have been told that to overcome an inability to sleep you must find its root cause, but this quest for an original trigger is guesswork. Was it self-inflicted in childhood, in my shared room with Tariq, or does it track further back than that, to infancy, to the womb, to genetics? One starting point is the concept of a 'sleep personality', and the idea that if you were an early sleeper as a child, you are likely to be the same later in life. I was born in London, but my family moved to Lahore when I was three years old, before returning to the UK a couple of years later. In Pakistan, there was vigorous, carefree slumber, on the roof of the house on the hottest nights, with the extended family in close proximity. It was sleep as communal ritual. Then the standstill after lunch when everyone lay down again in siesta. I remember my sister, Fauzia, sleeping beside me on these afternoons. There was no hint of insomnia until the move back to Britain when we found ourselves homeless, living in a disused building in north London for a while, crammed into a single room, before moving into a council flat.

In light of this, I see how my insomnia might be a reaction against the early chaos, with my exacting need for order and silence in adulthood, but that is my own armchair analysis. There are so many gaps in sleep science, so many unknowns, that I wonder if sleep is by its nature too mysterious to systematise, its correlations with childhood and personalities not quite as straightforwardly causal as we might hope. I have my two young nieces to stay for a sleepover one weekend. My flat is tiny and I am anxious about the lack of beds but, for them, it is an adventure. Martha, aged twelve, takes ownership of the sofa and her younger sister, Eva, eight, commandeers the chaise longue. There is initial excitement as they change into their pyjamas, but this turns into resistance against sleeping. At first I give in, but at 11 p.m., when they show no signs of settling, I order them to bed and switch off the light. The room goes quiet so quickly that I am in awe of their ease with sleep: as if they have free-fallen into it. I creep into the room to see Martha's legs dangling off the sofa, Eva curled in among her toys and blankets. I tumble into sleep that night too: it is as if their sleepiness is a vapour they have breathed into our shared air.

I do not know what time I hear the click of my bedroom door but I open my eyes to see Eva in front of me, so close I could reach out and touch her. It is too dark for me to see her face, but she is standing still. I ask her if she is okay. She doesn't answer but wiggles her body a few times, as if moving to music only she can hear. I close my eyes and when I open them again she is standing in front of the full-length mirror at the foot of my bed. It looks as if she is scouring her sleeping face. It is eerie and I am, for a moment, scared of this silently scrutinising Eva, so different from the high-energy chatterbox of the day. When I muster the courage to look out into the dark again, towards the mirror, she is gone, leaving the bedroom door slightly ajar.

How was *this* night personality formed? I think. And will her childhood somnambulism set a habit for Eva in her adulthood? When I ask her about it the next morning, she has no recollection of getting out of bed and laughs off the idea that she would have crept into my room and danced silently in the night. I am uncertain for a moment: did I imagine it? But her father, Tariq, had mentioned that Eva occasionally sleepwalks; I had simply forgotten about it, until now. Was the Eva who stood in front of me in the middle of the night another version of herself, unknown even to herself in the daytime? And what would happen if the two versions met each other? Would they recognise each other as one?

****

If science can't explain the grey areas around sleep, maybe art can shed a light; I am in a hangar-like space, with walls that seem to swirl around me. My nieces are there too. We are at the Van Gogh Experience, a virtual reality exhibition whose basement is lit up with projections of the painter's 'greatest hits'.

Giant sunflowers and almond blossoms float around the room, on walls and floor, a rising, dipping, spinning drift. It seems simultaneously as if they are orbiting us and we are riding a merry-go-round inside this room-sized moving canvas.

Martha and Eva are rapt. This show takes the concept of the 'art blockbuster' to another level, not only immersive but huge in scale, running across three floors of an east London warehouse. This room is its pièce de résistance; images of *Sunflowers*, *Irises*, *The Starry Night* all bob and shimmer as magnified, moving projections. The whole experience is, probably, dumbed-down sacrilege to art purists. I might not have come here without my nieces, yet I can't be cynical. The room captures all the wonder and naive joy of Vincent van Gogh's work. Eva *oohs* and *ahhs*. Martha is frozen in awe as a projection of Katsushika Hokusai's *The Great Wave off Kanagawa* swishes past our feet.

Hokusai's painting is said to have inspired *The Starry Night*, which now sails, galleon-like, into the room, with its oversized cypress in the foreground, its bright yellow stars that fizz like Catherine wheels and the expanse of swirling sky beyond. To my surprise, I feel a choke of emotion. I have seen the original painting at MoMA, in New York, with its tightly curved brushstrokes that already seem like they are in motion. Here the effect is crackling and kinetic.

It is surprising, given the painting's sense of joyous nighttime, that Van Gogh painted his post-Impressionist masterpiece in the midst of depression, after being admitted to an asylum in Saint-Rémy-de-Provence in the summer of 1889. He had suffered a severe relapse into mental illness and the following year he died by suicide, two months after leaving the clinic, in July 1890. *The Starry Night* was painted in his tiny east-facing asylum room, partly capturing the view out of his window but also drawing from a mix of memory and imagination to add details such as the village with its church spire and illuminated windows.

This is not Van Gogh's first painting of the night. His body of work shows an ongoing fascination with darkness. A year before creating this magnum opus, in a letter dated 16 September 1888, Vincent tells his brother, Theo, that he is doing six to twelve hours of non-stop work, often at night, followed by twelve hours of sleep. 'The question of night scenes or effects, on the spot and actually at night, interests me enormously,' he wrote. It sounds like a period of peaceful nocturnal painting, and sleeping. But the following year he was in the grip of a 'FEARSOME insomnia'. On 9 January 1889, weeks after slicing off part of his ear in a high state of anxiety, he writes to Theo about his torment. He is fighting sleeplessness with a 'very, very strong dose of camphor' on his pillow and mattress, he says, and he hopes it will bring an end to the insomnia. 'I dare to believe that it won't recur.' I read Van Gogh's hope as optimistic desperation. In my case, it has always returned. Yet, even in his 'insensible' state, Vincent tells Theo that he is reflecting on the work of Degas, Gauguin and his own art practice; he continues to think, paint, write letters, with the insomnia existing alongside his productivity.

The glittering night sky Van Gogh imagines beyond the confines of his asylum in *The Starry Night* is an embodiment of the way we so often think of the gifted artist at night: synapses fizzing, imagination touched by divinity, a compulsively unsleeping genius channelling a heightened state of buoyant creativity. Countless artists and writers have elected to work after dark, from Toulouse-Lautrec, documenting night revelries at the Moulin Rouge, to Franz Kafka, Philip Guston and Patricia Highsmith. Musicians, too, the Rolling Stones' all-night jams in the lead-up to their appearance at Knebworth Festival in 1976, for instance, or Prince, whose recording sessions could last across a continuous twenty-four hours. Certainly, if Van Gogh still suffered from insomnia when he was painting *The Starry Night*, it makes sleeplessness seem beatific – a curse turned gift.

His night paintings show how much colour and light he saw in darkness, even in the grip of the acute mental pain and psychosis that plagued his life. The night was not a blanket of black for him. In a letter to his youngest sister, Willemina, on 14 September 1888, he wrote of the night sky as being 'even more richly coloured than the day, coloured in the most intense violets, blues and greens'.

Being awake for between seventeen and nineteen hours causes the same kind of cognitive and motor impairments as the effects of alcoholic inebriation, according to a 2000 study by academics A.M. Williamson and A.M. Feyer. And being awake for longer than nineteen hours deems you significantly drunk, on a par with someone with a blood alcohol concentration in excess of the legal upper limit for driving. *The Starry Night* makes it seem as if Van Gogh is drunk in Technicolor. I recognise this; it is the way I have occasionally experienced insomnia, when I am so dizzy with tired wakefulness that some part of my brain must register the state as a lightness of mood. But more often it feels like heavy grey drudge. I leave the swirling room of the exhibition reluctantly. Its luminescent delirium is hypnotising. Stepping back into daylight feels like coming out of a state of exhilarating sleeplessness.

Just as Van Gogh painted through his insomnia, so Louise Bourgeois got out of bed and started drawing. She suffered from sleeplessness throughout her life but faced a particularly debilitating bout of night-time anxiety between 1994 and 1995, during which time she made her *Insomnia Drawings* series. 'It is conquerable,' she said, and for her it *was* conquered, by filling page after page of a drawing-diary with deliriously repeated doodles and creating a series of 220 drawings of circles within circles, a mess of red biro scribbles that look like screams on paper, a clockface with its hands at one o'clock, a page with an expanding circle of severed fingers. They are so different from the monumental stainless steel, bronze and marble *Maman* spiders and other caged sculptures for which Bourgeois is better known. These abstract lines and loops are like small, sewn stitches and they cover the paper so completely that you imagine them continuing on and on, off the page, until the eyelids finally droop. I feel a peculiar kind of excitement upon seeing these images, with their agitating boredom and agitating alertness, side by side. Their wordlessness chimes with me, reflecting a noisy nocturnal silence that I instantly recognise.

Their bland visual regurgitations reflect the desolations of insomnia in the most unadorned form I have seen. There is none of the buoyancy of *The Starry Night*. The drawings are scribbly and bleached of colour, like anxiety made manifest on paper. Yet they helped Bourgeois unlock something within her, and they brought her relief. She describes their effect as a kind of 'rocking or stroking'. It sounds maternal, as if she is trying to placate a crying baby who refuses to sleep. And they contain an unwinding through repetition, like the rituals of some children with autism or ADHD – the watching of a familiar video clip, over and over, the repetition of which might be mistaken for anxiety but which, according to some findings, is a way to counteract the day's sensory overload and reach a state of calm. A rocking of oneself, in a sense.

The artist Lee Krasner also painted her way through chronic insomnia, around the time her mother and then her husband, the painter Jackson Pollock, died – the latter in a drink-driving car crash in 1956, with his lover Ruth Kligman, who survived, in the seat beside him. Krasner's *Night Creatures* series has some similarities to Bourgeois's drawings, featuring repeating, abstract patterns, but washed in an earthy sepia brown. The patterns are insect-like, as if a swarm of tiny creatures is scuttling on the canvas, or as if ants are crawling across the retina. I am inspired by the images. Rather than seeking escape or avoidance of their sleepless state, Bourgeois and Krasner stare it in the face, and it stares back at them, an abyss of maddening monotony. It is one of the paradoxes of insomnia that I relate to both Van Gogh's spinning delirium and its opposite in these images. Both states feel just as valid as each other, and I have sometimes felt them contemporaneously, as opposing forces pushing and pulling in the same sleepless night.

****

There has only been one instance in my adult life when sleep became easy. Or rather, it became compulsive – as much as the insomnia was, and it felt perhaps even more disturbing. I fell *into* sleep. No, not fell but hurtled, like being pushed into a bottomless well. It happened when Fauzia died in 2016, at the age of forty-five, of undiagnosed tuberculosis. She had been admitted to hospital with an unknown illness, and lay wired to a ventilator in intensive care. When the hospital called to say she had had a fatal brain haemorrhage one morning, the shock of it was too much to take in. So I began to sleep. No amount was enough and I felt increasingly worried by the long, blank nights, which did not bring relief but became as strangely burdensome as the insomnia had once felt.

I would be in bed for twelve or thirteen hours at a time but with no sense of rest or recovery when I woke. Perhaps this phenomenon was a miniature variation on the 'resignation syndrome' that the neurologist and author Suzanne O'Sullivan writes of in *The Sleeping Beauties*. She travels to Sweden to meet refugee children who have fallen into coma-like sleeps, sometimes for years, after their families' asylum applications are rejected. She calls that phenomenon a 'sleeping sickness'. That is what my sleeping felt like, forced somehow, and enervating rather than restorative. When I spoke to my doctor about it, she recommended small bursts of activity, to encourage my body back into active mode again, but even when I took her advice nothing changed. The more I slept, the more I felt filled up with fatigue. And there was the uncomfortable sense, too, that sleeping so soundly in the face of grief might be judged inappropriate by others. Friends kept asking: 'Are you able to get any sleep at all?' and I couldn't tell them I was sleeping like never before.

Dr Brigitte Steger, associate professor of modern Japanese studies at the University of Cambridge, speaks about the ancient Japanese notion of sleep as an emotional act, born out of feelings rather than will. In the Kamakura era, dating from the ninth to fourteenth centuries, the aristocratic men and women of Heian (present-day Kyoto) suffered from insomnia brought about by troubling emotional states, often grief. A family death, an emperor's illness, the absence of a lover, all inspired a sorrowful state of insomnia, which infused the poetry and literary diaries of this period. In an online seminar on historical perspectives on sleep and wellbeing, Steger describes how this insomnia was perceived as a mark of the depth of feeling of whoever was going through the sleeplessness. What I experienced in my grief was the opposite: sadness that required a narcotically numbing sleep, which was both an expression of grief and a protection against being awake to feel it.

What happens to the mind when you sleep so much? Can it do damage? The science suggests that it does: habitually sleeping for more than nine hours over a period of twenty-four hours can lead to health risks such as depression, obesity, Type 2 diabetes and heart disease, which are, paradoxically, exactly the ailments associated with a lack of sleep. I would wake up in a profound state of alarm about Fauzia's death, unable to make sense of how the doctors could have missed her diagnosis, how this ancient disease could kill in the midst of such modern technology. There was also, increasingly, a confusion about *where* I was sleeping. The over-sleep left me unpinned from my physical location. I would awaken wondering if I was in my adult life, in my own flat, or in my childhood home, in the room I later shared with Fauzia as a teenager. I would feel the dimensions of that room as I rose out of sleep, sensing Fauzia in the bed opposite mine, our parents in their bedroom next door. These confusions came regularly, my sleep saturated with a yearning to return to a place where I might seek Fauzia out.

As a teenager, I was hugely influenced by Fauzia, copying her tastes in the way that some younger sisters do. Maybe it is why I fell into such deep sleep after her death, in another, paler imitation of her absence from the world. When I stayed the night in my family home, sleeping in the room where she had lain in her last days before her death in hospital, I noticed a different quality to my over-sleeping. It felt more restful, less blank, with the sense that I could go on sleeping, peacefully, as a way to be close to Fauzia and her perpetual state of repose, which now seemed to belong to the room.

Haruki Murakami's novel *After Dark* features two sisters, the younger, Mari, mourning the older sibling, Eri, who is in a coma-like, seemingly narcoleptic state. The book takes place over a single night in Tokyo as Mari roams through the city, meeting its nocturnal characters – a trombonist, a Chinese sex worker, the manager of a 'love hotel' (a kind of brothel). All the while Eri lies in a trapped and mysterious slumber. It might be an undiagnosed illness, a psychological condition or even a radical protest at the world and her place in it – we are never sure.

Mari refuses to see her sister as 'dead', even though there seems no prospect of Eri's waking up. She looks at her sister's face and thinks that 'consciousness just happens to be missing from it at the moment: it may have gone into hiding, but it must certainly be flowing somewhere out of sight, far below the surface, like a vein of water'. This is how I saw Fauzia as she lay in hospital, after her haemorrhage. Even though we were told she'd remain on a ventilator for twenty-four hours as a formality before being pronounced dead, I kept watching for her to twitch awake, sure that it would happen. It seemed as if she was in a deep sleep, albeit so submerged by it that she had become unreachable. If we could keep her on the ventilator, which breathed in lieu of her lungs, for one more week, month, year, then there might one day be a movement of the head or hands, a stirring back to life. She looked oddly content, her lips in a half smile, all anxiety drained from her face, and it comforted me to see her this way, absorbed in such pleasant unconsciousness.

There is a magnetic quality to observing others asleep, maybe because it has a puzzling vacancy at its core: the sleeping person is there, and yet elsewhere. Where have they gone? It is the same question you might ask yourself when someone dies. I come across Andy Warhol's 1964 film, *Sleep*, which features his sleeping lover, the experimental poet and performer John Giorno. The film consists of over five hours of pieced-together footage, the camera sometimes trained on Giorno with a wide lens but also in extreme close-up. We see his magnified chest, rising and sinking, his nakedness when he turns his back to the camera and his eyelids moving as he dreams. I only watch the grainy film for the first hour and it is both tedious and captivating; at first it seems like the camera is looking at Giorno with the adoring gaze of a lover but gradually its perspective becomes more searching and obsessive. Is Warhol capturing Giorno at his most elemental and unguarded? Or is there a fear of loss there – the lover present but also betrayingly absent? It seems like Andy Warhol is both studying the physical intimacy of Giorno's sleeping body and mourning his unknowability – and psychic removal – in slumber. Giorno becomes more distant, *less* known, it seems; it is slowly apparent that he is elsewhere, inaccessible to Warhol, a vacancy. My onslaught of sleep felt like a vacancy within – as if I had lost myself, and my 'sleep personality', in its depths.

Warhol's *Sleep* is informed, evidently, by his sexuality, the relationship he has with – the perceived beauty or otherwise –

his own body and that of his male lover. (Though it is said that he originally sought out Brigitte Bardot for the project.) But, historically at least, there is something in the artistic and literary portrait of a sleeping *woman* that seems less focused on the study of sleep than on the romanticised trope of passively beatific femininity. Hence, the trope of the pathologically sleeping woman in fairy tales, from Briar Rose, unconscious for a century because of a witch's curse, to Snow White, rendered prettily comatose by a poisoned apple. Can't a prone woman be a rebel in her sleeping state, like Eri might be? There is a suggestion in Murakami's story that she has purposefully taken herself to bed, and the coma is a choice, a refusal of some kind or a protest against the world, and her role in it. Neither is she waiting for a gallant awakening by a prince, it seems.

In her lifetime, Fauzia went through long bouts of over-sleeping brought on by depression. There seemed to be a rebellion in it, too. From the age of nineteen, when she first became seriously depressed, she began holing herself up in her room, sleeping for the night and most of the following day. She would wake up late and pad around in a bathrobe, as if hungover, refusing to go to college, or find work: she was wilfully unproductive. In the medieval era, the act of daytime sleeping, for men and for women, was seen to harm one's reputation. Many still regard it as slovenly and it can be subversive for exactly this reason. For a woman, especially, to refuse to get up and assume her role in the world – which may be one of monotonous domesticity, of caring for others, or of participating in the tedious, lower-wrung machinery of capitalist productivity – it might be a defiant way to say 'no'.

What might look like inertia, or passivity, can be an active summoning of inner strength, Bruno Bettelheim suggests in his psychoanalytic interpretations of fairy tales in *The Uses of Enchantment*. He speaks of Briar Rose – Sleeping Beauty – not as an example of meek femininity but as an adolescent 'gathering strength in solitude'. Her sleep is a temporary turning inward in order to foment, mobilise and psychically prepare for the battles of adulthood to come.

A glassy-eyed, self-medicating woman in Ottessa Moshfegh's novel *My Year of Rest and Relaxation* also 'hibernates' in her New York apartment. She is a Manhattan princess, narcissistic and hard to like, who does not want to experience any of life's sharp edges. Yet there is something I recognise in her overwhelming desire to disconnect from the terrible reality of the world. She plans to sleep for a year and wake up cured of her sadness, and she is. My sleep wasn't a cure but the maelstrom of over-sleep did eventually lift and leave me feeling less numbed to my own sadness. I was glad to be returned to myself, and to my insomnia, an old friend, missed.

****

There is evidence to suggest that women sleep differently from men and feel the effects of insomnia in discrete ways. Professor Dijk cites the familiar list of causes, from lifestyle to social class, wealth and genetics, but he has also found sex-based biological factors, with differences in the brainwaves of women and men when they sleep. Women intrinsically have different circadian rhythms, which are on average six minutes shorter than men's cycles; they experience more deep (or 'slow wave') sleep and may need to sleep for longer; while a mix of social factors, from breast-feeding to lower-paid shift work, means they face higher levels of insomnia.

Other findings support the notion of gendered sleep, and show that a lack of sleep may have a greater impact on women's cardio-metabolic health than men's. In 2023, scientists at Columbia University's Irving Medical Center found that even mild sleep deprivation significantly affected women who were used to getting adequate sleep, with insulin resistance rising by more than 12 per cent overall, and over 15 per cent in pre-menopausal women, leaving them more vulnerable to type 2 diabetes.

Sleep science makes a significant connection between hormones and sleep for women in the throes of menopause. About 50 per cent of women who suffer with insomnia as they approach menopause are thought to sleep for less than six hours a night, and many do not recognise it to be a biological symptom, which arguably makes it a more bewildering experience. The cumulative effects of this sleeplessness can be so intense that some have questioned whether they might be linked to UK female suicide rates, which, according to a 2023 ONS report on suicide in England and Wales, are at their highest between the ages of fifty and fifty-four.

This brings another kind of insomnia for me, almost exactly as I turn fifty. It creeps duplicitously into my night, so I don't recognise it; I fall asleep quickly but am awake again at 4 a.m. with alarm-clock precision. This is not the organic and woozy 'biphasic' interruption believed by some to have been common in the centuries before electric light, in which communities were said to have a first and then a second sleep through the night, getting up to work or chat in between in a brief window referred to as 'the watch'. My brain is pin-sharp, as if the sleep before has been entirely restorative and I am ready to start the day, except there is a move towards a certain line of thought, a search for the fault lines of the previous day, the urgent address of an old argument or decision far in the future. And it is, in its scratchy insistence, so much like Bourgeois's scribbled red balls and Krasner's insects that I wonder if they were experiencing menopausal sleep disruption while creating the works.

Where younger insomniacs struggle to fall asleep, those in mid-life might doze off quickly but wake up in the middle of the night as a result of hormonal changes, and it is in these 4 a.m. 'reckonings' that they encounter the night-time brain, says

Dr Zoe Schaedel, a menopause specialist with a particular interest in sleep, who sits on the British Menopause Society's medical advisory council. 'Our frontal lobe [which regulates sensible, logical thought] doesn't activate as well overnight, and our amygdala [the brain's command centre for irrational feelings such as fear, rage and anxiety] takes over.' So the very nature of 4 a.m. thinking is different: in the daytime, it is primarily logical but at night, we become more rash, anxious, catastrophic. That sets off its own physiological reaction in the nervous system, with a surge of adrenaline and cortisol, as well as rising heart and breathing rates. The physical sensations are essentially a fight or flight response, specific to this twilight time.

It is some relief to have a scientific explanation for my new state of wakefulness, but there is also a distant, dissonant reminder of my father's illness in Dr Schaedel's mention of the frontal lobe and the amygdala. I know already how the latter undergoes radical changes for those with frontal-lobe dementia. It reminds me of my father's free-floating fear when he clutches my hands and feels that something alarming is about to happen, or tells far-fetched stories that remind me of his gothic imagination – the secret services are after him, the skies outside are on fire. Is it, I wonder, out of the amygdala that ghost stories arise? It is curious that this part of the brain should become so active in the night during menopause. There is something enlivening in the connection it hints at between my father and my 'night' imagination which I can't quite grasp, returning me to the question of whether my night, and sleep pattern, are connected to my father in more ways than one.

Owing to a reduction in the sleep-promoting hormone, melatonin, quality of sleep declines for everyone as we age, but women are hit with a chaotic onslaught of changes in levels of oestrogen too, which influences mood and wakefulness.

There is an irony at play in these shifts: in the reproductive years, fluctuating sex hormones are often the cause of insomnia for women, whereas it is the *lack* of these hormones in menopause that leads to the same problem. Menstruating women experience sleep problems as well: the biggest disruptions come just before a period, when oestrogen and progesterone levels are dropping, and again during ovulation, midway through the cycle. I have known this sleeplessness, the night before a period, so overpowering that it can only be born of biology, and in the days after it, the falling into thick, deep sleep, as if the release of blood brings a psychic release too.

I have not had children, so haven't experienced the sleeplessness of early motherhood, brought on by night-time feeds and the dramatic drop in progesterone after giving birth, but friends describe its crushing exhaustion, although a few talk of the serenity of pre-dawn feeds and a wakefulness that is intimate, contemplative, precious. Some menopausal women do not mind the night waking either – or at least they have adopted strategies and given purpose to it. One tells me she reflects on her day, another takes a walk in the dark, another might go out into the garden and watch the break of dawn. These positive effects tend to be predicated on being able to sleep in the following morning, or going to bed earlier the following night. Women at the lower end of the economic spectrum can't afford that luxury, and even though I cannot count myself among them, I still feel cornered by my mid-life insomnia. There are never enough days to catch up.

Between the waking, there is a welter of dreams, so many it seems like someone is changing the channels on a TV set. Where have all these stories come from? I can never recall the dreams but I know they are packed with incident, and sometimes with the sense, within the dream, that this is a continuation of plot and action picked up from the night before. Is this kind of dreaming also a function of mid-life biology? In *Mapping the Darkness*, Kenneth Miller speaks of how dreams are triggered by the pons, a part of the brain that controls breathing, heartbeat and other functions essential to the body. Dreaming makes up around 20 per cent of all sleep and is key to health. A lack of non-dream sleep is not as harmful as a loss of sleep containing dreams. One scientist testing this theory found that 'continual REM deprivation – in rats, at least – could be fatal if kept up long enough', according to Miller's book. Rats aside, this has a certain poetry to it: not dreaming can seriously harm our health. But what does it mean to have such a mountain of dreams, heaped up, one on top of the other? I wonder if it is related to the speed of my day, the quantities I fit into it. Is the tumult of dreams excess luggage, carried into the night?

Dr Schaedel says this apparent barrage of dreams is not an assault at all but an illusion, which can be explained by sleep architecture in menopause. Slow-wave sleep mostly occurs in the first half of the night and is central for biological restoration and memory. There is a reduction in this deep, non-dream sleep when oestrogen drops. So women start sleeping more lightly and waking up in the latter part of the night, in the shallower REM – or dream – phase which gives the impression of dreaming more, because you are waking up in the midst of them.

Still, I am wrong-footed by this second life in my head, this middle-aged night, as busy, as complicated and as exhausting as the day. It leaves me drained by all its drama in the morning, as if I left my body in the night and entered a hectic parallel realm in the darkness, like the twelve dancing princesses in the Grimm Brothers' fairy tale, who slip out of their bedrooms through a trapdoor to wear out their shoes with romance and revelry. That door might be a gateway to a fantastical other life, as it is for them, or to self-knowledge: a glimpse of the unknown self that takes on life, or takes over it, in the night.

When insomnia is at its most agitating, engaging the brain visually may be a way to lull ourselves back to sleep, says Dr Schaedel. This idea makes better sense now of how Bourgeois described her scribbling as 'stroking'. Maybe she instinctively knew this science, and her body – or creativity – understood what it needed for its own soothing. Maybe I would find my own recurring patterns on paper if I did the same thing, I think, and so I put a notebook beside my bed. I open it up the next morning. I know I have had a maelstrom of dreams but, when I try to discover them on paper, it is like a stuck sneeze, a lost voice. I write a few words down, but I am left straining for more. A few snatched images come back, but far more float out of view, unreachable. The next morning I can recall even fewer details, although I know I have dreamed heavily. So my odyssey of dreams evades any attempt at codification. They are determined to remain mysterious, on the other side of daytime.

Chapter 5
To dream

Maybe it is better that way. That our dreams, and night selves, remain over there, safely separate. What would happen if the trapdoor opened both ways? So that it offered not only an entry point for the twelve princesses to slide into their dreams, but for their dreams to sidle up through the trapdoor of night and stand, dripping in darkness, before their sleeping selves? Their nightmares too, for that matter. And what if these night spectres remained on the 'wrong' side of the door once they had passed through it, refusing to leave at the first sign of light?

I have felt one instance of this incursion – a porousness between my sleeping and waking self when I was in my mid-twenties. For a time, the trapdoor was flung open and my nightmares yawned out of it, to stand in my bedroom, before me, or so I felt. I was living in Teesside, as a lodger in someone else's home, in the late 1990s, and I had a series of recurring nightmares that seemed as if they had crashed through their discrete world and entered into a solid existence in mine. I had just finished my journalism training course and had jumped at a job offer as a trainee reporter, in Middlesbrough. I didn't know where the town was on a map but I was excited to find myself there, in the north-east of England. A few weeks in, I had found lodgings in a terrace house near the leafy suburbs but still only a short bus ride from the office.

I have always been nervous of sleeping in new spaces – hotels, spare rooms, even in houses I have bought and claimed as my own. Slowly, though, a space becomes mine. Except this one. The danger didn't announce itself immediately. At first, I was simply ecstatic to be here, out of student life and in gainful employment, although this town felt like it was in the doldrums, or a state of grieving. The north-east had once been a booming centre for steel manufacture, but its industry – the labour that had kept it afloat – was in sharp decline. Teesside looked like it was being hollowed out, dotted with mausoleums of a once glorious manufacturing past: the derelict ICI site in Billington and Wilton, now a wasteland of disused office buildings; the Tees Transporter Bridge in the centre of Middlesbrough, which was a wonder of engineering when it opened in 1911, but since had become the town's number one hotspot for suicides.

A clam-like Mirpuri Pakistani immigrant population lived in the town, discrete and secretive from the wider community, and the local newspaper on which I worked was reporting a series of gruesome suicides by Asian women – many of them young brides – who were drinking bleach or setting themselves alight. Bristling alongside them, in their own fulminating enclave, was the white, working-class community. We were, as a nation, in the midst of 'cool Britannia', but this corner of Britain seemed marooned in another more melancholic era. I felt alive to the adventure of this first job, but also grateful for my 'visitor' status among the volubly angry white community and their silently suicidal Pakistani counterparts.

There was something melancholic about the house I lived in, too, which I didn't pick up on straight away. It belonged to a woman in her thirties who had become debilitated by ME. When I first went to visit, she led me around the house stiffly, with the aid of a walking stick, her complexion papery white with illness. I followed her into a cosy kitchen and then a cluttered front room with a mantelpiece lined with dusty miniature Buddhas, Hindu elephant gods and many-limbed goddesses. Large, coloured crystals dangled from the room's ceiling, like glass spiders hunkering in its corners. She explained how these crystals released positive energies, and that was helpful for her

ME. I had grown up with a mother who had inherited a keen interest in homeopathic and non-allopathic medicines from her own mother, as was customary in Pakistan among her generation, and she had gone through a phase of buying crystals for their health-enhancing properties. She'd tell us jade was good for healing this ailment, lapis or amethyst for that one, so I felt comfortable enough among the glass spiders.

Upstairs, she took me to the back bedroom and said it would be mine. It was sparsely furnished, with a small fireplace and a square view of the back garden. A long corridor connected this room to hers, which had a coloured flag draped across its entrance. It was a Tibetan motif to ward off evil spirits, she told me. Her openness to, and homely display of, other belief systems made me warm to her. She had been delving into alternative therapies to find a way to manage her ME, she explained. She was on sick leave, worried about the cost of her bills, and needed a lodger to make ends meet. I should make sure to switch off corridor lights to save on energy costs, she said. I had grown up doing this so I knew I could adapt to her rule, and to the dark of her house.

I moved in the following week and at first nothing happened. I worked at the *Evening Gazette* and cycled at the weekends, coming back to the lodgings full of the gusty air and wide-open vistas of the North Yorkshire moors. But I began to feel cramped. The landlady was a domineering presence and wanted us to spend time together in the evenings when I only wanted to be her lodger. I would come home later and head straight up to my room. Slowly, I tuned into my discomfort at being there. Maybe it was the house's coldness, or its sense of permanent night due to the lack of overhead lighting. It's nothing, I told myself. I was in a new town, in someone else's home. Still, when I noticed that my bedroom door had a lock, it felt like a relief. I started sliding it shut before bedtime. Maybe locking the door was a way to claim this part of the house as my own, I thought.

Once in bed, I'd hear the draught in the corridor outside my door, so fierce that it butted against the shaft of its lock. I wondered, in a state of half-sleep, if someone was rattling it. Was it the landlady, wanting to know if I had returned home? Surely not. I came to feel thankful for the lock. Perhaps this was what it was for – to protect against the angry draught outside. I tried to push the sound out of my head, remind myself that this was an old house with cold currents even in the daytime, but the rattling got louder over time, as if intent on drawing my attention, the knocking sounds so much like human knuckles rapping on wood that I felt like calling out, 'Who's there?'

Then, one night, whatever had stood knocking outside slunk in uninvited. The noise outside stopped but this new silence brought with it the sense that something had crept under the door and was now hovering in the room at close quarters. The air felt charged, as if it bore the weight of someone other than myself. Again, I tried to dismiss this as imagination but it was an unsettling thought in itself: what had happened for me to have imagined this, and then for it to feel so palpable?

The idea of sleeping in this unpredictable darkness became filled with unaccountable risk, so I'd leave the light on at night. Still, I imagined the presence padding to my bed and leaning over to watch me as I slept, and I'd flip my eyes open the minute I felt myself nodding off. The corners of the room became incrementally, inexplicably animated. A university friend who had visited me when I'd first moved into the house had just held her first exhibition as an artist and had brought me a gift – a painting of a woman holding a large, glittering fish. It looked like an image arisen from the sea, so beautiful it took my breath away when I first saw it. The woman had snaking orange-red curls, the fish a bloodied hook through its gasping mouth. It looked alive, just, but agonised – its fins splayed, its rimless eye already glassy although its scales glistened silver, magenta, turquoise. Its entire body shone with thick slicks of paint that gave it the look of permanent, oily wetness. I had hung the painting above the little fireplace and now I began to feel the swirl of the woman's red hair, the cold of her alabaster skin, the glare of her eyes, each time I passed it. When I switched off the light, I felt her continuing to stare, and then imagined her stepping out of the canvas to make her way towards me, like Sadako, the demon with a curtain of hair across her face, who climbs out of the TV in the Japanese horror film *Ring*. Maybe it was *her* presence I felt at night. Or perhaps some other unseen thing that had inhabited this room before me, with which I now found myself in mutually hostile communion. Once that idea occurred to me, it grew steadily bigger.

A few months in, I was badly sleep-deprived and I began to have recurring nightmares. In my sleep I felt awake but unable to move, with a great weight pressing down on my chest. It was pinning down my arms and pushing all the air out of my lungs. These episodes became more frequent and intense until one night, as the weight descended on my chest, bulldozing the air out of it, I saw a tiny pair of pink hands flash bright in the darkness. They were the size of a newborn's and I was staggered that something so small could exert such enormous force. I felt a spark of tenderness but that quickly turned to terror. Was the great weight I felt exerted by a *child*? Had a baby inhabited this room once? Had a baby perhaps died here? I wanted to ask the landlady, but the question seemed so unreasonable and I knew that its answer might have terrified me more. I became afraid of sleep itself: if I stayed awake, I wouldn't be ambushed by the crushing weight, and the unknown force that exerted it. So I lay in bed, simultaneously desperate to sleep and to stay awake.

I carried on returning home later and later, dreading the room and its darkness. The final fright came six months in, when I got back just before midnight, switching on the light to see a small black bird, perhaps a baby crow, standing silent and watchful on the desk, in the centre of the room, its feet spread flat on the wood.

When I moved abruptly back to the door, it remained still, following me with its eyes, its head cocked. There seemed such a preternatural calmness around it that I half expected it to speak. The lack of sleep over so many months might have left my mind wobbly and unreliable, but at the time this felt like the solid, familiar world colliding with another reality, no longer ambivalent knocks and sleepy imaginings but a winged creature of jet black feathers and shining, inscrutable eyes that were as hard as zirconia.

I fled down the corridor to wake the landlady and splutter out my story. I stayed outside while she went into the room and I expected her to come back out to say there was no bird inside but instead she slid out to get a blanket so she could gather it up and let it out.

'Maybe it came in from the window?' I said, but she told me the window was locked and she would need to find the key if we were to open it.

'It was so tired it dropped to the ground,' she said, afterwards.

'Where did it come from?' I asked, and she pointed to the chimney, saying it had probably fallen down and scrambled around the room in panic until it had exhausted itself and stood waiting, where I found it, for rescue.

Whatever its source of entry, to me the bird was a sign the invisible thing that had insinuated itself into the room was now announcing its presence in no uncertain terms. It took me three days to find another room. The landlady seemed shocked by my sudden departure and I don't remember what reason I gave. I didn't tell her that I was too scared to be in her home for another night longer. A few weeks later, I noticed that the painting my friend had given me, of the red-haired woman and the fish, wasn't with the rest of my possessions. I contacted the landlady. I had, I remembered, taken it down and put it behind the wardrobe out of fear. Perhaps I left it there, I said. But, no, she told me, nothing of mine remained. Still,

I imagined the painting continuing to hang above the fireplace, the room's draught whipping the woman's wet red ringlets around her face, the fish clasped tightly to her chest, with the tenderness of a mother who is either mourning its imminent death or smothering the life out of it, as a mercy killing.

****

Even at the time, I knew what I was experiencing in Middlesbrough was sleep paralysis, while simultaneously believing there was more to it than that. I have recounted the episode many times to family and friends. In each retelling, I have tried to decode my terror, but instead encounter the story's confusions anew. Did I really hear the angry knocking? Why did I become so afraid of the painting, which was after all a gift from a friend? Wasn't the bird proof of something beyond sleep paralysis, or was I attaching one thing to another and constructing a scary story out of it? Opposing beliefs can co-exist in your mind, and I both believed and disbelieved that there was something sinister in the room. Perhaps that is the nature of irrational fear: it has the ability to exist alongside the rational, and chip away at it.

Friends reacted differently. 'Are you even sure there was a bird there?' said one. Of course, I told her, my landlady saw it, and she struggled to get it out of the window. Maybe she was doing that to placate you, because she saw how distressed you had become, my friend said. I wasn't willing to entertain that notion. It was too chilling. But yes, of course, the charge I felt in the room must have been the weight and dread of my fear, building night after night. However much I believed this was a straightforwardly happy and productive new phase of my life, there were pressures around me. Maybe I felt more threatened, more alien, in this unfamiliar environment than I had admitted to myself.

The phenomenon of sleep paralysis is relatively under-researched but it has an exact science behind it, and its key symptoms match those I experienced: a mistaken sense of wakefulness while still asleep, the feeling of a weight bearing down on your chest, an inability to move, and an overwhelming sense of a menacing presence nearby. A series of physiological stages takes us into deep sleep before the rise back up into the 'dream' phase, otherwise known as REM. The cycle repeats over the night, the REM periods getting longer each time. It is when we are in REM that our limbs are paralysed by our brain, to stop us acting out our dreams. The disorder comes in this phase of the sleep cycle, when breathing and heart rate slow down, and brain waves change their patterns.

Sleep paralysis can strike just once or recur nightly for years, and research suggests that it affects a tiny minority – under 8 per cent of the population – with two kinds of people more susceptible, according to a 2011 academic study by Brian Sharpless and Jacques Barber: students (28 per cent of cases) and psychiatric patients (almost 32 per cent), with a slightly larger proportion of women reporting such experiences. Its classic causes include those I was unwittingly grappling with: the unfamiliar new home and the loop of stress and sleep deprivation that is known to exacerbate the condition. When I read other people's testimonies, they sound like a mix of hoax, paranoia and psychosis: baroque reports of red-eyed monsters, talking cats, shadow-men or aliens looming in the room. My story of tiny hands and baby crows could sit comfortably among these outlandish accounts.

Christopher French, emeritus professor and head of the anomalistic psychology research unit at Goldsmiths, University of London, says evidence suggests that the phenomenon is inherited. 'We know there is a genetic component and a tendency for it to run in families.' This reminds me of the research which shows that sleep is rooted in biology, but it also chimes with notions of spiritual 'second sight' as a quality passed down, from parent to child.

In its most benign form, sleep paralysis is nothing more than the inability to move while sinking into sleep or emerging from it, says Professor French. But often it comes with more disturbing components: sleepers can feel the keen sense of a malign presence in the room, which may manifest as a fantastical or otherworldly being. The intensity of the experience activates the amygdala, the part of the brain which controls our perception of threat, so even knowing you are in its grip does not take away the acute fear. While dreaming is fraught with unknowns, says Professor French, what *is* known is that perception, hallucination and imagination emanate from the same area of the brain.

My father comes back to mind. He has told me many times that he is visited by his parents at night. They stand over his bed, he has said, and it's not clear from his account if he is seeing them while he is asleep or awake. Whether they are classified as dream visions or hallucinations born out of his dementia, they are powerful antidotes to his profound forgetfulness. His parents, consigned to oblivion in the daytime, rise up in the night from some undamaged recess of his brain. Are they more clearly sensed when his brain switches to a night consciousness, and the amygdala is triggered? It sounds like a childhood tucking-in ritual – a soothing mental picture like the rocking motion of Bourgeois's drawings. It is, whatever its cause, a reminder of incontrovertible parental love.

Superstitious thinking has accompanied the experience of sleep paralysis down the ages, sometimes with fatal consequences. Professor French posits the theory that historical accounts of witchcraft involving visions in the night might in fact have been sleep paralysis episodes experienced by the accuser, including those testimonies presented in the Salem witch trials. While the physical processes of sleep paralysis – the illusion of being awake, the inability to move, the feeling of a weight on the body – are universal, the visions seen are bound up with local cultural tropes, such as the *mara*, the ancient Scandinavian name for a tormenting or suffocating spirit that attacks a sleeper and is often depicted as a horse.

The most common mythologies around the disorder in the West stem from the ancient Roman notion of the incubus – a male demon believed to lie on a sleeping woman in readiness for sexual intercourse – or the succubus, its female equivalent. Brian Sharpless writes of how some instances of sleep paralysis manifest as sexual assault hallucinations; he looks back at historical accounts of alleged assault during the night to find the scientific features of the disorder present, although of course not all nocturnal assaults are merely dreamed. But in these cases of sleep paralysis, there is the disturbing illusion of acts of sexual violation taking place. Professor French has documented numerous such contemporary accounts, which are experienced as rapes. What is especially unsettling is the physicality, he says. To the women, the nightmare feels like a real violation. In medical circles, the phenomenon of 'incubus disorder' – when someone is convinced that they have had a forced sexual encounter with a non-human force – treads on similar ground, although psychiatrists suggest this is, in fact, an instance of psychosis rather than that of a sleep disorder.

Henry Fuseli's 1781 painting *The Nightmare* is famously interpreted as a depiction of sleep paralysis, although it would not have been called that at the time of its painting. But it sums up the queasy sense of violation that Professor French has documented. A Swiss-born artist who settled in London, Fuseli had a fascination with dreams and visions. *The Nightmare* features a woman lying supine (a position that leaves you more susceptible to the disorder), with her arms and head tipping off the bed and an imp-like creature squatting on her chest. The head of a horse floats in the chiaroscuro gloam around her, suggesting a stalking menace nearby.

In its day, *The Nightmare* so captivated the public that Fuseli produced at least three different versions of it. The art historian Christopher Frayling writes of how the image divided opinion when it was displayed in the Royal Academy's summer show of 1782. Audiences were scandalised and seduced in equal measure, with over 55,000 people turning out during the exhibition's two-month run. Some hailed it as a 'sublime' evocation of nightmarish terror while others said it was a tawdry, sexually depraved crowd-pleaser.

It is easy to see why the painting stirred such antagonistic feelings. It is resonant with gothic lustre and spectacle, its red velvet backdrop resembling theatre curtains. The woman might be sleeping, or swooning in post-orgasmic languor. But equally, she might be dead. Some see a coded quasi-bestiality in it – the sense that sex has taken place with the hairy creature resting on the woman's midriff. Fuseli, at the time, had been rejected by Anna Landolt, the woman he loved, who had become engaged to another man. An unfinished portrait is sketched on the reverse of *The Nightmare* which some suggest is Fuseli's drawing of Landolt, and critics have seen a likeness to Fuseli in the impish creature who squats on her chest on the front. So both sides of the painting together create a double-portrait: a disturbingly accurate depiction of sleep paralysis and also an angry fantasy by a spurned lover who seeks to crush the woman he once loved: you might read it as a kind of historical revenge porn.

****

Science tells us we can be asleep and awake at the same time, as implausible as that sounds. There are 'localities' in the brain that are awake when other parts are in repose, says Dr Leschziner in *The Nocturnal Brain: Nightmares, Neuroscience and the Secret World of Sleep*. So sleep is not always a 'global' phenomenon but one in which 'deep sleep and full wakefulness lie at the extremes of a spectrum'.

I recognise something important in this contradictory duality. The liminal state that I experienced in Middlesbrough, wavering on the borderline of wakefulness and sleep, is a reminder of the multitudinous state of being. We are a multiplicity of selves, one part sometimes clashing with the other or lying in ambush, keen to contradict or disprove our own truths. I didn't really think the room was inhabited by anyone other than myself, but was also absolutely convinced that it was. Even now, knowing the science, I feel the weight of both truths, theories, stories – whatever I choose to call them.

In sleep paralysis 'different parts of the brain are clashing', says Dr Leschziner, and this, if taken as a metaphor, aptly expresses the contradictory beliefs that are simultaneously held, felt and denied. I know the disturbance in Middlesbrough came from within me, but the idea that there was something in the room itself does not leave me. I think of contacting the landlady again, but discover she moved out long ago. So I write a letter: 'Dear Resident, I lived in your back bedroom over two decades ago . . .' I keep the details vague, but even as I compose it the letter strikes such a peculiarly opaque note that I expect no reply.

A message arrives a few days later; it is from Jo, a nurse, and Brian, a science teacher. They have two teenagers and the eldest, Holly, aged sixteen, sleeps in that room. They are friendly, curious, and they invite me to visit them. We discover that we have a mutual friend in common, Michelle, a former journalist and friend from my *Evening Gazette* days who went to school with Brian. Middlesbrough is a small enough town for such a coincidence. Michelle says she will meet me off the train and take me to Jo and Brian's house now, my former lodgings then. The night before, I am surprised to find myself unable to sleep. Just as I begin to drift off, I wrench myself awake and stare out at the untrustworthy dark. After all these years, the fear still has a hold.

The street looks much as it did twenty-five years ago. Smart terrace houses, some with stained glass details in their front windows. But inside, when Jo opens the door, the house has been transformed; it now has a cool Scandi modernity to it. Walls have been knocked down and patio doors installed so that light pours in from the garden. There are fresh flowers on the kitchen table and a trendy blackboard which reads: *Welcome, Arifa!*

Jo and Brian are warm and open; they would have to be, I think, to allow a stranger to enter their bright, airy home with her peculiar story about its past. For a while we sit talking in the kitchen. They never met my landlady, but took over a property they felt was dark and dated. They gutted much of it, and when they give me a tour of the rooms downstairs, I am left wide-eyed by the changes. It is not so much the physical renovations that surprise me. It's that the atmosphere of the house feels so different.

I tell them my story, beginning with the sleep paralysis, and Jo says she has suffered from it too, mostly as a child and then as a nursing student in Oxford, where she met Brian. She has worked through the night in various hospital units, and is familiar with the slow, grinding fatigue that such work brings. When I ask them about any odd instances in the room upstairs, they are not instantly dismissive. There was an incident with a bird, a year after they moved in, Jo says. She was painting the chimney breast in the back bedroom when Holly, then two years old, heard a noise inside it. A pigeon had fallen down it and, because the chimney was stuffed with newspapers, it couldn't escape. They got it out eventually, but it died as soon as they released it. 'It fell straight to the ground,' says Jo, just like my landlady's description of the exhausted bird she released from the room when I slept there. They also found a starling in the front room, Brian says. His father covered the chimneys with cowls after that. Their neighbours have done the same thing; trapped birds are not uncommon here.

Holly did go through a period of hearing unaccountable scratching – 'like an animal's clawing' – coming from beneath the floorboards in the room, but this could have been down to the problems they had with mice over the years. The more I listen, the sillier I feel for coming here with my tale of tiny pink hands and baby crows. Jo waves away my apology: 'I think our brains want to make a story from things we don't understand.' Still, I am unsettled when they suggest I go up to the room on my own. The household's two cats are toasting themselves by a heater just outside it. Inside, I feel a noticeable drop in temperature, but it does not look like the same room at all. It is full of bright, sparkly things: a wall plastered with pictures, a guitar propped against the fireplace, and a cloth bag printed with the words 'Let's Fill This Town With Artists'. I stay a while, hearing the others murmuring downstairs. The cats continue to sleep. There is nothing to be scared of here.

It is when I have left Middlesbrough and arrived back in London that the visit sets off a train of thought: how difficult I found the landlady and her controlling maternal care, which left me feeling like a forcibly adopted daughter. It must have been why I took to spending so much time in my room. She wanted more of me than I was willing to give. When I told her I was leaving, she burst into tears, crying with an intensity I found curious. We simply weren't that close. She said her tears were because of the loss of my rent money, but I am not sure I believed it was as simple as that.

What is clearer to me now is that, just as I was going through an anxious time, so she might have been too, trapped in the house by her sickness. Maybe I picked up on an abstracted sense of that unhappiness, and I felt it as a threat to me, somehow, as I lay half asleep in my bedroom at the opposite end of the corridor from hers. And then, just as I am getting ready to go to bed back in London, the painting my friend gave me flashes into my mind. The woman's swirling red hair, the same colour, I realise, as the landlady's, and the sickly white pallor. That woman, staring out of the dark at me, was my watchful landlady. *She* is the presence that I found so unsettling. Imagined terrors, I think, so often turn out to be domestic and mundane. The house is not languishing in sickness, nor is it filled with the dark anymore, because Jo and Brian's sunny family are in it now. It has become light, warm. *Welcome, Arifa!*

The sleep paralysis comes back once more after that. Decades after Middlesbrough, I go to sleep and feel a shapeless presence expanding towards me, hostile in its pinioning of first my arms, then my torso, coming to a heavy rest on my chest. There is a familiar yet still elemental fear, but it is not all I feel. Alongside it is a prick of anger at the brick-like thing pressing into me. This feeling is tiny at first, but it grows and grows as the weight bears down suffocatingly, until I am no longer fending off an attack. I have become the aggressor, seeking to do violence. I feel incensed by the nameless force, I want to overpower it. Slowly the weight lifts, as if in retreat, slowly I wake up, still fizzing with anger, and then surprise. What had seemed so monstrous, perhaps all the more so because I knew it rose from within me, could be challenged and resisted; I could enter the liminal space between day and night, sleep and wakefulness, and push the darkness to the other side, back into its underworld.

Part 3

Midnight wandering

Chapter 6
Street theatre

My early family life was itinerant, furtive in its poverty, and shaped by lessons in invisibility that were welcome because, as a child of immigrants in the late 1970s and '80s in the UK, it felt safer to remain unseen. When we returned to London from Lahore, in the winter of 1978, we found ourselves homeless and hiding out in a derelict building in Hampstead, in the hope that no one would notice us. We *were* noticed and housed more securely in a first-floor flat in Primrose Hill, where my mother still lives. But in those months of secret destitution, I learned how to move through the world as a child, unnoticed.

We had so little money that our flat remained unfurnished and it took years for it to look like a home. Going out felt like freedom and walking was what we did as a family, often after dark. We'd observe the night's winding down, the rush of people after the eleven o'clock pub closures, the dog walkers and the surreptitious, shadowy goings-on. My parents had an unhappy marriage but would reach an entente, going out together to walk around the park and returning with a camaraderie between them that was rare in the day. They would tell us what they'd seen in the neighbourhood as if wandering around the streets contained an inherent drama.

One night, they returned rattled and breathless because my mother was convinced she had seen a djinn on a dark turn in Primrose Hill park. My father said he wasn't sure, but she was adamant. It was just a few years after we had emigrated, and if I felt homesickness after leaving Lahore, at the age of five, my parents must have felt it so much more acutely. They'd left Pakistan reluctantly because my father couldn't find a good enough job to keep us there, but once in London, they seemed to turn their backs on it, as if they felt betrayed, never taking us back for holidays. Maybe my mother could not disentangle herself from that past as cleanly as she would have liked, because here was a haunting that had followed her almost four thousand miles to her adoptive home. Or maybe the djinn was a manifestation of the fearful forces she felt around us in our new anti-immigrant environment – a sense of being stalked by them in the night. Either way, it was not the first vision my mother reported seeing and as children we guffawed at or disputed her accounts, yet we seemed to believe in them too – the same contradictory doubleness I found in my own haunting in Middlesbrough, so many years later.

Our flat was always cold and badly lit, it seemed, and my brother, sister and I were more scared of this darkness, inside, than that beyond it, outside. Our parents didn't tell us then, or for years afterwards, but the previous resident had been an elderly woman who had died inside the flat. Because the space remained unfurnished for so long after we moved in, it kept its unhomely, emptied out quality, as if we were temporarily camping there, rather than inhabiting it more fully. At night, especially upstairs, around the bedroom that I variously shared with Fauzia and Tariq, the darkness seemed to expand and acquire a spaciousness in which shadows gathered shape and solidity.

Fauzia would whisper of all the things she saw in its dark corners. There were two old women who stood just outside our bedroom. She had seen them with knitting needles in their hands, muttering. Maybe our stint of homelessness in Hampstead had left her, as the eldest, more affected, seeing danger lurking where there was none. But then, Tariq saw an old woman slumped in that same corner. He was eight, and by then slept in the box room downstairs. He had come up to go to the toilet when he saw the figure, hunched in one corner of the hallway, close to our door.

He was so scared he slept with our parents that night, but neither me nor Fauzia were told of what he saw until many years later.

I ask him about it now, and my brother recalls the woman vividly. She was tiny, shrivelled, and wearing a ratty shawl. She seemed not to see him. It didn't feel to him as if she was a threat, rather that he had momentarily crossed wires with another, equally solid but discrete world. His certainty puzzles me because he is such an unlikely candidate for supernatural sightings. I had assumed that he was the least affected by our departure from Lahore and the desolation of the squat, that he was too young to have absorbed the anti-immigrant hostility around us as fully as Fauzia and I had done. That assumption might have been wrong and he could have been more frightened of this new world, and home, than I realised.

More recently, when I see how my mother has aged, how frail she looks at eighty, I find myself skittering into magical thinking, wondering whether Tariq might have channelled a vision of our home, with our mother in it as she is now, living alone. Did he see a ghost of the future? Or maybe the flat's previous resident was still exerting herself as its rightful occupier. The hunched old woman remains a puzzle, remembered every time I pass that corner in the flat, even now.

Then, the darkness outside felt comparatively safe, the streets emptier and more neutral after dark. So we carried on walking. It was a habit passed down by our father, who talked often of his childhood ramblings in Shimla – explorations into nature with his brothers, and playfully aimless wanderings that lasted the whole day. He spoke with such a nostalgic ache, the stories carrying the unspoken trauma of that early loss. My father had originally arrived in London in the 1950s as a twenty-something, and he'd encountered many other similarly single men from the Caribbean, the Indian subcontinent, Poland, Yugoslavia who had all travelled to the UK to forge new lives. He spoke vividly about this time too, and of these men, when I was a child. Because he had little money, he spent much of his time walking in public spaces, exhilarated to be in this iconic capital city, even while remaining pushed to its fringes. All the photographs we have of him from those years, when he was renting single rooms in west London boarding houses, are outside: on street corners and in parks. He stands, snappily dressed, in front of a flowerbed in Golders Hill, or on a bench in Shepherd's Bush. There is no photo of him inside.

Those pictures have a bittersweet romance to them, conjuring the tight group of Windrush-era Caribbean men from Sam Selvon's novel *The Lonely Londoners*, who came to the 'mother country' only to encounter a British population who did not want them there, and who were rising up against 'foreigners'. Like my father, Selvon's posse walk around the landmarks of the city, by day and by night, barely able to believe they are Londoners, however much they are reminded of being outsiders in it. Selvon knits their radical joy with pangs of disappointment, disconnection and loneliness so lyrically. It is easy to imagine my father as one of them, walking the night for pleasure, finally able to roam the country that held out its hand to him in invitation, only to whip it away on arrival, in the invisible safety of urban darkness.

As children, he took us on epic wanderings that lasted almost the entire day. Whenever he could, he would drag us back out in the evenings, after dinner. Stories often accompanied these walks, and they became more gothic after dark, with a thrilling, fairground fear to them. I don't remember any one story, but they all featured demonic creatures that terrorised their victims: djinns that stood under trees and took possession of souls, daayans that ripped into human flesh with bare hands and ate their innards. Walking became its own night-time entertainment, always accessible, free and democratic. We would weave through the neighbourhood, slowing down when we got to the well-heeled heart of Primrose Hill, peering into the big bay windows of these Georgian homes and drawing our breath at the scenes of refinement and comfort within, extravagance way beyond our means.

This was how we observed the world, and there was an illicit wonder to our voyeurism. We would move on for fear of being spotted, although we never were, and there was again a sense of being unseen in the night, outsiders in more ways than one. To walk in any area we chose, however wealthy, was a leveller; there was no street off limits. For us, as for Selvon's men, this walking became its own pleasurable pursuit. We were the city's awkward new inhabitants, but its far more confident night-time tourists.

Just as trauma can be passed down, joy can be inherited; I felt my father's passion for walking as my own, and I think Fauzia and Tariq did, too. Walking at night remained a ritual in adolescence, but now without our parents. Fauzia and I went out together as teenagers, and we grew to trust the night. It is ironic, given how scared my father was of the dark inside, with all the forces he imagined roving in it, that he should be so assured when walking out in it. My inheritance of these two opposing factors has its own double-edge: the city's darkness has never scared me, despite its evident, well-documented dangers. Fauzia and I absorbed, through our nocturnal adventures, my father's unquestioned male entitlement to the outside darkness, impervious to the fear of predation or attack; it was only later on, as an adult, I 'learned' to feel this fear.

For us, it was the day that presented the greater predatory dangers: walking to and from school, we would often be ambushed by 'flashers' – baleful, middle-aged men in raincoats who looked possessed and would stop us to tell bizarrely winding stories that we didn't want to hear. They resembled the comical perverts we saw in Benny Hill's TV sketch show in the 1980s, but they still terrified us. We never met them at night, and it might be one reason why those walks felt safe. Fauzia and I would walk arm-in-arm, murmuring to each other about what had happened in the day, how fed up we felt, who was to blame. Our walking had no journey plan. We turned onto the next street and then back around again.

I wonder where Tariq was during this time; he tells me that he was out, too, taking off into the darkness after dinner with his gang of neighbourhood friends, many of them children of Greek, Kurdish and Bangladeshi immigrants. They'd romp around Hampstead Heath, an unruly span of parkland: 'You couldn't be seen, so it was more exciting,' says my brother of these excursions with the posses of local boys. Some nights, they would walk to the West End or Leicester Square, observing its hedonism but too young to partake in it. Or they'd sit and talk in the dark corners of Primrose Hill park: 'We even had our own bench,' Tariq tells me. As they got older, they started going up to Kite Hill, which overlooked both his boys' school and the girls' school that Fauzia and I went to next door, and which is close to my home now. They'd enter into the bracken-filled woodland behind the hill that is canopied with birches. There, they'd collect firewood to light small fires, only stamping them out and scarpering when they saw the light of the park keeper's Jeep. My brother's fire-lighting misadventures sound like my father's stories of Shimla. 'We'd only go home to eat,' he says, and the memory amuses me for his gang's feral independence. They could only have been eleven or twelve at the time. His present-day circle of friends still includes several of those boys; they have never lost touch. It is as if a brotherly alliance was formed in those night-time rituals. There are gangs of boys in the same park now, straddled between childhood and adolescence, loitering in the dark. I see them not as threats or social menaces but as a benign wolf pack, forging friendships in the thrill of the city's night.

I started going out on my own when Fauzia refused to come with me. Slowly, her life began to veer off course. She got into trouble at school for misbehaving, and started staying in for days on end, too depressed to leave the house, then dropping out of a prestigious art school because she lost all confidence in herself. By her late teens, she was battling an eating disorder which dogged her for most of her life, becoming more acute as the years wore on, and always growing more compulsive at night. Often she'd pay me or Tariq to go around the corner and bring back a bag of food from the late-night supermarket. I'd drag myself out reluctantly to do so, but then I'd push on for a longer walk, becoming energised by the night. I don't remember any single route but there are isolated snapshots of memory from which I could piece together a nightly circuit: leaving the house after 10 p.m., the sense of release from the cramped, overheated family fray, where my parents were forever pitched in battle, and then the freedom of the dark, bigger and more elastic the further I ploughed it.

Virginia Woolf writes of needing a pretext for a walk in her 1927 essay 'Street Haunting: A London Adventure'. She decides she needs a new pencil, so ambles across town with that sole purpose in mind. It gives her a focus as she dips imaginatively into the minds of those she passes on her journey, which is the actual purpose of the walk. In my trips, I drifted along the same roads many times a night, circling back on myself and never venturing far. I didn't have an aim, like Woolf's pencil, nor did I walk to observe the world like an urbane flâneur, striding the streets to record their kinetic sights. In *Wanderers: A History of Women Walking*, Kerri Andrews draws pen-portraits of notable, maverick female walkers whose wanderings are full of discovery, daring and exploration, from Elizabeth Carter, an eighteenth-century 'rambling genius' who walked the Kent east coast, to Anaïs Nin's bold strolls across Paris by night in the 1920s and '30s, and Cheryl Strayed's 2013 backpacking odyssey along the Pacific Crest Trail.

But then there is Dorothy Wordsworth, William's sister and a poet herself, whose walking seems different from the rest. She had a habit of looping her favourite paths circuitously in the day and then again by night. Andrews speaks of the value in this repeating movement when Dorothy relocates to the Lake District with William, to live in their original family home, Dove Cottage, in Grasmere, from which she had been exiled following the death of her parents, and which had to become known to her afresh in adulthood: 'Becoming acquainted with her new home meant, for Dorothy, walking and knowing it in every mood and every light.' She walked over favourite paths repeatedly in the evenings and on moonlit nights, feeling safe to do so because they were so intimately familiar. I see my own hamster-like circuits in Dorothy's walks, which help to ground her in her environment as she experiences it anew. The retreading has a ritualised purpose, and is not, as I had thought my repetitive circuits to be, an unambitious meandering that lacks the curiosity or brio of those other women walkers in Andrews' book.

Perhaps, after our emigration, the walking was a seeking, of sorts. In Pakistan, I had felt certain of myself. In London, I was quiet, shy, unsure of my place in the world. The circling of the streets in darkness was a way to re-find myself, each step leading me closer to calling myself a Londoner. Once I got into my stride, I'd feel released, and then transformed. Tariq tells me he would often do the same thing, walking the same roads over the course of a single night. Or, he'd knock for Ian, a friend of Hungarian and Irish heritage who lived on the same housing estate, and together they'd take a bus to its last stop and then catch the same number bus back home, straight away. They might do this several times a night, travelling in loops, no destination in mind, the purpose not arrival, nor return, exactly, but the repetition of the ride itself. For two or three hours every evening, they'd sit on these buses, sometimes not talking, he says. Through these circles, the back-and-forth of the ritual, Tariq and Ian were taking in the sight of the city by night, but also claiming their place in it, just as I was doing in my walking circuits. Touring the night was a way of learning to feel at home on these streets and, ultimately, to find our way towards becoming Londoners.

****

For decades afterwards, I became too busy to walk. I felt it was a waste of time to wander the streets as I had done, growing up. There was a vagrancy about it, a slow-paced sense of killing time, which didn't match the speed of my adult life. Kite Hill, the park up the road, had long since become uninteresting. It was filled with yapping dogs and bored crows pecking at the grass. But in the summer of 2020, when the world came to a standstill during the Covid pandemic, I began venturing to the park again, just for exercise at first. The days were hot and long, every evening exactly the same. Soon the walks became longer, extending into the night, and I would often come back home past 1 a.m. In our new socially distanced reality, this was a way to congregate while remaining safely apart. Tariq and his family were the same. When I phoned them in the evenings, they'd switch the call to video and I'd see them as shadows or silhouettes, eyes flashing as they walked through empty parkland, dimly lit streets, overgrown graveyards.

It felt liberating to be out in the park, in communion with my past. I would leave my house after dark, when the streets were almost empty, and as I walked I spotted other women. We barely looked at each other, but I felt reassured by their presence. There were so many things to fear in the pandemic but, for me, being alone outside at night was not one of them. On the way up to the hill, nestling on the park's fringes, was my old secondary school, now mostly hidden behind high, prison-like gates, with the same bike sheds at one side and the door to the old block that I thought I'd long forgotten. The walk along the hill itself was a sharp, breathless one but rewarding in its panoramic view of the city, stilled below miles of moving sky, as handsome as a postcard. Why had I remained indifferent to the park's proximity for so long? I wondered, as I began walking my old teenage circuit around the school, and the hill.

The Scottish author Linda Cracknell writes about returning to familiar paths in *Doubling Back: Paths Trodden in Memory*, and how this repetition has led her to intimations of her past, present and future selves. The act of re-treading old or well-worn routes across landscapes is, she says, a simultaneous glancing forward and backward to who you were, are, might become. It is both reminder and discovery. It also offers an encounter with an area's greater historical past, and connections with those who have trodden those paths before you. Dorothy Wordsworth writes similarly about the sense of meeting ourselves by retreading routes – in her case the paths of her childhood around Dove Cottage.

The park's walkways certainly bring memories crashing back: traipsing across the flats beneath the hill every morning, head down, to get to school on time; running the steep circuit around it for PE class and cramping with stitch on the skid down the hill; slouching around the tennis courts with mannered insouciance as a self-conscious sixth-former. But even though the park's big candyfloss clouds and mobs of crows are virtually unchanged, I do not think it familiar, exactly, nor do I even feel as if I am walking the paths I trod in my past. Too much has happened since then and, if anything, there is a clashing congregation of selves, one looking at the other, in judgement. The person I have become is glancing askance at the crushingly shy thirteen-year-old in the stuffy pleats of school uniform and royal purple tie, and then the boyish, bookish sixteen-year-old, hiding under layers of sports clothes in the height of summer. If those spectres were to spot me now, as I am, what would they see? A middle-aged stranger, privileged beyond recognition, who would be judging them just as harshly in return, I suspect.

But there *is* a strange synergy between the old nocturnal meanderings of my younger years and my work as a theatre critic now. Both interactions are observational and occur after dark. While every theatre in the land was shut that summer, my wandering across London might have been an attempt to fill the spaces left in my life. I felt newly at home in this night, looking at its dramas with fresh eyes.

It's close to midnight in London and I am staring out of the window at the first of the year's full moons. It is a Wolf Moon, to invoke its Native American name, orbiting to fullness at 11.48 p.m. Bruno Bettelheim, in his reading of 'Little Red Riding Hood', likens the story's wolf to nocturnal danger and speaks of the night devouring the day in the wolf's attack on Little Red Riding Hood's grandmother. I think of this as I observe the cold, lupine quality to the moon's returning stare tonight.

I am aiming to get to Waterloo Bridge but have to fight against the pull of the warmth and light inside to usher myself out. As soon as I'm on my way, I'm glad to be freewheeling my bike along empty roads. The cold air is astringent and blasts me awake. I have cycled to Waterloo innumerable times, so the route is familiar: the empty wastes of high street along Kentish Town, the down-and-outs of Camden with plastic bags, cardboard and bedding under their arms, the empty office blocks that stand like brick sentinels, their strip-lit windows gazing blankly out at darkness.

I slow down when I see the familiar coffee shop at the turning onto Waterloo Bridge and begin to walk, my bike rolling beside me. This is where Charles Dickens began his night walks over a hundred and fifty years ago, leaving his home in Bloomsbury in the early hours and wandering the city for hours on end. A lifelong insomniac, Dickens walked from the docks to the betting shops, hospitals, morgues and workhouses, sweeping past prostitutes, street children, thieves, carousers, law enforcers, Bedlamites and pie-men, and documenting everything he saw in a series of night writings. He spoke of these fast-paced walks as solitary acts of 'self-exhaustion', a flight both from his everyday life and from himself.

I have come out to retrace his route, having followed his circular journeys on a modern-day map of London with my finger. He walked a brisk pace for miles each night, sometimes all the way to Kent, observing all kinds of gloomy sights along the way and describing this bridge with particular ghoulishness. Tonight, it has an air of dereliction, with just a few tourists wearing bum-bags and lone commuters walking with a rushed forward purpose. The night population is largely male and they either take darting glances as they pass or walk head down, inattentively, seemingly in a zombie glaze.

I feel an apprehension in being out on my own at this time that I would not have felt a few months ago: the pandemic pause is almost over, the city's machinery is whirring back to life. The benign nights of lockdown are gone too, it seems. The danger is back; it's business as usual.

In Dickens's day, this bridge was a ghastly place of suicide, murder and black, muddy depths. 'The river had an awful look,' he writes in his 1860 essay, 'Night Walks': 'The buildings on the banks were muffled in black shrouds, and the reflected lights seemed to originate deep in the water, as if the spectres of suicides were holding them to show where they went down.' There is a sinister imagination at work here, and, reading his description, I can see where Dickens's stories came from. I wonder how much this city darkness inspired his fiction, and his ghost stories in particular.

Behind me on the bridge I feel an approaching figure; I twitch, turn around and am surprised to see it is an older woman, small and slightly bent, whose leisurely pace strikes me as odd for this time of night. But the presence of another woman is always a comfort after dark. She stops to look at the water, which is nothing more than a flat black sheet, before taking a few steps and pausing again, as a tourist might in daylight, when there is a clearer view of London's skyline and its landmarks to point at and admire. I look away and when I turn my head back to her I realise she is ahead of me, but still dallying, craning her neck over the bridge. It strikes me as peculiar that the woman is pulling a shopping trolley behind her. Is she one of life's strays, not wandering for leisure but out of necessity, for want of somewhere safe to rest? A fog has lowered over the river and I try to follow her path but the woman, as solid as the bridge a minute ago, is gone. I wonder if she quickened her pace or if I have momentarily tuned into another frequency, like my eight-year-old brother did in our family home, and glimpsed one of Dickens's ghostly visions: a past jumper, forever drawn back to the water.

Maria Martins, when I spoke to her about observing London from whichever doorway she was guarding that night, described a specific community of people who emerged between the hours of 3 a.m. and 4 a.m. They'd appear just as the clubs were closing and revellers were spilling back out onto the streets: a mix of pickpockets and homeless people, but alongside them was a more troubled contingent who seemed to be suffering from poor mental health and would suddenly become visible, still awake at this time, come out just to be among a crowd.

'It's a crazy time of night,' Maria had said, and she was right, because the hour between 4 a.m. and 5 a.m. is officially the night's most abject, when suicide rates peak. It is the setting for Sarah Kane's play *4.48 Psychosis*, which features a depressed psychiatric patient plotting her death for exactly 4.48 a.m. – the time is said to be that at which Kane recurringly awoke, and the play is often seen as Kane's theatrical suicide note, given her struggles with mental health and depression; she took her own life in February 1999, soon after writing it and before it was first performed. Its central character debates the reasons for not living anymore with several people in her head. Her arguments are considered, composed, not fevered or illogical, and the time of night gives her reasoning a chilling lucidity: 'at 4.48/the happy hour/when clarity visits/warm darkness/which soaks my eyes.'

She comes to mind as Maria Martins describes the motley, post-club population; these figures of the night could just as well have roamed the streets of Dickensian London, too, I think. They seem eternal, familiar in their loneliness, and their inner wrangles with the night's darkness. I carried on walking at night after leaving home for university, until life became too busy, and whatever the walks had given me was lost. I'd always thought Fauzia had given it up too, but after she died, I found out that she had, in fact, continued. When I inherited her diaries, I read them and was surprised to see entries that spoke of walking the streets at night, when she wouldn't be observed. In one passage about New Year's Eve, she wrote of watching the crowds as she walked, and in her melancholic account I saw a push and pull in her desire to become part of the night's bustle but also to hide in its darkness. I think of the dispossessed people Maria observes converging around the nightclubs as they empty out. Had my sister been among them? The woman on Waterloo Bridge comes back to me, adrift under the full moon, and I wonder if she was Fauzia, re-enacting one of her old night walks, or maybe come back to keep watch over me in the dark. In a letter dated 23 May 1791, Dorothy Wordsworth wrote, 'I am particularly fond of a moonlight or twilight walk – it is at this time I think most of my absent friends.' I feel sadness when I read these words, for my abandoned sisterly walks with Fauzia.

Waterloo's misty unreality has spread across the skyline and St Paul's Cathedral looks like a faint pencil drawing scribbled next to the luminous buildings on the other side of the river: the Oxo Tower, the National Theatre, Queen Elizabeth Hall, all blaring red, pink and blue lights against the dark, dense expanse of the Thames. I watch these buildings for a while and it looks, disconcertingly, as if *they* are floating, the water between them thick, deep and concrete still. The cold air has begun to feel like tiny shards of prickling glass on my skin, so I leave Waterloo Bridge and head for home, after – I urge myself – a quick circle around town.

I hit the corner of Covent Garden where Dickens wrote of seeing men sleeping under their cabbage wagons and the usually prowling children, whose criminality perturbed him so much, asleep in baskets. Instead of Victorian wagons and cabbage sellers, I find a convoy of trucks and the low hum of roadworks around the central cobbled square. Two people lie next to each other in sleeping bags in the doorway of a smart boutique, just off the square. A third approaches them with some flattened cardboard tucked under their arms and eyes me warily, not chancing to settle down until I quicken my pace and walk past. The workers that dot the streets around the square are centuries away from Dickens's nightwatchmen, paupers and tykes. But the three figures in the doorway of the swanky shop are more timeless; he would surely have recognised them, perhaps written about them in his articles or folded them into his fictive tales.

One of his most excoriating articles on Victorian homelessness is 'A Nightly Scene in London' (1856), in which Dickens describes how, on a rainy November night in Whitechapel, he finds five homeless women outside a workhouse, sleeping in sacks: They were motionless, and bore no resemblance to the human form, he writes, and he repeatedly compares them to rags and bundles, to convey how society dehumanises the destitute and dispossessed.

Dickens goes into the workhouse to inquire after their care and is told by a defensive warden that the place is too full to accommodate them. So he gives a shilling to the first woman, who simply takes it and staggers away. 'I have seen many strange things, but not one that has left a deeper impression on my memory than the dull impassive way in which that worn-out heap of misery took that piece of money, and was lost.' Dickens's coin seems almost unwanted, as if it will only prolong the burden of pained existence for this woman, whose homelessness has turned her into someone apparently less than human, grappling with the monotony of survival in her diminished state. Dickens notes the lack of thanks with neutrality, but still there seems to be an almost embarrassing honesty in his recording of this moment. Of course, we want to be thanked for our charity

– even when our coins are no solution for suffering. And we are puzzled, as Dickens is, by a misery so profound that there is no light or shade anymore, only a flat, black hopelessness.

I think back to the third homeless person I passed in Covent Garden, who only wanted to settle down to sleep in the shop doorway without my intruding gaze. There is the flashing knowledge that those who may be trapped in this world do not want to glimpse my passing sympathy before I melt away into my far more comfortable night.

Chapter 7
Strays and waifs

For a while, in her twenties, Fauzia became homeless. She had plunged into a depression that left her increasingly angry at our parents, and she left home with nowhere to go. I was away, working as a journalist in the north-east and experiencing hauntings of my own, but I was told she was living in a hostel while waiting for a permanent home and then, I'm not sure why, that she had left it. Perhaps she felt a threat there or maybe she was in too chaotic a state of mind for the rules and regulations of a hostel. She lived on the streets, I learned, and at her hungriest she went through street bins for food. I hadn't known this, but my mother told me after Fauzia died, when we began picking over how she could have contracted TB, circling over the possibilities. Had she got it, we asked ourselves, in this short but desperate period of her life?

I wonder now how she spent her time on the streets, especially at night, whether our childhood habit of walking at night had left her any better equipped to be out in the dark, or even if the experience of squatting in a derelict building made homelessness more known, if no less dreadful or frightening. It can't have been easy for her then, for anyone now, and women in particular, to navigate the dark this way.

****

Tina, from afar, might be mistaken for one of Dickens's desolate heaps of rags. She is often pitched up opposite the local supermarket, her eyes downcast, but sometimes she is actively begging. She is so diminished in size that her clothes seem to swallow her. Her face is sunken, her skin weatherbeaten, which, against the smallness of her frame, gives her the disconcerting look of an elderly child. She sits with her back against the plant pot that the council has installed to prettify the high street, barely taking up any space.

From a cursory glance she has the generic, crumpled look of homelessness, but when I begin to pay more attention, I see her flamboyant eyeliner, metallic nail varnish, shimmery blue eyeshadow. The makeup gives her an odd but distinctive glamour. For a while, she remains in my peripheral vision. She does not look directly at me either, so it seems as if it is she who is choosing to ignore me, rather than vice versa, and there is a hardness to her stare when she does look up that warns me off from speaking. She knows those times when I will give her change, even before I seem to know. It is as if she has learned to read people from her pavement vantage-point view of the world as they stride past. Maybe she can glean whether a passer-by will bend down or walk on. But if she reads my body language, I begin to watch hers, too: sometimes she is coiled into herself, other times she sits with back straight, her face soft and open.

Gradually, we make eye contact and start talking. Tina is nothing like Dickens's resigned heaps. Sometimes I see her glowering as she sits, as if seething against her homelessness. When I crouch down for a chat, she shows me the dirt etched along the creases of her palms. 'Look!' she says, holding her blackened hand up to me in outrage. Her anger is the opposite of the resignation that Dickens describes in his encounter with the woman outside the workhouse: it is rousing, righteous, demanding accountability.

I have read about women dealing with periods on the street, staunching monthly blood with anything they can find, but such matters are the smaller indignities, it seems. Tina tells me about the physical pain she's in, how doctors have told her that her organs are not functioning as they should. She has had a slipped disc, a bleed in the brain and her right arm has not been fully functional since she had a stroke some time ago. She talks about the men who rip her off or those who prey on her, and the cumulative effects of the cold and the rain. Her tone is enraged, as if the weather itself is an injustice. She crams words at speed and I wonder if she thinks I might lose interest and walk away if she were to slow down.

One day, she is especially distressed. A man had sex with her and refused to give her the money he'd promised for it. Another time, she has had to sleep the night in a bin – one of the big green ones for recycling, she says, almost shouting in disgust at being forced to do so. She shows me an oversized wooden safety pin that she keeps in her bag to defend against attack on nights when she is most exposed. The safety pin looks like a children's toy. I ask if I can bring her anything for the next time I pass. She thinks for a moment: 'Black eyeliner.' I'm surprised by the request. It doesn't sound like a necessity in the face of all the urgencies, but maybe that is the point. The desire for something beyond emergency and need. Beyond mere survival. I intend to buy an eyeliner pencil but I don't get around to it, perhaps because I think the request is not serious enough. She does not ask for it the next time I see her, either, and to my regret, it becomes a forgotten conversation between us.

There are days when Tina is full of smiles, keen to chat. She is forty-six, she says when I ask, and her answer shocks me, though I try not to show it. She looks much older. Still, it is testimony to her survival: the average life expectancy of a woman sleeping rough was forty-one in 2020 – five years less than the average of just under forty-six for men, according to the 'Making Women Count' 2022 rough sleeping census for women in London, produced by the Single Homeless Project (SHP). She has had six children, five of whom survive, she says with evident pride, and then, more matter-of-factly, tells me that one child still talks to her.

I take my father out of his nursing home occasionally, in his wheelchair, and when Tina sees me pushing him along the high street for the first time, she runs up to us, animatedly. I warn her he doesn't like to be touched, and that he can become alarmed if people get too close, but she doesn't listen. I tense and wait for him to jerk his arms out at her or cower, but he beams in a way he rarely does with strangers. She hugs him and it is a genuine embrace. She looks pained when I tell her he has dementia and she bends down to tell him that he must never feel like he's not normal. She repeats it until he smiles again. When she looks back at me, she has tears in her eyes.

She tells me she once featured in a TV documentary and finds a clip of it on my phone. She had been living on the street for two years by then, she says. She looks much younger and less ravaged in the footage, though with the same steeliness of tone and manner, which might have been cultivated in order to survive on the street: it's a posturing fearlessness. The TV crew call her by a different name and when I query it, she tells me that it is, in fact, her real name. Tina is what she goes by on the street.

There is another woman sitting on the pavement in the film, who has men intermittently approaching her, somc in friendship, others to ask her how much money she has, where she lives, where she is going next. As day turns to night, the woman begins to look cornered, even with the film crew at hand. She is invisible to some, and all too visible to others, a woman on her own with nowhere to go.

I watch the film clip again when I get back home. At first, the traffic bothered her the most, Tina tells the camera, but now she can't sleep without its hum. She speaks about how she once had her own place, but lost it, and how much harder it is for a woman to live rough. 'You trust no one but yourself,' she says in her tough way. She talks about one homeless woman who hanged herself two days before the interview for the documentary, and another who was attacked but didn't report it to the police. 'There are things that can happen to a woman . . . If you look vulnerable, they will eat you alive.' Is this why

Tina looks so fierce? Maybe her anger is the flip side of fear; fear adrenalised and turned outward. A front, like the name, to keep herself protected.

It is common, I learn, for female rough sleepers not to sleep at night. It leaves them too exposed, so they take repeated journeys on night buses or sit up in 24-hour cafés and railway stations, where they can. 'Women are at great risk of harm sleeping rough on the streets, so this will tend to be a last resort. [They] will exhaust all other options or sleep in more hidden locations,' states the SHP. One of the other options is a hostel, but as treacherous as it is to sleep rough, it is not uncommon for many women to feel more vulnerable to predation there. In 2021, a record number of domestic abuse survivors became homeless – almost six thousand in England, according to the Department for Levelling Up, Housing and Communities – and it is a dreadful irony that, after fleeing abuse, many find themselves at risk of male violence or intimidation in emergency accommodation. Because there are not enough dedicated shelters for those fleeing domestic abuse, and too few single-sex hostels, many women feel better hidden on the streets.

Female rough sleepers might hide or make themselves invisible by sleeping behind benches, in alleyways, under the camouflage of rubbish heaps or beneath bridges. Some find refuge in disused cars, A&E waiting rooms, or woodlands. They hide themselves so well that even street counts miss them, with official statistics under-estimating the numbers of women living on the street by a significant proportion. 'A large percentage of people, mainly women, are the invisible homeless,' says Suzanne Morgan, an outreach worker who supports rough sleepers in Croydon, south London, and who has worked with marginalised women since the 1990s. The official calculation, that 15 to 20 per cent of rough sleepers are female, is believed to be a massive under-estimation. A pioneering project in 2023 revealed that the numbers could be more than seven times higher than this official count in some parts of England. Again, SHP – a coalition of homeless charities and women's organisations – carried out the first census of female rough sleepers in London in 2022; they found there were 154 women living on the streets, per week.

Experiences of violence and abuse among such women are near universal. The minute they begin to attract attention on the streets at night, they move on, some walking around the city from dusk until dawn. Maybe the disappearing woman I saw on Waterloo Bridge was no apparition but someone without a home, roaming the streets with her possessions until the safety of daylight.

Women can easily disappear on the street, Suzanne Morgan tells me, because the system used to 'verify' the homeless works against their safety. 'To be verified, you have to be bedding down at least three nights in a row in the same place and an official has to come and see it. Then you've got to have an intimate conversation in a public street with someone you don't know. You're asked to give your name and national insurance number, tell them about your benefits situation, where you come from, if you have mental health issues . . .' The official walks away but the woman is often left feeling totally exposed, visible and vulnerable, Morgan points out.

Homeless men can prey on women too, and sex becomes a necessary exchange for many. Some use dating apps as a way to be inside, in the warm for the night, and to have a shower, possibly even breakfast, the next morning. This is essentially survival sex. 'A lot of the women try and pair up with somebody – a man – so they're protected, and he often trades them,' says Morgan, although the women do not always see it as transactional sex work, nor do they regard the men as pimps. They view them as boyfriends, allies and protectors. The most disadvantaged women are the least likely to talk about their situation and the extent of their suffering, because they have the greatest fear of being, for example, sectioned or locked up. Morgan has worked with first-generation Caribbean and South Asian women who have high levels of cultural or religious shame and guilt. The endpoint for many of the most vulnerable women is often addiction. It begins as a strategy against the pain of their situations, and becomes a compulsive, implacable driver. The intersection between homelessness, addiction and sex work has become more extreme since the Covid pandemic. The closure of ports limited the supply of crack and heroin, with fewer drugs coming into the country, and women taking more risks to feed their habits, with a knock-on effect, a few years later, of plummeting prices at this end of sex work – Morgan's team recently spoke to people selling oral sex for £2.50.

I wonder how addiction plays out in the night, if the darkness amplifies or even fuels it. I remember my sister's eating disorder growing more ferocious after dark. Dr Bhags Sharma, a consultant addictions psychiatrist, speaks about the diurnal quality of addictive behaviour. There is a primal instinct to sleep at night, but that gets displaced by the addiction. At the stage when addiction can be controlled, day and night are still separate, the day for abstention and restraint, the night for release. The latter offers the potential for compulsive and addictive behaviours to become much more powerful, he says, because the night is an uninterrupted, unsurveilled and solitary span of time. The addiction begins to take over when boundaries collapse: the day brings the effort of reining the behaviour in until it can no longer be contained, and the night spills messily over into the next morning, until the day/night distinction falls away into unending, addictive night. I saw this from Fauzia's compulsive eating, with its sharp midnight cut-off in the resolve to stop bingeing for good the following day, but which brought a frantic kind of glutting before then.

Tina's agitation was often heightened at night, just as the supermarket close to where she usually sat was shutting at 11 p.m. and when she hadn't raised enough money to ensure her safety for that night, whatever 'safety' meant to her at that particular time. She has never spoken openly about it to me, but Tina is a drug addict; her face and body give away that fact, and she refers to it, obliquely, when she tells me of the damage to her organs, of trips to A&E and of hospital admissions, but then she shrugs it off, as if it is par for the course. I follow her lead, not acknowledging it directly, simply telling her she's looking too thin and needs to take care of herself, medically. I offer to buy her food, but she's not interested. Sometimes I hear the hard calculation in her voice – how she will wind up freezing on the street if she doesn't amass the £8 entry fee for a hostel before midnight.

There are days I stay on the opposite side of the road, or sail past her on my bike. I hope she'll be okay, and I have faith that she will because, as wispy as she looks, Tina is tough, she struggles on. Gradually, I see less of her. Sometimes it is a relief because I haven't been able to help her. I have just listened to her stories. But she doesn't disappear. Just when I think she's gone, I see her shoulders hunched by the plant pot on the high street. It becomes a reflex to look for Tina. Whenever I see her after an absence, I'm reminded of her ability to survive. But the months stretch longer. I see others sitting outside the supermarket, and I imagine Tina's territorial anger if she happened to come by now and see them in her spot. But more and more, it is vacant. Soon, no one sits there. Maybe it is down to a new street-cleaning initiative by the council or police, I think, and I regret not buying Tina the eyeliner she asked for.

She is gone so long that I wonder if she is still alive. And then she is back. I see her from afar but she looks different. She is coming out of the bakery near the supermarket and I see, as I get closer, that her face has become miraculously younger. By the time I reach her, she is back sitting by the plant pot, tucking into a bread roll, and has the rest of her food laid out around her. 'Tina!' I say, as if she is an old friend, and feel a surge of warmth as she asks after my father. She has a new haircut, one side shaved, with a punkish quiff at the front. I tell her it suits her, and that she looks great. I keep staring at her young face, her changed body. Slowly I realise she has been in recovery; the council has even offered her a flat, she explains. 'I'm waiting to move in,' she says, and I am in awe of her turnaround. This is what she was doing all this time, when I thought she had simply disappeared. But after that, she begins returning with growing regularity until she is back to being there most nights, thinner again, and when I mention the flat she shrugs and says no more. I feel naive for having worried for Tina when she wasn't here at night, when her absence from this spot was a sign that she didn't need to be here. It was her return that should have disturbed me.

****

'Wandering is withering,' says a goatherd in Agnès Varda's 1985 film, *Vagabond*, which is about a homeless woman's last days. As if to prove the hard truth of those words, the film begins with the discovery of her dead body. Sandrine Bonnaire plays Mona, the itinerant young woman of indeterminate age and background whose body is found frozen in a ditch by an agricultural worker. The film is framed as a docudrama, so all those who came into contact with Mona in the lead-up to her death are interviewed, and her last movements are pieced together through their encounters with her, creating a jigsaw, with some bits missing.

It is clear that Mona is spirited and resilient, trudging across the fields and highways of southern France in winter, hitchhiking when she can, having adventures but also experiencing moments of desolation when she looks exhausted, thirsty and cold. We see her pitching her tent in woods where she is ambushed by a stranger and, it is intimated, raped by him, although the camera swings away before we can see it happen. Alongside this, we see a burning romance in a derelict chateau with a temporary lover, before she moves on, bunking in with a Tunisian vineyard worker at his dosshouse and then squatting with a murkier crowd of drug addicts. Mona drifts, floating among this underclass and between outsider communities, meeting other 'vagabonds', all of them male, many of them predatory, and it's clear she is swapping sex for survival. Towards the film's end, she meets a man who is preparing to act as her pimp. 'I have big plans for you,' he says, intending to take her to Toulouse so he can launch her into the porn industry.

So many of the dangers in Mona's daily life cohere with what Suzanne Morgan has told me about life for women on London's streets, from the exchange of sex for food, shelter or companionship, to the threat and reality of male violence as well as the draw of addiction. We find out, in the middle of this film, that Mona's real name is not Mona at all, but Simone. There are two identities, one from 'before' the homelessness, just as there are for Tina. In some scenes, Bonnaire looks so young that I wonder if Mona is supposed to be a child, but she has an adult toughness, which reminds me again of Tina, entering into male-only spaces and appearing so fearless in the face of all the unknowns. Like Tina, she can't afford to feel fear, or at least she can't let the fear be nakedly shown.

The film sets up the promise of getting to the bottom of Mona's life, but there are lacunae in the sequence of events which stop us from fitting together all the pieces. It is as if Varda is saying that female homelessness will always contain unknown, undocumented experience, and exploitation, however strong-willed the woman. Mona is found without identity papers; she has no birth certificate and no one claims her body. In her death, there remains a vacancy around this wandering woman, and I feel a deep sadness as the film moves from her exuberance and adventures on the road to her suffering at the end.

It is a keenly observed picture of female vagrancy, homelessness, wandering – whatever you call it. The homeless woman is, in a way, the consummate single, unprotected woman. She is the woman on Waterloo Bridge again. Perhaps she wasn't my sister but a projection of myself, as I fear becoming one day. Maybe my childhood shuttling, from one city to another, and the early dank, dark home, sank further into my bones than I realised. But it's not only that. I am unmarried and childless, as Fauzia was. I have never felt reason to be otherwise. It is freedom to me. But I feel a certain kind of vulnerability creeping in, as I get older. Or rather, it is the dread of future vulnerability or loneliness. The fear does not spring from an absence in the here and now. My life is full of people, sometimes too full. It is a more existential fear of maybe, one day, becoming the vagrant on the bridge, exposed to all the world's dangers.

In Varda's film, the vagrant life is one that Mona has chosen for herself, or so it is suggested. It is her version of freedom. A former secretary, she says that she prefers to live this way, over the hamster-wheel of office existence. At one point, the goatherd gives her a caravan and land on which to plant potatoes but she rejects his offer of domestic security, determined to remain outside the system, it seems. Some call her a hippy, others a dreamer. A maid wishes she could be as 'free' as her. Are we being encouraged to imagine that Mona is on a quest for freedom, and, if so, is this romanticising female homelessness? I'm not sure; there is little romance to her end. She has the same puzzling duality as Murakami's sleeping sister, and Moshfegh's tranquillised New Yorker – I can't quite work out if she is a rebel or a victim.

Maybe Varda is questioning whether a woman can ever be wholly free outside the bounds of convention, by day and night, and living on her own terms, without dying or being killed. Yet, she gives us the answer right at the beginning, in Mona's frozen grave. The message is clear: for all the renegade daring and glimpses of romance in a woman's bid to live on her own terms, she is all too likely to wind up dead in a ditch.

Part 4

Night terror

Chapter 8
Dead night

I walk through the pandemic. It is the height of summer when I meet up with a friend in her twenties. As we hike across Hampstead Heath, past the ponds and the splayed groups of socially distanced people, she tells me how her peers have taken to meeting up in this park, and staying there until well after dark. It's the only way to be together, she says. What has surprised her is that she prefers this to the socialising of pre-pandemic days. There are no complicated plans made on WhatsApp, no anticlimactic nights out and no fear of missing out because nothing else is happening. Just sitting and talking for hours in the park's emptied dark, in their own sparking corner, as if around a campfire. Sometimes they bring food, whatever they find in the fridge. She wants to keep on gathering this way. She tells me that her whole social group is dreading the end of lockdown and a return to the old, expensive nightlife of cramped bars and clubs.

I am often in the park too, albeit tramping up Kite Hill more often than the Heath. I am in company, despite being alone; even after midnight, Kite Hill throngs with life. Teenagers chat loudly around portable speakers, girls walk with linked arms in the dark, smoking and laughing, the park keeper's Jeep watches over the night's activity from a distance. The streets, by comparison, are emptier and, when I don't want the sociability of the park, I circle my home, head down, just like old times. I feel no fear, even when a street is badly lit, even when I see the shadow of a stranger advancing. I remember my childhood walking. It floods back, one foot after the other, a moving meditation, the journey in darkness opening up more space inside me. These streets are mine, I own them.

But then, in the hushed city, freshly filled with birdsong and the soft tread of lone, late-night walkers, a thirty-three-year-old woman is raped and killed. The abduction of Sarah Everard happens on a spring evening in early March 2021, as she is walking back home after dinner at a friend's house in south London. She takes her usual route – the safest and brightest roads from Brixton to Clapham. At 9.27 p.m., she is picked up on CCTV. She stops using her phone at 9.28 p.m., after a call to her boyfriend, and she is not found until ten days later, in a water-logged woodland near Ashford, Kent. Her murderer has left her body here, or its remains, after raping, strangling and burning her.

Afterwards we find out that Wayne Couzens was a serving Metropolitan police officer, and that he had a history of indecent exposure that stretched back to 2015, but had evaded arrest and conviction. Kent police force apologises for this failure. The Met expresses its feelings of betrayal at the discovery of this monster in its ranks. The Mayor of London says city streets are not safe for girls and women, while a North Yorkshire police commissioner warns that women should be 'streetwise' to avert another such incident. The murder leads to an exposé of men with histories of sexual assault in the Met, but they are labelled 'bad apples'. The police brutally breaks up a candlelit vigil for Everard, organised after her body is recovered. I take in the news footage, watching the officers fume at the women who have convened there.

For a while, we hear about other women who are randomly killed in or around London: Sabina Nessa, a 28-year-old primary school teacher, left beaten and strangled a few months after Everard while taking a five-minute walk to a pub one evening; Zara Aleena, a 35-year-old aspiring lawyer, sexually assaulted and murdered the following year on her way home from a bar. Their deaths are a reminder. Of course, how could I have forgotten? The parks, the city's bright centres, back streets and well-worn roads are not filled with the fantastical monsters I have grown up hearing about in folk tales or imagined in the Isle of Sark's safe, dark night, but the very real hazard of murderously angry men. I am chastened, but these deaths do not make me more scared to be out in the city's darkness, not exactly. I summon the old teenage imperviousness, but I can't ignore the fact that there is a new apprehensiveness, and a surging anger, too. Keep walking into the darkness, I tell myself. The city is still mine.

****

It is a warm Friday in August, early evening, and I am standing outside Whitechapel tube station. It has been years since I came to this corner of east London, and I am surprised by how thoroughly it has been gentrified, no longer home to the Bangladeshi immigrant population and white working classes of a few years ago, but full of shiny bars, money and buzz. The station itself has morphed from a sooty old period building to a glass and chrome edifice.

I am here for a two-hour 'Jack the Ripper' tour. I wait opposite the station entrance, as instructed. The walk will wind its way around the back streets of Whitechapel, stopping at each spot at which the Ripper's victims were killed. I hesitated before booking a ticket. I have known about these walking tours for years, and thought them tasteless, catering for tourists with a morbid fascination for a faceless nineteenth-century psychopath. But I am following a certain line of inquiry after the actions of Wayne Couzens cause a national outcry. There are important differences here, though: the fact that Couzens has a name and a face makes him mundane in his evil psychopathology. It is clear he is a failed human being. But the Ripper keeps his lustre through his mystery; it gives him a disturbing sprinkle of celebrity stardust, to which these Ripper tours attest. Who was this monstrous Moriarty-style genius who managed to evade capture and persist in his murderous mission?

The others on my walk start arriving and we stand in a convivial huddle. There is a middle-aged Canadian couple who have sold all their possessions to travel the world; a younger Italian pair flying to Barcelona tomorrow; a husband and wife from the suburbs. 'He loves this stuff,' says the wife, good-naturedly. I warm to them all. They seem so amicable in their openly gruesome interest. Our first stop, on Durward Street, behind the tube station, is a newspaper stand. We collect around it to stare at the empty paving. This is where Mary Ann Nichols was found, lying on her back in the dead of night. It is an early August evening, the light still bright, and the paving so spick and span that it might have been freshly wiped down. There is nothing to see now, of course. We have convened around a vacancy, but the description of what once occupied this space – Nichols' body, skirt raised, throat cut, eyes wide open – is so graphic that the absence of any sign of its violence feels conspicuous.

It is almost one hundred and forty years to the day since Nichols' murder, and every last vestige of the crime-riddled, poverty-infested neighbourhood of a century ago has been expunged. Despite this murder-trail tour, the street, like the station, is exorcised of its grimy past, and I wonder if the Ripper lore might even add to the area's cachet. Our guide, a one-time actor, tells us that Nichols was found at 3.40 a.m. on 31 August 1882 by a man who mistook her body for a piece of tarpaulin, which bears echoes of Dickens's bundles of rags. She had been on the street after being evicted from her dosshouse on nearby Dean Street for not being able to pay the nightly fee of four pennies. What is extraordinary – and one of the many details that give the Ripper's serial killings their intrigue – is that she appears not to have cried out or put up a struggle. Was it because she knew her attacker? Our guide tells us he keeps an open mind about Jack's identity as he walks us towards the site of the next murder. It feels like we are inside a life-sized game of Cluedo and, in spite of myself, I start to play along. The footage of Sarah Everard comes to mind; how her killer pulls over in his car, approaches her, starts talking. We know now that he was telling her, at this point, that he was a police officer, and we see her getting into his car, willingly. Was Nichols' killer parading as law enforcement, too? There is a theory that suggests this, our guide says. The group is already well-versed in the killings and the men pick over the fault lines of the various theories, batting them to and fro, the women chipping in every now and again.

In 1888, when the Ripper was still murdering his victims, an adaptation of Robert Louis Stevenson's *Strange Case of Dr Jekyll and Mr Hyde* was staged at the Lyceum Theatre, a stone's throw from these back streets. The writer Bram Stoker was working at the theatre, alongside the actor Sir Henry Irving, who is said to have been the inspiration for Stoker's vampire count. The guide suggests that the Ripper mythology might have had a bearing on Stoker's creation of Dracula a few years later, in 1897. It is a strangely tangential intrigue, but one which transposes the actions of a mortal murderer into the realms of the supernaturally monstrous. It nudges something in me, and I wonder if fears – of imaginary, diabolical creatures feeding off the blood of women in this case – are not as far-fetched as they seem, but are warnings of what reality might hold, and whether that is why my father's scary stories continue to hold purchase in my mind.

Our tour takes in the locations at which five bodies were found: after Nichols there was Annie Chapman, Elizabeth Stride, Catherine Eddowes and Mary Jane Kelly. Chapman was attacked in the early hours. Her stomach was split open, her uterus, parts of her bladder and vagina removed, and her intestines placed on her shoulder. The killer performed a similar kind of disembowelment on Eddowes, whose body was discovered the same morning as Stride's, on 30 September 1888. He also mutilated her face with slashes across her eyelids and cheeks, severing her right earlobe and nose. These women were labelled the 'canonical five' – a perverse moniker for its religious overtones, especially given the associations with prostitution that the press conferred upon the women, with all the judgement and prejudice that followed, and a reminder of the sensationalised language with which the Victorian media reported their deaths.

I am chilled by the fact that the Ripper's later victims were out alone at night during this 'autumn of terror', as it was dubbed. Surely, with the hysteria around them, they must have known that a serial killer – of lone women – was on the loose and in their midst. They were no doubt driven outside by necessity, the guide suggests. Judgement of them was unequivocal, nonetheless. Why were they out? The press and police reached a unanimous conclusion: they were plying their trade as street walkers, selling sex. That story stuck. Our guide does not buy into the theory that they were *all* prostitutes. It is bold of him to say so, I suppose. Hallie Rubenhold's 2019 book, *The Five*, a victim-centred counter-narrative which claims there was no substantial evidence to connect three of these five women to prostitution, raised voluble dissent from some Ripperologists who seemed desperate to maintain that these murdered women were sex workers. Their outrage at her revisionism seemed to be led by the charge that her argument was ideological, not based in historical fact. But Rubenhold *did* draw a compelling, factual picture of these women as rough sleepers.

The sun has set now, and there is little street lighting around us; the CCTV footage of Sarah Everard's last walk comes back into my mind again, with all the obscured dark corners of her south London journey, even though we know that she chose the safest, lightest route home. The feminist design co-operative Matrix, which worked on social housing projects in the 1980s and '90s, argued that cities were quite literally 'man-made' – architecturally planned and designed for men's comfort, wellbeing and safety. So many artists have proved this, intentionally or otherwise, such as Edward Hopper, whose paintings show solitary women within the grid of a city's narrow back streets, or obscured by jutting buildings, the artist tracking their movements, watchfully, from above or behind. There is the strangest feeling now that *we* are being observed on these dimly lit streets. Maybe it is the Ripper's shade gliding behind or in front of us, triumphant that this infernally dark corner of East London has become forever his.

We cross Brick Lane to our final stop at Spitalfields, for the site of Kelly's murder, and it brings the most appalling account of violence. Her body was discovered not outside but in bed, her throat cut to her spine, her organs emptied from her abdomen and her face disfigured beyond recognition. Chunks of viscera were placed by her body, including her kidneys and a breast under her head, with other bits of her on her bedside table. Importantly, her heart was missing, presumably taken as a grisly memento. I feel sickened, but also naive at not having known this. The Ripper hashed up his victims' bodies with a cold, precise rage, evidently so vast and yet so forensic in making parcels of meat of the women's flesh: a controlled orgy of butchery. The aggression, though, lays bare an unparalleled terror of women; the particular mix of hatred and fear that has been found to lead to such violent misogyny. Here was a man so fixated on women's reproductive organs, so resentful of their life-giving capability, that he set about obliterating them. Were his vicious eviscerations an expression of deep self-loathing too? The unconscious desire to crush the organs that had given birth to him? Of course we cannot know, I am just getting sucked into creating my own narrative amid the others being batted around me.

Two hours later, the tour is winding up, but the couples are still asking questions. I am worn out and impatient for it to end. The theories take us in circles but achieve no closure. I realise that the endless speculation is precisely what Ripper fans come for: this is the ultimate true crime, unravelling onto these streets ad nauseam. Going on a tour that traces a murderer's deeds, step by step, feels like the most macabre of parlour games dressed up as criminal history. Our guide tells us that this walk is by far the most popular of the many the company offers – everything from Dickens's London to Harry Potter. Up to two hundred people have been known to book at any one time and by midsummer Halloween night is sold out. It is so popular that there are competing tours, too: we see a gang of at least fifty people, led by two men who talk jauntily while holding up illustrations. My own walk stays with me, creating discomfort not so much around the long-ago crimes but from what they tell us about our streets now, and about ourselves. They remind us of what comes of women who 'dare' to go out at night, even if the story is not presented in that way. To remember the Ripper is to keep that warning alive.

A few weeks later, I encounter another murdered woman, this time on canvas. I am a few miles south-west of Whitechapel, at the Tate Britain, where there is a Walter Sickert retrospective. The Munich-born artist moved to England as a child in 1868 and tried his hand at acting – even securing small parts in Henry Irving's theatre company – before becoming an artist. By the early twentieth century, he was part of an artistic movement influenced by the work of Vincent van Gogh and Paul Gauguin, which came to represent English Post-Impressionism. Its members, including Lucien Pissarro and Wyndham Lewis, were labelled the Camden Town Group in 1911 because of their habit of meeting in Sickert's north London studio.

Sickert painted everything from the theatre stars of his day to female nudes. At the exhibition, I encounter his theatrical paintings, which are full of musical-hall performers and clowns. I am struck by the prominence these paintings give to the audience. There is a clear fascination with looking at people, unobserved, while they are looking elsewhere. As someone who sits among an audience most nights of the week, often alone, observing the people around me, I recognise my world in these faces and its everyday act of voyeurism. Sickert is capturing audience behaviour as its own performance. Some eyes are wide, childlike in fascination, other mouths are slackened in boredom. There are backs of top hats, mussed hair, ribboned bonnets. It is these smart, dishevelled or unsuspecting spectators, caught in the artist's eye, that give the paintings their drama, rather than the dainty ballet dancers, ruffed clowns and Pierrots on stage.

In the next room are street scenes, several at night, such as *Maple Street, London* (1916), a painting with a woman walking in the gloomy dusk light. She reminds me of Edward Hopper's lone, introspective wanderers. The woman here looks indistinct, with large buildings and sky towering around her. She is being observed without realising that someone – the artist, or an unseen stalker? – is watching, which makes her more exposed, and vulnerable to attack. Beyond this room are canvases of naked women from Sickert's infamous Camden Town Murder series. The temperature drops with every work in this sequence, the dread rising picture by picture. The explanatory text on the wall describes how the work, created between 1907 and 1908, was inspired by the real-life murder of a young woman, Emily Dimmock, who was known as Phyllis and lived in Camden. In September 1907, she was found naked in her bed, with her throat slit while she slept. The killing left the public scandalised, not unlike the Ripper murders, perhaps because no motive could be found, and maybe also because she was known to be a part-time prostitute.

Sickert's series reprises the image of a half-clothed woman reclining on a bed, while a man stalks the corners of the canvases. One painting, with the innocuous title *Summer Afternoon*, shows a naked woman in a bare, cell-like room, lying on a bed with an arm behind her, while a man in a flat cap stands watching. There is a charge between them, the man tense, as if making a dark calculation, while she looks sleepily unaware, in a pleasurable daze. There is a slight arch to her back, which carries a hint of carnality, but there is ominousness too, a stillness before the frenzy, as if the physicality of sex is soon to become entwined with an outburst of extreme aggression.

Other paintings in the series feature more couples, always a nude woman in a dingy room with a fully dressed man nearby. The threat of violence lies just off the canvas, in the blank wall between each painting. There are some naked women on their own as well, and the explanatory texts celebrate the gritty new realism that Sickert developed in these images. What alarms me is how these women are being looked at; I feel the contained aggression in the gaze. Their nakedness is explicit and almost warped, with misshapen breasts and legs splayed open. They are unforgivingly, *brutally*, exposed, pinned and pressed to a page, like insects, framed for display. I stare at their indistinct faces and feel a shiver: their eyes are voids and their mouths inchoate black holes.

Sickert's name famously features among the list of 'gentlemen' suspected of being Jack the Ripper – he was in London in the 1880s, when the Whitechapel murders were taking place. Standing before these images, I can see why. Emily Dimmock's violent death took place fifteen years later, and these paintings show little sympathy. That is what is so disturbing – Sickert's flinty gaze as he peers unemotionally into these seamy, stripped-down bedrooms, presenting a real-life Victorian 'snuff' show in a chilly pause just before the frenzied finale. Is he assuming the gaze of the killer for artistic purposes, or is this dead-eyed ruthlessness his own? It contains no love, no empathy, no human appreciation. Instead, there is the unsavoury implication that these grimly sexualised women are willing victims, arching their backs at the prospect of their imminent deaths.

I am as disturbed by this art as I was by my Friday night Ripper tour. Both present stories containing blood-curdling horror, not predicated on the irrational or supernatural but real-life tales of men turned into monsters by the darkness, women into their victims. These men stalk the streets I have dared to think I own. Just because the love of walking at night was passed down to me by a father, it does not make me a man walking in the night, to those who see me in it. Fear is rational, and danger, in *this* context, is not a feeling but a fact, an inverse of what I felt on my night walk on Sark. It is an unsettling paradox that stories like these remind us to fear men at night, but they also tell us in so many other ways that they are our protectors – the good men we know, love, marry – who walk us home or collect us from the train station after dark. If I don't have such a guardian in my life, where does that leave me?

I feel like I have entered the hostile, unprotected night, or am standing on the brink of it, rather like that cat's cradle of trees on the Isle of Sark, a few metres in front of me, that I did not want to venture into because of the chaos I imagined inside. I feel the same desire to turn away now. Do I turn back, or find company, to brave the darkness together?

Chapter 9
Reclaiming darkness

A grassy plot overlooking a side street in a suburban corner of Leeds looks eminently unremarkable. There is a row of houses at its back, a children's playground and a scatter of benches. I am sitting on the other side of the road, with Al Garthwaite. We are both staring at the plot, although there is nothing to see. Reginald Terrace, in the city's district of Chapeltown, bears no hint of its past, but in 1977 it was convulsed by another 'Ripper'. This green is where the body of a sixteen-year-old shop assistant was found at 9.45 a.m. on 26 June. Al was thirty at the time and living in a commune a few roads along. Back then, this was the site of an adventure playground and it was two children who found the body of Jayne MacDonald, who had a broken bottle embedded in her chest. After going to a dance, she had missed her last bus home the previous night, and so became the fifth victim of Peter Sutcliffe, a serial killer who murdered thirteen women and attacked seven others from 1975 to 1980, usually with a claw hammer and a kitchen knife.

Al, now seventy-seven and the city's outgoing Lord Mayor, has lived here since 1973, campaigning on everything from abortion rights to unequal pay. She was part of the Women's Liberation movement when Sutcliffe was at large, and co-founded the original Reclaim the Night movement, organising the first UK-wide march to take place on this spot, a few months after MacDonald's death. We had planned to walk the route she marched in 1977, but there is a wind whipped with sleety rain outside so we are driving it instead. On our way to Chapeltown, which was then a down-at-heel enclave, with a high concentration of sex workers, Al describes its changed topography, pointing to buildings that have vanished, others that have taken their place: the now disappeared Gaiety Pub, where Sutcliffe drank; the Hayfield, a meeting place for the area's British Caribbean community, which has since turned into a community centre; Cantors Fish Bar, which has been here for over a century; and Spencer Place, a side street where Sutcliffe went to pick up sex workers.

The murders were committed widely across West Yorkshire which is why he became known as the 'Yorkshire Ripper'. *This* Ripper lost his mystique when he was finally caught in January 1981, and turned out to be eerily ordinary: a man from Bingley, working as a long-distance lorry driver, who had been interviewed and dismissed by the police nine times. The investigation, the biggest hitherto in the country, was for a long time stymied by the assumption that the killer was solely targeting prostitutes. Until he was caught, women were warned not to go out at night, least of all in Chapeltown.

If Peter Sutcliffe were the only man in the world to be frightened of in 1977, then women further afield, in numerous towns and cities across the country, would have had no reason to march as they did, Al says. 'But they knew that if they were going home from work or an evening class and something bad happened to them, then they'd be asked, "Why were you out at this time, dressing like that, on your own, taking that route?"' Her words send me momentarily back to my night shift at the nursing home in Barnet, and a conversation with its activities coordinator, Kaye Campopiano, a vivacious woman who, it turned out, had once been a child performer. She recalled those glory days as she showed me around the home. She had acted alongside Jodie Foster in *Bugsy Malone*, she said, and when she was fourteen, Laurence Olivier had visited her in her dressing room to congratulate her on her performance in a West End show. It was a strange life for a child, she said, and then mentioned how often she would get stopped by the police on her way home, after an evening show. 'They would always ask me what I was doing out at that time of night, why I was there and where I was going.' That judgement again that any woman alone after dark, even one as young as Kaye was at that time, is seen to be making an incursion into space not meant for her. Or that her presence in the street at night is a kind of vagrancy, which brings back the hostile reactions to Mona's wandering lifestyle in Varda's film. Why was Kaye there and where was she going? the police asked. How could she justify her presence in the dark?

A conference called the International Tribunal on Crimes Against Women, held in Brussels in 1976 to address the rise of night-time attacks on women around the world, had sparked a forest fire of protests across Europe. The first Reclaim the Night walk was inspired by marches in Germany. Al Garthwaite had read about them, but the idea for a UK march was floated at an Edinburgh feminists' conference, and Al's colleagues from the local women's movement came back talking about it. 'We had become aware that there was a serial killer around here by then, and I said, "Why don't we have a march in Leeds?"'

So, on the night of 12 November 1977, at 10 p.m., a group convened on the plot where MacDonald's body had been found, brandishing placards and flame torches that Al had ordered from a novelty store in London. A second cohort met at Woodhouse Moor, another grassy area near to which the body of Sutcliffe's final victim, Jacqueline Hill, was later discovered. She was a university student, aged twenty, attacked less than a hundred metres from her home. The action was coordinated with a blaze of other marches across the nation on the same night.

Even then, it didn't immediately feel like the start of a movement to Al. It was a small gathering, fewer than a hundred women converging at City Square, in the centre of town, leaving passers-by puzzled by their demands. 'We chanted slogans and had leaflets which said we had the right to walk outside at any time of night. We gave them out to whoever we passed.' But most people responded with astonishment. It was a given that women didn't go out after dark, that they were inviting trouble if they did, and no one could see the value – or the point – in protesting against it. 'It was incomprehensible, as if we were protesting about needing air to breathe. I don't recall any hostility from passers-by, only this bewilderment.'

After Sutcliffe was caught in January 1981, there were still women who feared going out alone, after dark, even after he was imprisoned, Al tells me. 'There are many in that category.' It is sad to hear of women tormented by a ghost. I am reminded of Linda Cracknell's notion of how treading well-worn paths can lead to encounters with our pasts, and intimations with the history of the path itself – what has happened there, at other times, to other people. The history of *these* particular urban streets contains a psycho-geography of collective fear and terror, based on real enacted violence. Its shadows evidently remain; for some, they are forever forced to walk alongside them.

The terror might more ordinarily be classed as an internalised legacy. The aftermath of Sarah Everard's murder invoked the same self-regulating fear, with many women reminded that the dark was not a place of safety for them. A friend, Kate, accustomed to going out on her own after dark, said many female friends became too afraid to go jogging at night, when they had loved doing so before. She felt there was a fundamental inequality in that fear. As the mother of a fourteen-year-old daughter, she didn't want the psychological effects of Everard's murder to limit her teenager's freedom.

I ask Al if she felt afraid to walk around Chapeltown after dark at the time. She did change her behaviour, somewhat, after the body of Wilma McCann (Sutcliffe's first victim, a mother of four whom he killed in October 1975) was found, she says, but she wasn't cowed, exactly: 'You can't let fear dominate.' I have heard those words before, on a night walk I took with the novelist and nature writer, Melissa Harrison, earlier in the year. She moved from south London to a Suffolk hamlet almost a decade ago. Rural darkness shocked her at first. Even though she grew up in semi-countryside, on the outskirts of London, she hadn't experienced anything quite like this. The night would begin creeping in from around 3.30 p.m. in the winter months, and if she hadn't chopped firewood for her stove by 6 p.m., she'd have to do the job in pitch black, or else go without the warmth of a fire that night.

The decision to live so far from family and friends, and on her own, was partly motivated by an unwillingness to let fear make her life smaller, she told me, and I was in awe of this decision to occupy spaces that were apparently not meant for her. She had been doing it in smaller ways in the lead-up: going into what might be called an old man's pub and having a drink at the bar by herself, for instance, and remaining unwavering in the face of the awkwardness her presence in this exclusively macho drinking environment presented.

Several years on, although there is still an adrenaline charge to walking across fields in darkness, she feels no danger and the satisfaction of an unmediated relationship with the natural world outweighs any potential risks. There are so many delights: she sends me footage she has filmed of nocturnal life ambling in the woodlands around her home: a trio of badgers play-fight, lurching from side to side as if drunk. A mouse zips across the screen and muntjacs scour for food with eyes like lasers. Kate, who grew up in a Devonshire village, has told me similarly beguiling stories of finding nature in the dark: she'd go badger watching with her mother as a child, and remembers the excitement of sitting in a tree, wearing a head torch, and watching the woods stirring to life below. It conjures a lovely image, of mother and child entwined, observing the night from their arboreal eyrie, like human hawks.

Towards the end of my conversation with Melissa, I had asked if she had ever taken a sharp object out with her, a pen-knife maybe, just in case danger should arise. That would only open up the imaginary possibility, she had said. Then, the darkness would become perilous and her freedom in it would be diminished. 'You grow up with the [fearful] stories but you have to choose whether you want to live inside those stories or not, and it *is* a choice.' Fearful stories again, I think, but now the suggestion that we have the choice to allow them to occupy us, or otherwise. It is not a matter of whether or not we believe the stories, but that the storytelling is a necessary part of living inside or outside of fear. Melissa is saying we can decide, in the fact of one awful story, to remind ourselves of other stories of the night, as a way to roam freely in it.

A different story about Chapeltown can be told, too. It is not *only* the site of trauma, I realise, as Al and I trace the path of the inaugural 1977 Reclaim march. It is a geography of female resistance and strength. And of not one woman walking into darkness, afraid, but of many women, hand-in-hand, as each other's protectors. Al has carried on campaigning for women's night safety, and the city has a host of initiatives in place including a customised walking safety app and an anti-stalking phone-line. Still, many women and girls feel judged by what they wear when they go out at night, says Al. A survey, conducted by Women Friendly Leeds in 2021, yielded gloomy findings: 97 per cent felt that simply being a woman out after dark affected their personal safety, while 40 per cent said they 'dressed in a certain way to try to minimise risk'. Al finds that depressing. Yet, I think, a *certain* reclamation has been made. If we meet the ghost of Sutcliffe's victims in the streets of Chapeltown's past, we also encounter Al's fierce band of protestors, spread across the road with their flaming torches, retreading the paths that Sutcliffe haunted and changing the history of this concrete and stone paving with a movement founded across it. And if

Chapeltown's night encapsulates a man's murderous rage, it also resounds with these women's footfalls.

That movement has evolved since Al's foundational work in the 1970s; its profile dipped by the 1990s, but was revived by academic and activist Dr Finn Mackay, who in November 2004 organised a march through the London Feminist Network that turned into a full-scale, nationwide Reclaim the Night movement with annual marches attracting thousands of people over subsequent years. Then, in 2021, after Sarah Everard's murder, it was reborn as Reclaim These Streets, a distinct movement in its own right, not acknowledging the back-story of Reclaim the Night, but galvanising a new generation into urgent activism. Alice Jackson was among them, and speaks of a pivotal moment at a vigil in Edinburgh. It was March 2021, she was a final year university student, and had gone there with her friend, Rho Chung, who took up the bullhorn to address the crowd. 'Rho said that if anyone ever needed any support to get home safely then they were somebody others could rely on.'

Out of this idea, they founded Strut Safe, a telephone helpline that keeps lone people company as they walk home. I am shocked when Alice tells me of how many young girls ring, alarmed by the unwanted, often blatant sexual attention from men on their way home from, say, an after-school club or swimming practice. 'You, as a helpline listener, are with them in a moment when they realise they will always move through the world differently [as females]. There's nothing more heart-breaking.'

Alice was attuned to the night's danger from a young age herself, she says, and she tells a story that leads uncannily back to Sutcliffe. She grew up in rural Yorkshire in the early 2000s, near to where he had carried out his murders. Alice's mother arrived in Leeds as a student a few months after he had been caught. She knew a friend of a friend who had been murdered by Sutcliffe, and felt that the atmosphere in the city remained fearful. The inheritance of that generalised fear became its own lesson for Alice, who would make her way home from school when her parents were working late. The school was an hour away, in York, and after the train, she would take a bus, which dropped her off at the top of a hill. It was the nearest stop, a mile away from home, and on the nights Alice wasn't able to get a taxi from the station, she would sometimes walk this last mile from the bus stop, in darkness. Sutcliffe had attacked a woman close to Alice's route home, but she had escaped by running into a field. So Alice was instructed, at the age of thirteen, that if she got off the bus to walk, she must cling to the darkness of the hedge, on the other side of the road, in the hope that such cover might provide a refuge against potential harm.

Here was yet another path blood-soaked by past night terror. How unnerving for a schoolgirl to prepare against the possibility of attack, and how frightening to be stalked by a psychopathic spectre on your journey home from school. Alice showed a necessary pragmatism – and courage – as a teenager uncowed enough to be alone after dark on this path, but it is hard not to see her apprehension as a continuation of Sutcliffe's tyranny, perpetuating its power through its infamy. Is this what Melissa Harrison meant about inhabiting some stories over others, when I asked about carrying a knife? That factoring in measures for self-protection was an acknowledgement of fear which contained a submission to it? I imagine the 'possibility' Alice talked about growing bigger in her journey's darkness, filling all its shadows, although I also think she was sensible in taking the course of action she did.

Of course, a woman might also carry a knife in the dark not as self-protection but to command fear in others, out of vengeance or sport.

****

I go in search of the demon women, vampires and witches, who are driven by such bloodlust. I remember them vaguely from the stories I grew up hearing. Are they avengers, protectors? I try to pin down their symbolism but I can only recall flashes of detail from my father's tales: they take possession of women's bodies and then seduce men, killing them and feeding on raw liver torn out of their insides. They are indestructible, irredeemably evil, and never brought down.

When I seek out their cultural origins, I find that, in Indian folklore, the daayan is a witch with supreme powers of sorcery and a will to do evil, but there is also the mythic figure of the churail, a supernatural entity whose lore is often conflated with that of the daayan, though some scholars dispute that they are interchangeable creatures of the night. Once I know this, I remember how my father would use those two terms interchangeably himself. The distinctions between them are opaque: the daayan could adhere to the Western concept of the witch, I'm told, while the churail is a non-mortal figure, or ghost. It makes the daayan of my childhood imagination all the more unknowable. Both are motivated by vengeful anger, and originally believed to be victims themselves, in a previous human manifestation, when they were invariably lone, unmarried, widowed or deemed in some way aberrant, and met their death after being terrorised or overwhelmed by forces beyond their control.

In *Ghosts, Monsters and Demons of India*, J. Furcifer Bhairav and Rakesh Khanna, a husband and wife team of writer-publishers of translated Indian-language folklore and graphic novels, describe how these female demons are reborn from the souls of bereft, needy outsiders who suffered great loss or were heinously mistreated in life: women who died in pregnancy, or young wives abused by their husbands and in-laws. Resurrected as churails, some disguise themselves as human for years, getting married, having children, and slowly, implacably destroying entire extended families, one member at a time. Bhairav and Khanna say that 'the first aim of these vengeful ghosts is to seek and destroy the father or family members who ill-treated them'. But once they have been eliminated, they find new prey, especially unmarried young men and new mothers. So even though their fantastical powers are born of apoplectic rage at the injustice meted out to them as mortals, they acquire an endless appetite for revenge in this supernatural form.

There are circles upon circles of fear and violence within the mythology of the churail, though; however terrifying their strength in their non-mortal manifestations, the women who are suspected of being witches, in real life, especially in rural communities, are made powerless by the charge, often facing deadly consequences if they are accused by their neighbours, enemies or family members. It is an inverse equation: a woman suspected of being possessed by an all-powerful demonic spirit often finds herself made powerless, cast out, tortured or killed.

Between 2001 and 2016, India's National Crime Records Bureau listed 2,468 murders where 'witch accusation and persecution were recorded as a motive'. Those who stand accused are unmarried or vulnerable outsiders and also women of independent means with inherited land or money. Suspected witches have been burned, hit with hot iron rods, had teeth or hair pulled out, and much worse. In the most extreme cases, they are beheaded. I read shocking case studies in *Witch Hunts: Culture, Patriarchy, and Structural Transformation* by feminist scholar Govind Kelkar and economist Dev Nathan. Hari Bai, a widow from a farming community in Rajasthan, is tied up by men who try to throw her into a well. Odisha, from Mayurbhanj, who is unmarried, is first ostracised by villagers and then, when two local girls die on the same day, is blamed for these tragedies and strangled to death. Dalia, a Dalit from Chhattisgarh, is married at thirteen but when, at twenty-two, she has not become a mother, her husband abandons her, her in-laws accuse her of eating children, and she is beaten to death.

It is horrible to read accounts of dangerously wealthy widows who become targets out of jealousy for their fortunes, and of single women who become victims of whispering campaigns branding them diabolical for their childlessness. I recognise the isolation of being a single and childless woman in a culture that regards that specific status with suspicion and threat. At least these slaughtered women's resurrections in myth contain power and fury, I tell myself, although that myth might, in fact, fuel fear-mongering in reality: the churail is so villainous, such a force of destruction in society, that she must be brought down at any cost.

There are many more grisly stories in Kelkar and Nathan's study, but among them is an uplifting case of thirteen women accused of witchcraft in Jharkhand, who draw together to become a self-sufficient, dignified community of outcasts. They live outside the villages from which they have been expelled, but refuse to be cowed in the face of their persecution. This group seems to have found a way to rescue themselves and become one another's protectors. A kind of liberation, I suppose.

****

It is close to Halloween and I am talking to three theatre directors about a female-led horror festival they have curated. The idea came to them in lockdown, when they set up a WhatsApp group called 'The Gore Girls' in which they shared their love of horror. They are aficionados and speak of the many awesomely awful women in the genre in a flurry of references unknown to me. One mentions Ana Lily Amirpour's 2014 Persian-language American film, *A Girl Walks Home Alone at Night*, the others nodding vigorously, and they return to it so many times that I seek it out to watch.

It is artfully shot in black and white, taking place entirely at night and in a surreal underworld of industrial wasteland filled with the wretched and the damned. It features an innocent-looking young woman in a black chador who has the same gamine look as Jean Seberg in *Breathless*, and a man called Arash, resembling an Iranian James Dean, who becomes infatuated with her, though she remains coolly removed. She is doe-eyed and unassuming, and the story seems like a kooky romance at first, so it is genuinely frightening when she reveals herself to be a vampire and pounces on the first of her victims.

After that, when we see her scouring the streets at night, we assume she is seeking out any human being as prey, but gradually it becomes clear that she is a self-appointed vigilante – quite literally a caped crusader, cleaning this dissolute town of its bad men, and a protector of outsider women, including a sex worker she befriends. She selects her male victims carefully, sniffing out the violence in them, and directing her terror at the Peter Sutcliffes and Wayne Couzens of this world. 'Are you good?' she asks a boy one night with such foreboding that it looks as if she is about to tear him to bits if he indicates he isn't.

If women's visibility at night has historically been judged as improper and unsafe, then this film inverts that idea. This woman is the upholder of moral good, and the men she passes on the street are the ones in potential danger, although they see no threat in her because she appears so fragile, so wide-eyed and devout. I watch with dread, but also excitement, as she glides along dark roads on her skateboard. It looks like she is levitating, her eyes empty black holes from a distance. I feel a stir of recognition: this is how I imagined the daayans in my father's stories; she is just as he described them.

She is terrifying in her feeding frenzies, turning into a vulpine thing that growls and squats on all fours. It is horrifying and magnificent when she first reveals her fangs, biting off the finger of a drug dealer and stuffing it in his own mouth. She is simultaneously the stuff of nightmares and dreams: a furie exacting revenge in the dark, but also a girl out alone at night, able to walk freely and without fear. She makes me wonder: to take on the monstrous, do we need to become monstrous ourselves?

When I asked Al Garthwaite if she had been scared to walk alone, after dark, in Chapeltown while Sutcliffe roamed free, she told me of a recurring dream she had during that time. Less a dream than a fantasy, she had said, one that had played over and over in her mind in those years of terror. She would imagine going out for a walk at night and finding Sutcliffe in her local park. She told the story as 'her' finding 'him' rather than vice versa. She saw herself turning towards him, picking up a brick and bashing his head open with it. A brick might not be an effective defence against a man who lurks in the shadows with a claw hammer in real life, but as a wish fulfilment of crushing a dark force by summoning a greater, darker, more overpowering force of your own, it was a liberating fantasy to live inside.

I come across another liberating fantasy, of Carmilla the vampire, a queer outsider created by the Irish writer Sheridan Le Fanu in 1872, twenty-five years before Bram Stoker invented *Dracula*. The scion of an undead dynasty in Austria, what is so surprising, and radical, about the story for its day is its barely concealed subtext of lesbian desire, even though male authorship of coded female queerness obviously brings its own complicating politics for contemporary readers. Carmilla always targets a woman, usually a lone daughter, first reeling her in with an intense friendship that becomes indistinguishable from romance, then invading her dreams to puncture her throat and suffocate her before moving on.

The book's narrator, Laura, becomes her unknowing prey; she tells us how she is both drawn to Carmilla and repelled by her, as if tussling with illicit desire. 'I was conscious of a love growing into adoration, and also of abhorrence. This I know is paradox, but I can make no other attempt to explain the feeling,' she says.

Carmilla is the opposite of Amirpour's vampire: she is uncomplicatedly, amorally villainous, making no effort at social conformity even in her incarnation as a mortal; she wakes up well after noon, never goes to church and sneers at the sight of a funeral cortege. Le Fanu gives her unfettered freedom to do bad. Her killings seem entirely born of appetite, they are a necessary meal. And although, like Dracula, she is hunted down and killed by the men in Le Fanu's novella, there is a tantalising sense – even after Laura and her father discover that she is a vampire, and her coffin is found, torn open, her breathing and unaged body plunged with a stake and then beheaded, burnt, with her ashes thrown in a river – that she might still have found a way to carry on living. In the final paragraph of the book, Laura feels that she sometimes starts from a reverie and 'fancies' that she hears Carmilla's footfalls at the drawing room door. You wonder if a part of her will always remain unkillable, in Laura's fantasy life if nowhere else. Le Fanu cannot quite destroy her; maybe Carmilla has seduced her own creator. The story is, covertly, a celebration of the monstrous feminine. Like Amirpour's vampire, she resembles the daayans in my father's stories.

But those stories were not in themselves about liberation, or empowerment. That is not how they were told to me. They weren't so much tales about the charismatic villainy of the witches, like Le Fanu's Carmilla, but warnings about an animated dark that was populated by unknown, unquantifiable forces, told to inspire a very real fear of darkness. The witches could have been fairies or aliens or an eerily animated dress, surfing the night's shadows to float across the room on its own, like I imagined at my guesthouse on the island of Sark. What was as frightening as the stories was sensing my father's fear and awe as he told them; it was as if they were channelled from outside him. This may simply have been because he was a gifted storyteller – an actor, in a sense, living his characters. But then why would he remain so scared when the lights were switched off, plagued, as he was, by a lifetime's fear of the night?

It is hard to stare into the face of absolute darkness. This is what I discover when I seek it out. There is Sark, with its natural dark sky, and Melissa's Suffolk landscape, with its sharp moon shadows. There are rooms darkened with blackout curtains and photographs sent by friends of the polar night in Lapland. But still the light is liquid, pouring in through cracks, diluting the texture of the darkness so it is never a pure black pitch. I find it, eventually, down a Victorian mineshaft in Snowdonia. It is in the former pit village of Tanygrisiau, which was once a thriving centre of the nation's slate industry, but is now filled with heaps of waste slate which, from a distance, look like mountains of ash. The former quarry burrows deep into a hillside, and now operates as a novelty hotel. I have not read the small print and find out only once it is underway that it is a demanding descent: abseiling across steep drops, climbing up man ways and wading through tight passages of water with a group of fitter, younger people. Miners who worked here from the mid-nineteenth century until 1970, when it closed, would have trekked much deeper simply to begin their shift. Conditions were said to be so abysmal, with five hundred men and boys packed inside the pit's narrow chambers, that it became known as The Slaughterhouse.

We keep descending and just before heading into the chamber that has been converted into a sleeping area and canteen, our guide tells us to switch off our helmet lights, to see what total darkness looks – and feels – like, for a few minutes. This is the kind of subterranean dark that can't be found above ground. I switch off my torch, and find myself inside Dylan Thomas's 'bible black' night, from *Under Milk Wood*, so thick I can feel its heaviness hanging on me, so total it is like instant, total blindness. I wonder if there are shades even within this pitch black, if it becomes denser the deeper beneath the earth's crust you go. I wave my hand in front of my eyes and see nothing other than the same wall of darkness. I might be scared if I were alone but this experiment feels more like a game with the group chatting around me.

The guide tells us we weren't built for this unnatural state of dark. It is a shade to which our eyes can never adjust, and it triggers a fundamental upset in the mind. Those who became lost or isolated within it would begin to hallucinate: the distant drip of water in this mine would start talking, the rocks would lurch towards you. It sounds scary, ridiculous and thrilling, a blackness like a blank page you fill from the darkest recesses of your imagination – or the irrational cerebral centre-point of the amygdala.

It stays with me. I am surprised by how soothing it felt, and how safe. There were no shadows, no sense of animation, and ironically, nothing for my imagination to take hold of and interpret, despite the fact that this total darkness triggers visions, given enough time in it alone. To me, it felt dead, comfortably untextured, like a thick, warm, enveloping blanket thrown over the eyes. I realise that the ghoulish forces I fear living within this kind of darkness – where there is nothing rational to fear, such as in my room at the guesthouse in Sark – are so often born out of suggestive shadows and gloaming light, onto which I can project my own meanings. Maybe what I fear most is an encounter with myself in this evidently safe darkness. Whatever unknown quantity floated around me in my rented room in Middlesbrough came from my night self, as unknown to me as Eva's sleepwalking self is to her. That is why the fear felt so unbeatable, so constantly present. It wasn't a matter of fleeing the room; it was that I couldn't escape this 'other' nocturnal, me.

These imaginary projections onto the night are not only about fear, though, I sense. My father has shown me how breathing life into darkness is a kind of storytelling, an active desire to consider the outer reaches of possibility and to conjure the fantastical. Bruno Bettelheim, in *The Uses of Enchantment*, says fairy tales bring an 'enchanted' quality to children's lives because they do not quite know how the stories have 'worked their wonder' on them. There is a beguiling mystery at their heart. The flat, black dark of the mine was strangely disappointing because it took all the conspiracy out of the dark – and the wonder.

The reason that I am scared of the dark – I think – is because I *want* to keep being scared of it. I want the dark to remain animated, alive with possibility and interpretation. Perhaps it is a way to keep hold of a child-like wonder. It is, too, a reminder of my father's storytelling, which gave value to the irrational as something to explore alongside all that is solid and certain in the world; the irrational, unconscious and not-quite-graspable is surely central to stories, and to the imagination.

In his illness, my father is no longer the storyteller. Maybe I have become my own; in imagining all that might be invisibly hovering towards me as I lie in a guesthouse in Sark, or a back-room in Middlesbrough, with the lights out, I am telling myself my own scary bedtime stories; another inheritance, perhaps.

This might be a far-fetched interpretation of my fear, yet it feels true, and freeing. It loosens a knot inside, and I feel as if I am passing through the terrifying dark, not any less terrified but more knowing, heading into the bright, enchanted night.

Part 5

Adult entertainment

Chapter 10

Late show

It is 10.30 p.m. and I am at a theatre in Lahore, to watch late-night Punjabi comedy. There will be two performances of the same production tonight: the first starting now, and a second running into the early hours of the morning. I am not staying with my mother's side of the family – the only relatives who remain in Pakistan – but in a hotel. It is my first time here alone, and I feel torn between wanting to claim the city as a place of belonging and my status as a Western tourist. I have instinctively assumed the latter position, maybe to protect myself against judgement or curiosity for being a single woman in an Islamic society, out alone at night. Although I see plenty of women on their own, they are mostly in cars if they are from the wealthier echelons, while those walking on the roadside, under the drumming heat or the fading light, are usually those at the other end of the social spectrum.

Lahore, I realise, is not a city I can pretend is home, though it once might have been. Rather, it is the original home of parents who are now too old or sick to travel with me, the birthplace of a sister who has since died but who I still associate with this city because of the happy, early years spent playing here together. Now, inside this darkened space, I find a whole new night of revelry that I have never before seen. This is not the city of my childhood. It is an adult world of late-night entertainment. The clientele of Punjabi comedy is very different from the usual theatre demographic, I'm told. When I mention that I'm coming to this show to people from the theatre community whom I meet in the day, they either raise an eyebrow or guffaw. I am intrigued by their reactions and eager to see how the drama will play out. It sounds a little like the variety shows of the old nineteenth-century music halls from the way locals describe it: broadly appealing entertainment filled with ribaldry and physical humour.

The venue is a former cinema, off a busy thoroughfare that throbs with nightlife. The theatre's façade has a faded colonial grandeur that is present in so many of Lahore's older buildings but alongside it, in the foyer, is classic Bollywood movie bling: an elaborately winding staircase, a delightfully florid blaze of cinematic images that range from scantily clad actresses to Mughal-era kings, musicians and dancers, plastered across flame-red walls. There is a whiff of tawdriness to the dimmed lights, the oversized leather chairs and the lovebirds' swing that dangles further in, which gives the place the feel of a nightclub.

I am with an English-speaking woman from the Netherlands who I met earlier that day and who has asked to come along. She has also newly arrived in Lahore, and is visiting for the first time; she is more conspicuously an outsider than I am: tall, blonde, white. We are greeted by a friendly posse of men, including the theatre manager, who shakes our hands warmly. The show we will see is like all the comedies of its genre, trading on puns and linguistic wordplay, he says. The double meanings will be lost on me because I do not understand Punjabi; only Urdu is spoken in my family home. Although the former is a regional language which shares some vocabulary with Urdu, it has its own twisty declensions of which I have little more than rudimentary knowledge.

Our hosts lead us into a cavernous auditorium which seems to go on for miles. I strain to see its back wall but it melts into darkness. We are taken to the front row and, from what I can see, the audience is made up exclusively of men. It is not unexpected, given how social spaces are sometimes split along gendered lines here. Maybe the women are sitting at the back where they are not so readily visible, I think. The show has already begun by the time we settle down. I strain to follow the dialogue and feel a twitch of concern for the woman beside me who speaks no Urdu or Punjabi at all. I wonder how much of the story she will pick up from the music and movement alone.

Three men are on stage, clowning around. Their jokes are punctuated by blasts of music, like a Vaudevillian clash of cymbals, every time they produce a punchline. There is a flow of relaxed laughter across the room. I catch random words which resemble Urdu and piece together a vague sense of the plot: it is a caper in which these men open a massage parlour to extract money from their clients. A glamorous woman in a red shalwar kameez is on stage with them, but she is a foil to the comedy. I have been told that women play a particularly active, quick-witted role in these dramas, ad-libbing with tart ripostes and witty puns, but this woman just watches the men with a wry, almost disdainful expression, refusing to join in with their high jinks.

She is an enigmatic presence, very different from the other, recognisably stock comic types – one man is portly, the other wiry and a third has styled himself as a Punjabi Charlie Chaplin, with a walking cane and an ostentatiously jaunty manner. There is a beaded curtain and a cheap, glittery sheen to the props that gives the show a down-market feel, although the price of a ticket begins at a thousand rupees for the back rows and rises up to five thousand rupees at the front – the kind of money a family further down the social scale might be able to live on for several days. There are other, cheaper entertainment venues dotted around the city which cater for blue-collar workers letting off steam, but this theatre is among the most expensive, housing the most stellar acts and with an audience consisting of zamindars, or wealthy landowners.

The comedy comes to an abrupt end and the auditorium darkens. I imagine it will continue in the same vein but the man beside me leans over and explains what is coming next: Punjabi plays are always interspersed with song and dance numbers, with up to five routines tucked in between the spoken drama. These musical elements do not relate to the drama per se, he tells me, but are there simply to please and entertain the crowd. The first song starts up and brings such a dramatic shift in tone that it feels as if we have entered another show. A woman shimmies onto the stage and begins to lip sync to a Punjabi song set to a disco beat. She is wearing an ornate shalwar kameez, bridal in ritzy red and gold, and she is accompanied by a bare-chested troupe of male dancers in sparkly jackets that match her outfit. The latter look like a boyband, young and pretty, with the bubblegum choreography of a pop video. She begins an energetic dance routine and the men move around her like a crew of camp Chippendales.

They could be an ensemble from a Bollywood musical, but there is a hint of lewdness to the routine that makes it different from any song and dance number I have seen in an Indian film. The bhangra blares out and the suggestive moves turn lascivious: the woman has been full of saucy smiles but now begins to gyrate, judder and pump her body. It is crude, comical, like something from an old-style *Carry On* film set to a bhangra beat, with the same tongue-in-cheek innuendo, it seems, but magnetic in its big, blaring theatricality. The men wriggle around the woman, and I realise they are not bare-chested but wearing transparent shirts under their glittery suits, which adds to the bizarre mix of the sanitised and the uncensored playing out on stage. It is like drag: extravagant, over-the-top, with a homoerotic undercurrent. What surprises me most is the gleeful mischief that the female performer exudes. Her eyes are bright and she sticks out her tongue, laughing uproariously when she spots me at the front of the auditorium, clearly amused by the sight of a woman sitting among the men. Her frankness strips away any sense of furtiveness.

I am bewildered and captivated by her floor show. I turn to the Dutch woman to see if she is as caught out as I am, but she is bristling and does not return my smile. Before the first song is over, she tells me she is too uncomfortable to stay. 'Poor thing,' she whispers, nodding towards the woman on stage, then surveying the men in the auditorium around us. The blood has risen to her cheeks, and she looks like she is either angry or embarrassed. I am confused because, despite my shock, I do not feel pity for the whirlwind figure who swaggers and rampages across the stage as if she owns it, the men following in her wake. I feel awed by her. But the Dutch woman does not see what I see, and she rustles up to leave, disappearing out of the auditorium.

Her disapproval seems to be a declaration – of feminist credentials? – and requires my departure too, so it seems. I feel a protest rising: how has she made such a quick and categorical judgement of the woman, this audience, this theatrical tradition – all before the show has barely begun? I turn around to glance at the faces that she scanned in the auditorium. Rows of men look back at me, not with hostility but something more inscrutable; I look back at them, with the wide eyes of a cultural tourist. I am more a foreigner here than I realised.

The comedy at the start of the evening is all but forgotten once the musical part of the night gets underway, and I realise that this is what the audience has come for. We never return to the three men in the massage parlour; they were merely the warm-up act. The first song sets other dance routines into motion, each raising the stakes in outrageousness, the music louder, the lights more delirious. Several women swoop in for the group dance at the end of the first act, rolling their hips with such brazen allure that they appear cartoonish. I am not sure if we are supposed to laugh or gawp or ogle; the auditorium is not raucous or boorish. Everyone is held in the grip of the performance.

This is another kind of enchanted darkness. A fantasy, acted out by the performers who occupy the stage. What would you call them? Entertainers, erotic dancers, or the Dutch woman's victims? I can't tell. Who *are* these women somersaulting across the floor, blowing kisses and licking their lips with such outré theatricality? Do they feel fear or anger at being looked at this way? Or indifference? I can't tell that, either. I hadn't expected to see them in Lahore, certainly not by day but not by night either, and so visibly in a public space.

Their presence has a different meaning here, I feel, perhaps naively, but to me it verges on the dangerous. The Dutch woman does not see this cultural specificity, perhaps, or she might think it an irrelevant detail. Her brand of feminism may cast these women unequivocally as 'victims' where I would question this universalisation. I instinctively think of the women as bold outsiders, and I am astonished that this sexually aggressive material is the stuff of mainstream entertainment in an Islamic country which still adheres to censorship laws that date back to 1894.

The director has arranged to take me backstage during the interval. I am keen to meet the women but at first I only encounter the men from the comedy who, I am told, are some of the most revered stars on the circuit. They sit smoking, as if waiting for a second act that will never come. The backstage area is as cavernous as the auditorium and, like there, it is hard to spot the women. We are about to leave when a dancer who has not yet performed is suddenly standing in front of us, eager to be introduced. She is small with a delicate, made-up face and an elaborate outfit, gorgeously gilt-edged. She has the same mischievous glint as the first woman on stage. I speak to her in my anglicised Urdu and she mimics it, jokingly. I carry on with my earnest questions:

'Do you like doing this?'

'Where are the women in the auditorium?'

'Why don't they come to watch the show?'

'They are further up in the auditorium, in another area,' she says in quick reply, and tells me there will be families coming for the second show, which starts after midnight. She loves her profession, she says, and answers all my questions nonchalantly, with no hint of embarrassment or apology. I meet another dancer who also works in TV and film. It's demanding but rewarding work, she says, and I learn that she is one of the show's highest-earning performers – a celebrity in her own right. These women are famed across Pakistan, and command huge fees.

I am told afterwards, by the men hosting me, that some performers trade in sex after a show is over, with the richest men in the room. I don't know if he is referring to the male dancers too, and I don't ask, but here are women who straddle the world of theatre and the sex industry, if in fact they *are* selling sex. I suppose it is not unlike the late-night floor shows in London. We are in a back office and the cheeriness with which these men greeted me at the start of the evening has given way to a more subdued mood. They speak quietly, as if embarrassed, and say that theatres book shows like this because of public demand. The manager nods along and they tut when I mention how well the women danced. I cannot quite distinguish between their admiration and censoriousness – they seem appalled by the show we have seen, yet also defensive of their right to stage it. It has passed muster with the state censor, which vets productions for vulgarity before every public opening, and it is not as lewd as many others, they say. If I want to see *real* vulgarity, I should go to one of the smaller, late-night theatres in Lahore. They boast about this production's starry cast of actors and, although they refer mainly to the comedians in the opening play, they acknowledge that the dancers are top-tier performers. That is undeniable. It is just that the latter might make some of their money from sex work too, they say.

I express my disbelief openly: dancing and singing publicly was once, long ago, associated with prostitution in South Asian culture, but I have questioned this correlation, and wondered if it is more rooted in prejudice and misogyny than fact. The film and theatre industries exist outside the usual social boundaries, with the sexes interacting in more intimate ways than they would do otherwise, so the morality of female performers might be automatically tainted. But these men are adamant: the trading begins as soon as the show finishes, and the richest zamindars in the audience huddle up to book whichever performer has caught their eye, thrashing out prices with their promoters in the darkened reaches of the theatre. As I leave, the men remind me again of the public demand for this kind of entertainment, which fills the auditorium to its rafters, night after night over a double-bill run that lasts for twenty-two days.

My own, immediate response to the show becomes confused with the strong reactions of those around me in the following days. The disapproval of the manager and his men, the horror of the woman who left, both lead to a negative judgement of the female performers, either as exploited victims or as morally corrupt benefactors. What about the possibility that they are neither, and that they even enjoy their jobs? Could this night work, in an Islamic country, facilitate a certain kind of public flouting of its religious morality? Prostitution is illegal in Pakistan, and sex outside of marriage, officially at least, a criminal offence. The women I spoke to backstage were not fearful but fierce. They were not a model of coy femininity, with eyes bashfully downcast, cowed by the stares of the men watching them. They traded on these gazes, staring them down from the stage. If sexual objectification is about whose gaze is active in turning the other passive, these women seemed to subvert that equation.

Soon after seeing the show, I meet Quddus Mirza, an artist and art critic in Lahore. He explains how there has been a slump in the popularity of cinema in Pakistan: Bollywood films are no longer shown in the country and local productions cannot match the Indian industry's bigger and better output, so audiences have dwindled. Venues such as this one are increasingly hosting theatrical shows rather than cinematic ones. The stars of these women have risen as a result. 'In terms of fame, they are equal to male actors. They might be selling their bodies, who knows, but they are also performing. It's not a binary equation of victimhood or empowerment,' he says.

The Dutch woman's disapproval continues to niggle, even so, until I come across a series of video installations featuring sex workers from South Africa, created by the artist Candice Breitz in 2017. In one part of the project, *TLDR*, several escorts talk about the work they do, straight to camera, in composed tones. These testimonies are so eloquent, so polished, that they sound like dramatic monologues. One woman explains how she chooses to do sex work because it is better than cleaning. Another says her body is her business, and that she can feel potential danger intuitively: 'If you hear your heart beat faster, don't take the client.' Another is snippy about her white clients: 'I don't know what is happening in their homes that men are running out for black pussy.' I can't tell if it is said in jest or in earnest. Clients are not just there to have sex, she adds, but to undergo a kind of healing. One man sends her lavish gifts, another professes love. A sex worker talks about her client with such shy tenderness that their relationship sounds like a romance. Then a stylish woman from Zimbabwe in a white cocktail dress begins reflecting on the way she is viewed by others, women in particular, how it is so often the case that privileged white women set the agenda and decide sex workers can't be feminists, and that they must be victims. How it is their word against her lived experience. It is so succinctly put, so clarifying.

Did the performance I saw with the Dutch woman press on an unacknowledged fear in *her*? What did she find so fearful – the men watching this spectacle of overt sexuality or the women's display of it? Or simply the reality of this side of the night, and the women in it, which some might not want to encounter? Rather than answer these questions, or address that fear, might it be easier to leave the auditorium, and leave these hyper-visible night-workers to their trade in darkness?

****

When I was twenty-seven, I visited Lahore for the first time since emigrating as a child. I went with my parents for a cousin's wedding and I was over-excited to be back in the city of my childhood, which had become an almost fictive inner landscape by then. I can vividly recall my disappointment on arrival, as I was carted from one home to another, to visit relations I had never before seen and with whom I could barely converse because of my then halting Urdu. I couldn't take off to sightsee alone either. My aunts made it clear it wasn't safe because so few women did such a thing at that time, and any dangers were immediately heightened for me because I could be readily identified as an outsider by my accent, my clothes, even my walk.

The trip began to feel cloying and claustrophobic, and I couldn't square this version of the city with the magical one I carried inside me, from those early years. My frustration turned to anger and I had loud, brattish exchanges with my mother about wanting to see and do things. So one of my mother's cousins offered to give me a tour of inner Lahore, a grid of narrow, higgledy-piggledy streets in the heart of the city, which marks its original, ancient dimensions. Huma was an artist, ebullient and unconventional, who took me through the old shopping quarter of the Anarkali Bazaar, filled with donkey carts, dim lamplight and artisans using medieval anvils. It looked like time had stood still here; either that or we had walked back hundreds of years into the past.

We arrived at the Badshahi Mosque, an opulent, multi-domed building from the Mughal era, and as we stood in one of its immaculately manicured courtyards, Huma pointed to a small swathe of the inner city covered in tarpaulin. That, over there, was Lahore's red-light district, she said. I was surprised that sex work occupied such a visible place within the nucleus of the city's heritage and tourism, but she told me that it had a history as illustrious as the sacred sites around it. The area had become known as Shahi Mohallah – the royal neighbourhood – in the seventeenth century, later renamed Heera Mandi, after Hira Singh, the favourite child of Maharaja Ranjit Singh, and sometimes called the Diamond Market, which had been home to high-status courtesans who entertained the men of power and influence in Mughal India. These women, called tawaif, inherited their status through family lineage and were extensively schooled in Khattak dance, poetry recital and singing, as well as the 'art of seduction', and often served as long-term mistresses to wealthy patrons.

The area where the tawaif had flourished had long since been reduced to a dilapidated matrix of broken roads and tatty music shops. The song and dance shows had become degraded, too, with live singing replaced by recorded pop, bhangra or Bollywood music blasted from tape-decks for a summary dance in shopfronts before the sex commenced in rooms upstairs. The trade lay still in the daytime, like a sleeping animal, but came to life at night, with some descendants of the tawaif still said to be operating alongside the less venerated community of ordinary sex workers. The British academic Louise Brown spent several years visiting the Heera Mandi, and followed the family of Maha, a high-status 'dancer girl' brought low. The neighbourhood is colourfully drawn in her 2005 book, *The Dancing Girls of Lahore*, and Maha is a vivid presence, as are her daughters, who are being trained for the same life as their mother. Her account captures so many of the paradoxes of modern courtesan culture: baby girls are highly prized, which is refreshing given the rates of female infanticide in some parts of South Asia, while 'female beauty and sexuality are openly celebrated', and women are the head of the household, as Maha is, controlling the finances and determining the fate of their children.

Since then, under the current government, the area has ostensibly been gutted of the sex trade, although there are still some areas and alleyways operating backstreet brothels, the most furtive of which is Tibbi Gulley, a narrow road where young girls are rumoured to be locked into sexual slavery.

In 2000 Huma had taken me to a restaurant called Cooco's Den, close to the Badshahi Mosque. It was owned by the artist Iqbal Hussain, the son of a twentieth-century courtesan who had painted a series based on the women of the Heera Mandi, including those who worked in the trade within his own family. His work had become famed for these honest and explicit portraits, and I remember the striking, large-scale paintings of the women hanging in the restaurant, which left me awed. They had direct, challenging gazes, with their hair uncovered and outfits in bright oranges and reds, like the performers at the Punjabi comedy.

Hussain's work had, by that time, gained international acclaim; the restaurant had featured in *Time* magazine and his paintings hung in the homes of Pakistan's super-rich. The road on which the restaurant stood acquired the moniker of Food Street with other restaurants setting up alongside Hussain's to cash in on its popularity. Soon, it swarmed with ambassadors, diplomats and tourists who made cultural pilgrimages to Cooco's Den in order to see Hussain's artwork. So these women on the restaurant's walls, and the red-light district itself, became sprinkled with Hussain's stardust: the ancient tradition of the tawaif given its modern-day renaissance, on canvas.

I found it heroic then, at the age of twenty-seven, that an artist had depicted these women with such flagrant disregard for the religious conservatism around him, and with such compassion for his subjects. He was an insider to the Heera Mandi, drawing from the world around him, and painting the women on such an epic scale, with bold glamour. I see things differently when I return, over two decades later. By 2023, the paintings of the courtesans have been removed from the walls of Cooco's Den because there has been a rift between Hussain and his nephew, who now runs the business. The family feud has been widely reported by the press over the years, but still Hussain's life is cloaked in mystery. Some say he is suffering from an unknown illness in Lahore, others that he left the city long ago and is living in Canada, others still that he is a recluse. His artistic legacy comes with similarly slippery mythologies: the market is said to have been flooded by replicas of his nudes so that it has become hard to tell the real from the fake.

But if Iqbal Hussain is elusive, his work is highly visible, and valued, in Pakistan. Some nudes sit in private collections, but many are accessible to the public, and he has had numerous retrospectives across the country. Quddus Mirza was taught by Hussain at Lahore's National College of Arts, where he was a student in the 1980s, and has complicated feelings about the Heera Mandi series. He thinks Hussain has 'exploited' the women by painting them, but recognises that he also knew and loved them. Many are now displayed in the Lahore Art Gallery, which has been closed to the public since the pandemic but allows entry by appointment.

Mirza and I are almost the only visitors when we go, and the walls around the entrance are covered with Hussain's canvases. The women look huge, all the more so in this emptiness. There are paintings of his sisters, mother, aunts and their children. These larger-than-life figures have a heavy-limbed realism, just like the ones I saw at Cooco's, years ago. Many canvases show everyday life for a woman being raised as a tawaif; there are some with teachers initiating girls into the art of music and dance. There are girls on the cusp of womanhood, sitting alongside goats, chickens, lambs. They are all livestock to the men who pay for them, Hussain seems to be saying. And there are casually naked women slouching next to men with banknotes, guns and bottles of whisky.

I see the skill in the images, the intimacy and the empathy. There is a refusal to sentimentalise the women, with an unvarnished baring of their fears. One woman is coiled on the sofa with her face in her hands, a foot dangling. Is she in the grip of unspoken torment? Is Hussain saying she feels guilty, or is she being coerced into this life? It feels strange to be looking at these women in an art gallery, all the same, as if I am a tourist of the sex trade, by only a few removes, like those who flocked to see the painted women on the walls of Cooco's in its heyday. One of Hussain's earliest patrons, Shehla Seegal, the wife of a powerful industrialist, was a voracious collector who became his star-maker, even giving him studio space. Others followed, with the cultural elite soon rushing to buy these images. It is an odd thing, to think of the women here gazing into the homes of the super-rich, and their owners gazing back. Is there a voyeurism there, an admiration, even jealous fascination?

This imagined exchange makes me think of the gulf between the women being painted and all those on the other side of the canvas. The artist, the buyers, onlookers like me. At the end of Louise Brown's book on the Heera Mandi, there is a passage in which Maha is modelling for Hussain. This vision stays in my mind, persistent, jarring. Hussain is evidently painting the area's sex workers with their consent. Yet while his work hangs inside museums, where are the women they depict now? Where is Maha and her daughters?

Some figures in the paintings are turned away from the viewer, in their own worlds. But others look out, straight at us. Hussain's sisters stand in a row, unsmiling in their wedding finery, as if forcibly on display. A row of solemn women are naked and flanked by police in full body armour; they also look at us, or at the artist painting them. It is implicit that they have been forced to strip but by whom, I wonder: the men paying them to dance, the police officers who are supposed to protect them, or the artist painting them in their nudity? They stare out with insinuation in their eyes. They are demanding the answer to a question, it seems. I am not sure how this relates to the dancers at the late-night show in Lahore, but it seems more furtive here. I am discomforted by all that lies between the women being studied and those undertaking the study, with the imbalance of power in between. What do these women feel towards their observers?

Chapter 11
Private dancer

When I was clearing out Fauzia's flat after her death, I found a collection of first-person accounts about sex work from the 1990s on her bookshelf. It included the essay 'Naked, Naughty, Nasty: Peep Show Reflections' by Vicky Funari, who had worked as a dancer in a peep show. Her performances took place behind glass, men on one side, women on the other. The set-up sounded so dated, yet Funari's analysis of the dynamics of looking, and being looked at, was so penetrating that she could have been describing the strippers, exotic dancers or sex-positive models of today.

Funari writes in diary-style entries about the men on the other side of the glass – the way they stare, the way she stares back, and what happens to her, and her body, in this exchange of glances. The looking, she makes clear, is not one way because the dancers are not passive objects. There is aggression and vulnerability on both sides. She holds the men who look at her in her own gaze, and she sees herself in multiples: as she is, as she is being seen by them, as other women have been, and will be, seen.

She follows the psychological chain reaction of these looks, writing of how, when she arrives for work, she gradually begins to see herself at a remove, turning into her own onlooker, and suspending her identity as 'Vicky' to become the peep-show performer, 'Naked Girl'. Although she is taking off her clothes, she describes it as an intellectual dressing up, or a putting on of armour through her nakedness. 'I construct a being who can see and observe and analyse, but who cannot respond or feel,' she writes.

'She is naked, but she is not exposed.' And when she sees a hostile customer at a window, she recognises the look immediately, thinking to herself: 'Okay, you hate me, I hate you, so let's just get down to business and make you come . . .'

I am at first shocked by the perception of mutually exchanged 'hate' between dancer and client. It certainly seems like the wrong reaction from a man who has paid to be there, to emanate hostility towards this purchased experience. I understand the woman's instinct better; the 'hate' may be a judgement of his desires and their fulfilment at her cost. But perhaps he can feel that judgement burning into him through her gaze, or maybe it is a circuit of contempt – he can only be here because she is here, and vice versa.

The hostility in these men's looking is distantly familiar. I have felt it myself, fully clothed, simply walking down the street in daylight. I saw it more when I was younger – the animosity of a stranger watching me do my makeup on a bus, as if disgusted by the act, or the look of contempt when I laughed loudly and uninhibitedly. These reactions left me perplexed. What had I done to inspire them?

Funari goes on to log the exchange of looks, and it is a complicated description of the power, and powerlessness, of a performer who is nakedly present yet removed from her nakedness. Funari's body, in her quasi-vacancy of it, becomes a receptacle for men's desires but this also gives her self-protection. Floating a few metres away from the 'you' who is being seen as a sex object is, I suppose, a way to resist becoming a sex object, although it also sounds like willed dissociation.

A dancer in Lahore talked similarly about a split self: between the dancer and the woman who, after a dance, provides 'room work', as she called it. I met her the day after my trip to the Punjabi comedy, in one of the side streets of the Heera Mandi. Of course, the area's sex workers hadn't gone away, they had simply become less visible. Even in the 1980s, when Zia ul-Haq's military adminstration thought it had driven them out of this dusty inner complex, they gradually requisitioned the Heera Mandi. The tawaif's tradition, clearly, had a claim to this patch of the city which was stronger than any government edict.

Nazree was the head of a household of four daughters, two of whom worked in the family trade. She was sixty-three, large bodied, and had an easy, ageless charm. She came from a multi-generational line of tawaifs, she said, and was raised to dance for a living. Her daughter, Hina, breezed in and out of the room in which we talked, as if she couldn't decide whether or not she wanted to be a part of proceedings. She was twenty-eight, with a self-evident glamour and a hard gravelly laugh. She would come into the room and curl up on the seat opposite me, only to uncurl and disappear when my questions turned to her.

Nazree told me her family story without much prompting; she was an elegant storyteller, not in a rush and with no embarrassment about her trade. 'This is dangerous work,' she said. Because the men could no longer come to them, at the Heera Mandi, they travelled to 'functions' – a private gathering out of town, a wedding party, a basement in a house filled with men – and could never guarantee how safe they would be in these unknown places. She described how they were usually accompanied by musicians, singers and several other dancers.

Hina had become animated when her mother began speaking of performing. She had spent nearly two decades learning to dance with 'gungroos' or ankle-bells and she considered this work a vocation. It required talent, and 'not everyone has it'. She waved away my admiring words about the Punjabi dancers I'd seen in the theatre the previous night, telling me their training could not compare to hers. She began learning classical dance at the age of ten, and still had lessons from the same teacher. 'Those women dance with their bodies' while she danced with her bells. 'If I have worked so hard to perfect my dancing, I want *that* to be the focus,' she had said, and showed me a video recording on her phone of a 'function' in which she was dancing, with a circle of people around her. It was clear that she differentiated this part of her job from the 'room' work. She identified as a dancer, someone who was proud of her skills and who welcomed people's gazes while she danced.

A few months after returning from Lahore, I travel to Amsterdam. I book a hotel close to the train station and when I get there I realise it is in the centre of the red-light district. Brothels were legalised in the Netherlands in 2000 but the district, De Wallen, has been trading in sex since it was built in 1385, with an estimated one thousand sex workers living there by the seventeenth century, rising to three thousand by the early nineteenth century.

Currently, the district hosts nine hundred sex workers a day, standing in four hundred windows to attract customers, and working out of almost three hundred rooms, with each one generating a nightly income of up to €300 for a permit-holding sex worker. I have grown up thinking of the Netherlands' legalised sex trade as the apex of sexual liberation but when I begin to read around the state of the industry now, I learn that its freedoms refer only to *some* who choose to be sex workers, not to those unquantifiable others who are trafficked and forced into the work by pimps or men who call themselves their 'boyfriends'. These exploited women remain indistinguishable, to look at, from the women who are freely exercising their rights; unprotected and invisible to the system.

I walk around the neighbourhood as dusk falls and the streets become filled with groups of men, flushed and gregarious. There is a buzz in the air, an open, animal prowling. This carnal aspect of the night – and the women who are the focus of its attention – so often remains invisible in the daytime, or secluded in its own enclave. But here, in this illuminated red night, it is not peripheral or furtive. It claims solid life and demands street space. There is honesty in that, at least. But both the men who look and the women who are being looked at stir up a discomfort in me that feels similar to that of the Dutch woman at the Lahore theatre. I feel myself first confused, then angry. It is, I decide, because the women here seem so passive. They emerge at their windows, in bras and knickers, and stand as if in a gym changing room. They have none of the swaggering, outlier spirit of the dancers in Lahore. Maybe they are simply comfortable that way, not trying to amuse, or perform. They are advertising for customers, I suppose, not there to put on a free show.

From among them, a figure steps into a large lit-up window. She looks different from the others, much more poised, and glamorous, like an extra from *Boogie Nights*, in a silver jumpsuit, split down the middle, with sequins quivering brightly. Everyone on the street turns to look. The rules of engagement, for customers or otherwise, demand that no one stops to stare in front of any one window, but I slow down in awe at this shimmering goddess of the red-light district. She stands with a hip cocked, as if she's a model in a photo-shoot. She faces dead ahead, impervious to the stares, and she seems to smile, slightly. She wears a pair of oversized sunglasses that look as if they are protecting her against her own blinding brilliance. Her eyes are the only part of her that remains obscured. I keep staring, trying to see where she is looking, slowly beginning to wonder if it is at us or if she is gazing beyond, bored of the passing adoration. Then a thought occurs: could she be one of Amsterdam's trafficked women? How would I know the difference, even as she smiles her dazzling smile?

'There is no standard sex worker,' Funari writes in her essay, and this is why it is so hard to make any generalisations around power, choice and consent when discussing sex work. I speak to advocates in the industry who confirm this. Lily works as a counsellor in Edinburgh, mostly for escorts and sex workers in the city's brothels, which operate as saunas or massage parlours. She has seen greater levels of satisfaction in women who specialise in sadomasochistic fetish work because the work is, by definition, so clearly boundaried and a dominatrix must assume sexual power, not be divested of it. Even if that power is performed as part of the financial exchange, its outcome is still often a happier one, Lily reflects. But the work across the board can bring all sorts of psychic damage, in how sex workers see themselves. A significant number of escorts are 'terrified' of their bodies, so much so that they can't face themselves in the mirror and no longer know what they look like. Even the highest paid escort is sacrificing her own desire for someone else's, she says, so if a sex worker starts to think about her body, she must necessarily acknowledge its trauma. This sounds further reaching than Funari's semi-vacancy of the body, disturbingly so. More a full-on abandonment, so that the sexual transaction can take place, but with the woman unable to wholly re-inhabit herself when it's over. To look in the mirror is perhaps to be reminded of this forced flight from oneself, and also the physical source of the repeated trauma.

It is not until some months later when I am looking through Fauzia's art portfolio that I see what might have interested my sister in Funari's ways of looking. Among the work she made is a series featuring naked women, embroidered on plain white cloth, colourfully stitched, who are all either looking at themselves in mirrors or looking at us looking at them, with a mirror reflection of their bodies in the backdrop. They seem to welcome our gaze, as they lie voluptuously across sofas and seats, not poised but sprawled and comfortable with themselves. Each woman has a different body shape and hairstyle. One has the cartoony look of Beryl Cook's larger, middle-aged ladies. Another resembles Édouard Manet's nude *Olympia*, who raised such controversy in nineteenth-century Paris because she was thought to be a prostitute; in my sister's version, she is much fleshier, and mischievous-looking. Some of the women wear no underwear, others wear thigh boots or ribbed stockings. All have a cat beside them, and each woman is grinning.

Are they sex workers? For some years, Fauzia lived in Edinburgh and had a friend who worked as an escort. Maybe these artworks were created then. If so, what are they saying? That you can smile in the face of your own objectification, like the shimmering woman in the Amsterdam window? Or that these women refuse to be diminished by what Funari spoke of as men's hostility and hate? Faced with a pornographic gaze, can you decide not to be objectified, to become bullet-proofed against it? Or, rather, to be objectified on your own terms, so that the baring of flesh is for your pleasure first? What gives these embroidered women their power? They seem to wholly inhabit their bodies, carefree in their physicality, their smiles embracing the viewer's gaze, full of their own naked joy and oblivious to the exchange of hostility or hate. They haven't had to absent any part of themselves, as Funari does in the lead-up to her peep shows, and it feels impossible for anyone's gaze to reduce them. Where have I seen this before? In Pakistan, watching the dancers of the Punjabi comedy. The sensibility matches so strongly, I feel as if my sister must have seen them too.

Or is it that she was freeing these beautifully stitched women from the hostile male gaze in choosing to depict their nakedness not as 'naughty' or 'nasty' but natural and at one with itself? The series beams with a sunny idealism which sits at odds with my sister's lifetime of depression. But the series is also a revelation, reminding me that women who might be mistaken for victims are not necessarily so. These embroidered figures present a different possibility, a hope.

Part 6

Thrill of the dark

Chapter 12
Up all night

I am on the lower deck of the N20 as it swings northwards from Trafalgar Square. It is 1.30 a.m. and the arterial central London street outside is abandoned in darkness. A quiet night lull fills the inside of the bus, with its dimmed lights and electric 'shush' of the doors as they open. There is an efficiency on the road that is never there in daytime, with little traffic and quickly changing lights. The bus driver, obscured in his dark glass compartment, slaloms down the street, like he is in a tearing rush to reach the end of his route. Other buses hurtle past, their illuminated destinations conjuring voyages into deepest suburbia: Enfield, Penge, Uxbridge. I am the only passenger, other than a sleeping man laid across the back seats. It is pleasurably meditative, steaming through the night like this, the bus rocking like a giant cradle as we go. I think of my brother's looping bus trips as a teenager when he would travel for the sake of watching day melt into night from the upper decks. The dark, out of these windows, allows my thoughts to clear, and my imagination to expand outwards.

But as soon as we hit Leicester Square, the after-party crowd clambers on and the bus explodes into roisterousness. The sleeper at the back shuffles awake, and I instinctively sit up straighter. Men in fancily patterned shirts sway on, chomping on chips and burgers. Women shout across seats with unbridled sociability, their heads still in the throb of whichever pub or club they've just left. One group is already in full debrief mode: 'We should definitely go back there . . .' I count the lone women as they get on. There are a few, some watchful, meeting my gaze, others in their own worlds. One is wearing an electronic bracelet that flashes colours when she gets off, then every time she swings her arm as she walks away. It looks like a rave accessory and a safety device in one. I follow the trail of its luminous blues and reds and yellows, lighting up long after the rest of her has vanished into the night.

There is fun to be had in city darkness, whatever the dangers. This bus encapsulates its enchantments: weekend hedonism with the promise of wantonness, mischief, joy, excess. It's all here, in the mussed hair, smeared eye makeup and hot, cheap food. This is recreational darkness, inviting us to seek out excitements the day simply cannot yield. I have become so attuned to working at night that I'd forgotten the pleasure-seeking, Friday-night feeling inside this bus. There was a time that it felt not only important but essential to party until the early hours of the morning, but this kind of night seems long gone for me now, with a peer group too tired or busy to come out, when I ask.

So I go out alone. Not in London but in Berlin, where I am told by a German friend, Barbara, that it is not unusual for women to go clubbing by themselves. She has done it. I resolve to do the same. I am in the city for work, staying on its outer western reaches, in Charlottenburg. It is well after 11 p.m. when I head out, but I feel no tiredness. In an online lecture series on medieval sleeping habits that I tuned into a few months ago, there was mention of a certain, emphatic kind of 'voluntary insomnia' and how, in Japanese literature, during the Heian and Kamakura periods of the ninth to fourteenth centuries, characters from the nobility indulged in this pleasurable nocturnal wakefulness by sitting on verandas to admire the moon, receiving visitors, playing music and telling stories. It feels like I'm doing something similar, but I'm jittery about my lone night odyssey nonetheless; it has been years since I last went clubbing, and I have never gone on my own before. I'm not sure what it means to inhabit this space, at the age of fifty-one.

I have decided to head to Berghain, situated in former East Germany and regarded as a high temple of techno. Its roots lie in the gay and fetish scenes of the late 1990s and it is not only famed for its sophisticated, state-of-the-art sound systems but also for its dark rooms, nudity and sexual abandon. It is the most pernickety of the city's clubs, with no photography permitted inside and a notoriously haughty door policy, with staff letting in just a fraction of the hopefuls who queue for two to three hours on a weekend night, and some past charges of racism among its bouncers. A few days before I get here, I send Barbara a photo of the outfit I've packed: 'They might ask you to take some of that off,' she messages back, and tells me I would fare better with more flesh on show, and an outfit with an edge of BDSM or kink. I blink at my reflection in the mirror now. I am wearing a chainmail dress, along with an assortment of mesh, fishnet, gold and leopard-skin. I look like a burlesque version of myself.

I squint for the taxi on the silent road outside my hotel but feel no apprehension. I am going to be delivered into safe, augmented, internal darkness, filled with sound and light – if I make it in. I have heard the stories about Berghain but never bought into its legend. Its owners, Norbert Thormann and Michael Teufele, refuse to be interviewed, but DJ Daniel Wang, who was at the 2004 opening of its original wing, Panorama Bar, has spoken of the ambition to 'create a club as a work of art'. Duly reclassified as an 'arts venue' in 2016, I wonder if Berghain's status as an edgy landmark is past its prime, now more of a revered institution, or tourist hotspot. Lady Gaga has performed there, Elon Musk queued up but never partied there. It is hardly cutting-edge. Still, I feel a butterfly nervousness as I get out of the taxi and come face-to-face with a concrete fortress, jutting into the midnight sky.

A former power plant, Berghain could be a brutalist museum, a Soviet prison or the Reichstag itself. Industrial sprawl lies all around it, entangled with overgrown grassland and an air of dereliction: fenced-off roads, a disused railway track, faded swathes of graffiti. Silent explosions of light detonate across its windows and the building throbs with a distant, deep bass, like a heartbeat pumping sound into the dead around it. There are a few people standing at the door, but not the long queues I have been told about. I'm confused. I was braced for a couple of hours of waiting, and hopefully making friends on the way in, but the iron stiles by the entrance are empty. The prospect of getting in so quickly is both alluring and unnerving as the bouncers come into view. They are nondescript, not especially fashionable, but numerous – around five – standing in a semicircle around the door. I have not given any consideration to what I will say, how I will present myself. Now, as I approach them, I feel tongue-tied and gauche, like I've forgotten to prepare for an essential part of an audition.

The hippest of the bouncers, a young Black man with an American accent and turn-up jeans, is speaking to the cluster of people ahead of me. 'Sorry, guys, not tonight,' he says, and points damningly to one man in the gang who is dressed in black, and looks innocuous. The group stands in what seems like stricken silence before moving slowly away. The bouncer turns to look at me. His face remains impassive, and I wonder if he thinks I am a straggler from the group he has just turned away. I want to clarify that I am here on my own, which I hope might count for something, but he keeps on staring and I feel, awkwardly, as if a judgement has been passed in his silence and I have already outstayed my welcome. I think of sweet, amicable Maria Martins, the bouncer I met at the door of the Gielgud Theatre for *Opening Night*, who told me stories of working at Heaven, a gay nightclub in central London. It was clear that Maria had supervised that door as a guardian, welcoming all but the obnoxious or anti-social. The door had been run by two women, she had said: Jo and Kaye. 'They were the best security

I'd ever met. They knew who was coming to make trouble and who wasn't.'

These Cerberus-like figures at Berghain seem to hold a very different role, one akin to casting, with an added sense of tyrannical whimsy. Withholding entry based on such enigmatic criteria seems like a bizarre nightlife model. The failure of so many to get in adds to the club's appeal and commercial lustre – successful entry endowing the chosen ones with specialness. Is this genuine inclusivity or is it uber-capitalism with a twist of canny marketing? If the latter, I am manipulated by it. I *want* to make the Styx-like crossing into this underworld, even though I don't know what lies inside it. So I stand in front of the man, pleading with my eyes, my smile. My outré outfit is covered up by my coat but he continues to calculate something beyond it. We have barely spoken and he has little to go on, as far as I can tell. Slowly the impasse ends, his face softens, and I am in.

It is unexpected, exhilarating. So much so, I feel unsure of what to do next. Unsmiling attendants chivvy me onwards, tape up my phone so I can't take pictures, and take €20 in exchange for a bracelet which grants me entry until 12 p.m. the next day. I am awed by the club's vastness inside, its hulking girdered steel, its stark industrial glamour. I sit opposite the cloakroom, lost. There are no signs to help navigate the floors, and the architectural layout seems designed to confound: corridors leading to dead-ends or openings into empty rooms. Eventually, I follow a group up a metal staircase with walls covered in layers of old billboards and flyers. East German samizdat might be buried in this mouldering, papier-mâché palimpsest.

Upstairs is a maze of even darker spaces. The central room is dungeon-like although it is lit up with occasional bursts of white and red strobe lighting which give off an otherworldly celestial glow. These lights were the explosions I saw in the windows outside. It is a Friday night and only the Panorama Bar is open; it is the original, smaller quarter of Berghain, which plays house music rather than techno. The bigger club in the rooms next door, across three floors, is closed until Saturday. The music hits me like a wave and my mood changes as I am submerged into it, its currents simultaneously pulsating and relaxing so that I feel as if I have swallowed an upper and downer in one. The crowd circles the DJ booth in unabashed worship.

I remember now, with unexpected intensity, how I loved this music once, and this world. Clubbing was a vital part of my life in the late 1980s and '90s, when the music inside the north London clubs I started sneaking into, from the age of fifteen, changed so fast that it felt like one genre spawning the next, from house to acid, techno, jungle, drum 'n' bass, each Friday night outing leading to the discovery of a new, irresistible sound. The bass here is so physical that it travels through me as if it were solid and I was air. Its beat, ranging from 115 to 130 per minute, is faster than the average resting heartbeat and I feel my pulse automatically quicken, my heart pump harder. It is a tidal wave of sound, so immersive it is impossible to resist. I feel fifteen again, electrified, in a first encounter with this high.

There is a scintillating moment in *A Girl Walks Home Alone at Night* when Arash asks if he can go back to her house. He is besotted and wants to extend their date further into the night. To him, she is a sweetly laconic girl in a chador. He has no inkling of her vampire nature. She agrees and we see them in her room, he in the back of the shot looking guileless, her face turned towards the camera, broodingly, it seems. She has shown herself to be a ruthless hunter of men up to this point so we anticipate, any minute now, that she will expose her fangs and he will be the night's meat. Instead, she puts on a record and they begin dancing, eyes closed, around her room. It is a lovely moment when they are no longer human prey versus demonic bloodsucker but two people, transformed together, dancing in the night. I imagine Ana Lily Amirpour's vampire swaying, eyes closed, among this crowd, her body in the grip of the music. She would not be out of place here.

For all the fugitive, frightening elements of the night, there is this: the thrill of convening together in euphoria. Dancing in this sparking darkness is as elemental as collecting around firelight, heady and hectic. How could I have forgotten how *fundamental* hedonism is to the soul, not merely as recreation but so much more? I've thirsted for it, for years, I just didn't realise it.

I take in the intersections of the crowd, the bar, the chill-out spaces, the unisex toilets which are almost as basic as the old hole-in-the-ground cubicles at the Glastonbury Festival. There are open cubicles at the back of the dance floor, which look like animal pens and double up as dark areas, I'm told. I buy a bottle of water and am taken aback when the barman is friendly. There is an instant, infectious energy up here, very different from the achingly cool cloakroom assistants and bouncers downstairs. People are smiling, happy, disconcertingly so. They stop me for conversation, some taking out their taped-over phones and asking to follow my Instagram account. The music is loud and yet we can chat without shouting. As they dance, they talk about the music, their jobs and lives. They tell me they like my dress, and ask me where I'm from, what brought me here. It is as if we are trusted friends simply because we are in this space together. I am suspicious for a while, but then it begins to feel like its own world, and I absorb its rules. I become friendly back, part of this house party.

Founded within queer and kink culture, it attracts mixed crowds these days, although this room carries a queer energy, filled with people of all ages and gender identities. There are many more men than women, some shirtless and wearing harnesses, one in a silver grass skirt, another in an animal mask, and several dancing with flamenco fans. The flamboyant mixes with the carnivalesque; nothing seems out of bounds, but nothing is threatening either. Is this what the bouncers sniff out, and curate for?

I see a woman who is naked under a mesh dress, and another in a swimming costume and trainers. For a moment I think of Vicky Funari, dressing up as 'Naked Girl' for her peep show. This nudity is so different, although it too seems like a performance, but without the mutually hostile exchange of gazes. There's equality and choice in people's looking here. The nakedness does not seem to be part of a currency, where someone has bought the right to stare at someone else, but rather a form of self-expression. There's a flaunting joy in it – the same quality I saw in my sister's embroidered women.

I move onto the dance floor and people make way for me. I feel oddly, instantly, at ease, in my outrageous outfit. Funari, in her essay, wrote about her nudity as her 'armour'. Had I wanted a kind of protection too, and so I came dressed in chainmail? I needn't have worried. The looks here aren't prowling. Barbara was right; there is nothing unusual about being a woman out on her own, and there is no sense of predation here, not for me, at least. I am relieved by this prevailingly queer crowd, maybe because I know there will be less appraisal, and less hassle, that I can just dance without feeling my freedom under siege from some other expectation.

But I wonder if this atmosphere might be intrinsic to the music itself – if its trance-like repetition offers an atomised high that drives you further into yourself, while simultaneously integrating you into the crowd around you. The music writer Hillegonda C. Rietveld believes that house music has a sound that is 'listened' to by the body, and that as a communal experience it brings a euphoric sense of dissolving: 'As subjectivity disintegrates, a sense of "the (objectified) other" disappears as well,' she writes in her book *This Is Our House*. The loud, un-self-consciously sweaty house clubs I went to in the 1990s had a push-and-pull between eyes-closed introspection, and the bigger collective experience, but I never felt prowled upon there either. And before that, as a teenager dressed androgynously, I wanted both to be among the crowd and not looked at, seeking the same meditative invisibility of my childhood street walks.

A Brazilian trans woman stops to talk. She has been coming here for thirteen years, she says, and introduces me to her group. A French NGO worker from Paris says hello as she rolls a cigarette; a woman from Portland on the dance floor tells me she has come on her own too. I keep catching sight of her over the course of the night and she never stops dancing. An Israeli man in a sequinned skirt circles back to me again and again, asking me more about myself each time. I wonder about these people: are they tourist clubbers? Do they have otherwise corporate lives? Have they come here to be something other than who they are in daytime, or do they become most fully themselves when they get here? And what is the wider meaning of this hedonism, beyond the intensity of the here and now, for them, for me?

A Slovakian food-truck owner points to the bottle in my hand and asks if I am planning on only drinking water, then asks if I do drugs. He is a regular, he says, and I wonder if he is a dealer, or a plant hired by the club to monitor guests. I ask him if he has ever been turned away from Berghain, for dressing the wrong way, and he shakes his head. The key to getting in is not putting on a 'costume', he tells me, but expressing your identity in your look. I think back to the bouncer's slow, silent appraisal of me at the door. Was he trying to ascertain if I was in fancy dress? Or did he see something in me that I hadn't quite seen in myself outside the club, but which now feels like a long-eclipsed, perhaps even forcibly buried version of me?

Because, once I have crossed the threshold and am inside this transfiguring darkness, I am no longer a responsible homeowner, journalist and carer of elderly parents. I am no more or less than my silver-black dress and gold eyelashes, the outfit itself presenting the possibility of becoming another 'me'. I feel this with an almost pharmaceutical clarity, as if the music has led me to this 'truth'. A scholarly study of Berghain in 2022 described it as a night-space that radically changed people's sense of self. Identity became porous and the architecture of the building itself impacted sexual orientation, Johann Andersson argued in his paper 'Berghain: Space, affect and sexual orientation'. Have the rooms and corridors unpinned my sense of self? No, I am both pinned and unpinned, deeper in myself but also part of this synchronised whole. Is this feeling of immersion both within and without a result of the music, or the darkness – or a confluence of both?

An Austrian man in a midriff top and Doc Martens tells me he has stayed at Berghain for days at a time. A Saturday entry bracelet allows you to remain in the club until Monday. There are beds, he says, and shower rooms. He walks me around and I come across spaces I haven't yet seen: more dim cubby-holes and a cage-like, bare room that has the look of an abattoir, where people stand talking. I ask him what he does for a living and when he tells me he is a postman, he says it with such remove that I imagine his 'working' self is still out there, delivering letters in the daylight world. He speaks enthusiastically of other festivals and clubs he has been to across Europe, ever more extreme in his stories of partying night upon day upon night again. This, it is clear, is where he lives his 'real' life.

I can see why. The highs of the day pale in comparison with the intensity of this rush, and I find myself feeling the urgency to come back and back and back again even while I am still here. The longer I dance, the more I feel suspended in the room's blazing darkness. With the curtains drawn, it does not feel like the day, not night either, but a third state: we are in a perpetual darkness, manufactured so it is thicker and more alluring than its natural counterpart. There are no mirrors in the bathroom and it has been hours since I saw myself from the outside. It is too dark to check my watch and any ordinary concept of time passing has long since dissolved. The club has conspired to render me so porous that even my body clock has been assailed. I am standing in the maelstrom of a timeless 'now'. Is this what hedonism is? A present moment so total that it becomes eternal, its nothingness claiming you entirely?

I am not sure how long I have been dancing because time is so bent out of shape. It is only when a woman taps me on the shoulder and points to a chink in a tall window's black-out blind that I see the outline of natural light around its corners. 'Look, the sun's up,' she says, laughing. She is right, it is morning outside, although from here it looks surreal, irrelevant. Maybe that's why she laughed. The sight of this natural light switches something in me, though. It is almost six o'clock in the morning. The music has swallowed up so many hours. Slowly, I wrench myself out of the enveloping timelessness, away from the hypnotic dance floor, and feel the regret of my impending departure.

I begin to leave the room but I circle back around a few times, until I finally go downstairs to the cloakroom. Even there, the mood has shifted and the attendants are smiling, as if we have become friends. The American who let me in is leaning against the iron stiles, his group of bouncers now thinned out, and we nod as I pass. The daylight is blinding and I am uncertain on my feet, physical exhaustion hitting me abruptly. I turn around and take in the building, still throbbing in its permanent state of partying night. I feel desperately disappointed to be outside, and I consider going back in a few times. I want to keep gulping down more of the music, more of the dark and its joyful abandon. I feel as if I have left friends behind. In spite of my tiredness I want to run back in. What is this? A desire for more hedonism? No, not exactly, I realise, over coming days. It is the wish to be among a community of people, to be part of a congregation in the dark, and to belong to that congregation, for that time. I see now how people come here not to be released but to be returned to themselves.

CHAPTER 13
Heaven

A few weeks after returning to London, I go to an immersive theatre production staged across several dimmed rooms and dark, winding tunnels. It is a show by the company Punchdrunk, which reimagines Barry Pain's 1901 short story 'The Moon-Slave', about a princess named Viola who is drawn to a secret maze to dance with delirious abandon at night. She is lured there by the full moon and it is a spirited act of self-assertion at first, to go to the maze, but it turns darker and more compulsive with every sighting of the full moon, which pulls her inexorably into the maze's centre to dance, as if against her will. Its siren call reminds me of Professor Dijk's study of lunar effects on women, its science throwing light on the moon's mysterious, magnet power.

We are given headsets on entry to the show and a pre-recorded narrative leads us into a bedroom which has all the sparkly detritus of a teenager's life: fairy-lights, posters, sheaves of poetry. It reminds me of the adolescent paraphernalia of Holly's bedroom in Middlesbrough, when I went to visit. We are instructed to lie on a bed, and the light fades to black. Viola's story, adapted by the novelist Daisy Johnson, has a Dionysian delirium to it; it hovers somewhere between waking dream, fairy tale and hallucination. 'The intoxication of the dance was on her,' we hear, and the story flips from a girl's discovery of dervish-like pleasure to a kind of demon possession. Viola disappears at the end, abducted, it seems: the only clue of her vanishing a cloven-hooved imprint in the sand next to her own slippered footprint. I see it as a story about disobedient femininity, of a girl choosing not to marry the prince waiting dotingly for her in a castle, but to stay on the outside, choosing to become the 'female monstrous' in her alliance with the devil. In my father's stories, she might be transformed into a daayan.

But I also recognise it as a warning against hedonism – its tipping from excitement to uncontrollable excess. It could be Pain's metaphor for addiction. I see Fauzia in it and my own compulsive tendencies too. I felt Viola's delicious mix of fear and desire in my pleasurable unravelling at Berghain; the instant, addictive pull of being there, the desperation to return as soon as I'd left, the fear of being swallowed into the depths of the whale, and the intense desire to never be wretched back up into the light.

The next day, in Berlin, it felt as if I had travelled to another realm the night before: a portal to another self, which was now out of reach again. Yet, the emotional intensity of the experience stayed with me. I couldn't stop talking about it, even when I saw people's eyes glazing over as I spoke of my club-night epiphany. I knew I was too old to be eulogising about the delights of all-night clubbing, that I would probably baulk at my breathlessness if I hadn't felt the thrill of the room. My feelings, even to myself, were embarrassing, like falling in love again after declaring love's ardour as nothing more than callow illusion. Just like the grip of Viola's dance, the closed universe of the club felt as important as the world outside, more so; a forgotten but significant part of myself rediscovered, an inner maze found, within.

Was Berghain its own dark kingdom with a maze at its concrete and steel centre? There was an opacity to the building, even when I was inside it. I came across roped-off areas with notices that they were exclusively for gay or non-binary guests, and I presumed these led into other rooms and hidden parties. Berghain grew out of the gay club Ostgut, as a safe, hedonistic space, and it seems to have retained something of that core spirit. The cordons I came across were proof of this 'original' centre, invisible in plain sight, a parallel world more extreme and intense than the rooms around it. I didn't see any signs for it but in the basement is a male-only 'play safe, dress dirty' sex club, Lab.Oratory, famed for its extravagant 'piss parties' and nights in which rooms are filled with mud, with partygoers role-playing as pigs.

So much counterculture has been sparked in the dark, manifesting as hedonism but containing its own radical politics. Queer night-time spaces have served as sanctuaries from the inequalities of the day, from London's eighteenth-century Molly Houses to the city's modern-day clubs like Heaven and G-A-Y, even as these clubs have become more mainstream. The writer Ed Gillett charts the history of dance music, and how its original underground scene pushed against daytime constraints and prejudices. Soundsystem culture was born out of exclusion and rooted in injustice, he argues in his book, *Party Lines: Dance Music and the Making of Modern Britain*. The origins of house lie on the margins, among those deemed 'outsiders'. Born out of Chicago's musical underworld in the 1970s, often played in squats, juice bars and unlicensed industrial spaces that could not easily be surveilled by police, it was taken up by African-American DJs; these first house clubs became inclusive partying spaces for marginalised Black, Latino and gay communities.

The foundation story around house music is one example of how the night allows those deemed 'outsiders' or transgressors to convene, create and take their place in the world in ways that the day doesn't permit. The search for belonging can take place in this dark more safely, I think, although the idea of belonging has always held equivocal meanings for me, as someone who is not part of the queer community through sexual orientation but who does not feel at home with nuclear family heterosexuality either, caught between Britishness and Pakistani identity. I live in between day and night in my work, and now I find myself suspended in mid-life too, where I waver between my younger self and this changing, older self, my mother's and my father's features emerging from my face when I look in the mirror. I have learned to live on the borders, in a kind of twilight space of belonging that I thought I liked, and found liberating. But what I felt was so seductive inside the darkened room and sparks of light in Berlin was the experience of belonging as a physical act. In the midst of a gathering, in physical proximity, united by breath and sweat and movement, in communion, made all the more ecstatic in the pulsing darkness.

****

When I visit my father at his nursing home and find him in a lucid state of mind, I often see him looking around his room, or at the row of patio doors if we are sitting in the back garden, as if he is trying to puzzle something out. When I wheel him around to the front of the home, to sit in the conservatory, he cranes his neck to look into every bedroom we pass, at the residents sitting or lying in their beds inside. Then he'll ask me if this is a hostel, or a prison. 'It's your home, Dad,' I say, but he looks unconvinced, as if my answer is more implausible than the other possibilities he has offered up.

I can see why he would be confused. This is his home, and it is homely in many ways, but it is also a holding place, of sorts. There is a sense of being uprooted, or removed, of no longer belonging to the world he inhabited before his illness, with all the old markers of who he has been obliterated, or reduced to nostalgic memorabilia, like the framed black and white photo montages on his walls that show the younger versions of him, us, his old home, his old life. They tell him who he used to be, and where he once belonged. Sometimes I think about taking these images down. Do they crowd around him in his room, insinuating that he is no longer that person? Do they leave a vacancy around who he is now, in the aftermath of the real, true, well version of him that they evoke?

I saw the same black-and-white picture galleries in bedrooms of the Hertfordshire care home on my night shift. I think how hard it must be to keep a hold on your place in the world, when it has changed in this way. My father is sitting within a pause in his life, and sometimes it seems like a post-life, from the outside, at least. But there are days when he remembers exactly who he is – and was – and looks utterly at home here, in this home, and within himself. It is a reminder for me that belonging, and being at home, is a feeling and state of mind as much as a place on a map. Other residents are equally vigorous, on their good days. I have made friends with several over the years. One of them is David Jackson, whose wheelchair I initially breezed past as he sat in the conservatory. He looked younger than most of the other residents, and I assumed he had early onset dementia, or another cognitive impairment, because he seemed so silent and impassive, always looking straight ahead.

When he turned his head and said 'hello' it surprised me. The next time, I stopped to chat, and I realised he was full of stories. He was originally from the West Midlands, or the Black Country, as he preferred to call it, telling me that the region had acquired its moniker in the Victorian age when its factories and foundries belched so much black smoke that they blocked the sun with their pall. Midday would have looked like midnight, he said. A place of permanent, industrial night.

David was fifty-four and had initially been sent to hospital with a serious chest infection. He had received no physiotherapy in the three months he'd lain in bed there and by the time he was well enough to be released, his legs had become atrophied. He had, he said, lived on the streets for most of his adult life, addicted to heroin for much of that time. Astonishingly, he had overcome the addiction, using methadone to wean himself off. He had been clean of heroin for ten years, off crack cocaine for six. The flesh around one half of his nose was missing – as a result of cancer – but he pointed this out in the same emotionally neutral way as he told me his history of heroin addiction. 'You feel like you're wrapped in cotton wool, nothing can hurt you,' he said, 'even if coming back down is like having six illnesses at once.'

Many months after we began talking, he told me he had once been a 'cross-dresser'. He came from a big working-class family with several sisters and began dressing up in their clothes, secretly, from the age of nine, enjoying the pleasure of his transformation. It felt good to be in their dresses, he said, but he kept what he was doing from everyone, until he was caught by his mother in his teens. He spoke of his shame and fear too, that his father, a building site shot-blaster, might find out. 'He would have killed me,' said David, although it sounded from his family stories as if he was brutalised by his father anyway, often beaten for no given reason.

He left home at fifteen and moved to London to be a trainee locksmith, but ended up homeless for the next twenty-three years. He never stopped cross-dressing, but this part of his life was always kept secret until his fortieth birthday, when he put on a skirt and went to the West End wearing it. What made him switch so suddenly? I asked, and he told me that a straight, male friend, also homeless, with whom he was squatting, had caught him dressing up. Rather than shaming him, he had readily accepted this female side of David's identity.

That moment set something free and, from then on, he moved between his male identity as David and his female alter ego, Davinia. He described himself in old-school terminology as a 'transvestite', telling me of the joy of being a woman, feeling most alive at night when he would go to a club called the WayOut, in Tower Gateway, east London, and where he could 'meet other trannies'. This world sounded like another invisible kingdom, or hidden maze. The club became a regular haunt and, gradually, he felt confident enough to walk there, dressed as Davinia. 'I remember seeing my reflection in a window one night and thinking, "Wow, this is what people see when they look at me."' When was the last time he went to the WayOut? I asked and he shrugged again. 'It was such a buzz, but it's probably long since closed.'

When I look it up, I find the club is still running, although not from its original home, but at a bar near Warren Street. It was founded in 1993 by Vicky Lee, and is now the oldest trans club in London. It has been a few weeks since my night at Berghain and I still feel brave enough to enter a not entirely dissimilar space on my own, although Vicky later tells me that – in the time-honoured tradition of queer clubs – many straight women come so they can drink and dance freely, without being propositioned by men.

The door to the club is closely guarded when I get there and I feel the tension around it; the bouncers are stopping everyone for a chat before they enter. It is very different inside, relaxed and intimate, with a mostly middle-aged crowd, around David's age or older. Everyone is dressed to the nines, except for a few men on their own. I imagine David here, smoking his roll-ups and watching the room. I half wish I had invited him along, but I have been put off by the logistical hazard of bringing him here in his wheelchair on my own, even if the care home had allowed it.

I take in the details, so I can relay everything to him when I see him next. There are two performers singing Amy Winehouse and Shania Twain covers on a raised dais, and an excitable social mingling in between songs. People smile at each other on their way to the bar, and maybe because I am on my own, some say hello, winding their arms around my shoulders, as if to tell me that I am welcome. The atmosphere in the basement, around the dance floor, is more tightly wound; it feels like a nervy high school prom, with men clasping their drinks around its sides, as they wait for the women to start dancing.

The club is its own community, says Vicky. It has brought innumerable people together, with sixteen marriages that they know of over thirty years. Some are openly trans, others simply curious. She points to a man in jeans and T-shirt, drinking at a table nearby. 'If I start chatting to him, he might tell me he's wearing stockings underneath the denim, or that he's attracted to trans girls.' Many trans women Vicky knows also work as escorts but come here to find a relationship; others turn up for a sense of community that can't be found openly, in daytime. Anti-trans prejudice has risen over the years, Vicky tells me, and it has never felt so dangerous to her as it does now. Where she might have taken public transport in a dress some years ago, she travels by car now for her own safety.

Since 1993, the WayOut has been through nineteen venues, moving on to the next when one closes, finding a way to exist, whatever the state of the world. Many come to the club in different clothes, to protect themselves; there are changing rooms and makeup artists so everyone can feel fully themselves inside. 'Once you're in, it's a sanctuary. Then, it's about joy and safety and self-expression,' says Vicky. I leave the club when the karaoke stops and the party is in full swing downstairs. The bouncers are now bantering with the women who come out for cigarettes, making way for the men who look at the ground as they enter, maybe for the first time. The club is in its element, at least until morning.

Once David has told me about Davinia, I hear him talking to others about her too as I breeze past, and his manner seems changed. He sits with legs crossed, holds his cigarette differently, and is louder, more playful. There is colour in his cheeks. Sometimes he beckons me over to tell me what he'd wear as 'Vee', his abbreviation for Davinia. Occasionally I see others squirming as he speaks, but he is impervious to their discomfort.

Then, it is as if the act of speaking about Davinia brings her back to life. I come into the home one Sunday to see him in a wig with girlish plaits. Every time I see him after that he seems more glamorous, closer to becoming Vee, in a miniskirt, lipstick, hairband, tights. The carers get involved, the manager bringing in a dress, the activities coordinator painting Vee's nails bright red. I ask about pronouns, as I'm walking in one day. 'It's always "she" now,' Vee tells me. It is as if Davinia has made her way here from the WayOut's celebratory darkness, into day, and that David has breathed life back into her through her stories.

Chapter 14
Lighting up the dark

It is midnight and I am in Leeds, in the middle of a moving crowd. People are throwing shapes around me, spinning on their heels, flapping their arms. I do the same, my rucksack jiggling on my back. I was freezing cold a couple of hours ago, now I'm hot-faced with my sweater knotted around my hips. I'm back up in the city, a few weeks after my drive with Al Garthwaite, for a mass public dance that started as the sun was setting and will go on until 1 a.m. The silent disco kicked off in this city square at 8.30 p.m., and a few hours later the crowd has become a huge, swinging body, unbounded. Electronic music fizzes into my ears and streams down my limbs.

This is another way to experience the night, and its 'dazzling' darkness. The dance is the culmination of a walk across the city which traced the route of the 1977 Reclaim the Night protest march, this time in celebration, with dance and music along the way. *Dance (All Night, Leeds)* was conceived by the artist Melanie Manchot, and similar versions have already been staged in Paris and London, adapted for each city. Here, the idea is to infuse communal joy into streets once defiled by Peter Sutcliffe's violence, and through it, heal the city's collective trauma. I think of the women from that time who Al said were scared to venture out after dark. I hope they're here tonight.

Al gave a speech at our meeting point, close to Hyde Park, where a small group had convened – mothers with teenage daughters, fathers with babies in papooses – but we collected people along the way, scooping them up as we walked through the park. A Chinese dragon skittered up front, its paper scales fluttering.

Skateboarders joined in, giving it the feel of a promenading street party. Stag parties and pub crawlers were momentarily silenced by the sight of our procession, which turned from fifteen to fifty to many more by the time we arrived at this square, in front of the city's art gallery.

I have been here since, dancing, and there are no dress codes, no bouncers, no artificially manufactured darkness. Above us, the night twinkles. I feel silly, self-conscious, and then, as if the bubbling fizz of the cold air has gone to my head, ridiculously happy.

When I met Melissa Harrison for our night walk in Suffolk, she told me that long before she became a nature writer, she was a clubber, working for the dance magazine *Mixmag*. Field raves were all the rage in Surrey where she grew up. She'd watch her older sister getting ready to go out at night, and then she started going to Ibiza every summer herself when she was old enough. The club scene seems an unlikely home for a nature lover, a packed dance floor at odds with organic open spaces, but these worlds come together in fields and at festivals, she said.

Although I am in the middle of the city, I can see what she means. Opposite me is a limber older woman with tie-dyed trousers and white hair, moving uninhibitedly. No one forgets how to dance, I think as a watch her, and doing so together feels like an ancient ritual in the open air. By midnight there are still quite a few of us. Couples clasping each other, friends swaying, and lone women weaving rhythmically among them, smiling at each other in recognition. We are safe tonight.

They remind me of Debris Stevenson, a playwright, poet, and one of the greatest enthusiasts for solo raving that I know. I first met her several years ago, when she staged a musical at the Royal Court Theatre in London. *Poet in Da Corner* was about her Mormon upbringing, queer sexuality and coming out, set to a grime soundtrack that she performed herself. In our conversation then, she had mentioned that she'd been dancing around the world, on her own, since the age of nineteen. There is something incredibly powerful about occupying the streets in this way at night, she says when we meet again, soon after I have returned from the outdoor dance in Leeds. 'You're less self-conscious in the dark, more embodied, and there's a wildness to dancing outside.'

People respond to her presence as a lone woman on the dance floor in different ways, but she has rarely felt afraid or inhibited in a club. I'm not surprised by this; she has a fearsomely steely quality about her. She will choose to be sociable at times, and to be alone at others. I think about this – being a woman, alone in the night, comfortable with that fact, asserting one's visibility. It is the opposite of what I learned to do as a child, albeit as a necessary form of self-protection.

The experience of being in a club, on her own, is made all the more intense for its uninterrupted, trance-like wordlessness, Debris says, and she could be describing the fever that Viola feels in the maze, or the fervour I felt at Berghain. Unexpected alliances have been forged on nights out alone; DJs have driven her home, and she has danced for six hours or more with men and women whose names she has never known. 'Sometimes I'm preoccupied, I just want to enjoy the music. Other times I feel incredibly connected to my sexuality in a way that is mine. I understand it, I feel empowered by it, I'm not doing it for you. It's for me.'

Here is the joy of the women in Fauzia's embroideries again. Even so, there have been instances of intrusive, objectifying, unwelcome encounters. She has been filmed without permission. There has been catcalling and times when she has felt overwhelmed by the attention, which at its worst is sexualised, hostile, sometimes physical. I feel chilled when she tells me of instances in nightclubs when she has saved women from dangerous situations: the sight of men forcing kisses on unconscious women is commonplace to her.

But, when the raving is good, it's transformative. She recounts parties from years ago with verve: a night called Baile LDN at the Hackney Social with Emily Dust DJing while seven months pregnant, her mixing so good that Debris was drenched with sweat; in South Africa, hearing *gqom*, a form of electronic music, and experiencing its inherently collaborative nature as people added their own exclamations and whistles on the dance floor; in Nottingham, where she did much of her early raving after finishing her waitressing shifts at 1 a.m. As someone with neuro-divergencies, she has felt the therapeutic effects of dancing together. Such movement is connected to somatic therapy, which focuses on what the body holds in. There is considerable science now around releasing trauma with shaking therapy, which is used by some factions of the military for treating PTSD, she tells me, although it has been used for hundreds of years in tribal practice before this. 'If you're shaking, you can't be tense.'

I listen, rapt, as Debris talks. Her passion is palpable; her stories full of poetry, courage, humour, verve. I want to carry on talking so I tell her about my trip to Berghain, how the DJs were so sublimely in command of the room, how spiritual it felt. I hear myself gushing, and my words sound corny, but there is no cynicism in her tone when she responds. She has felt transcendence on the dance floor, at festivals, at carnival or during a Pride parade. Travelling to an event and gathering together in this way feels like a pilgrimage to her.

Hearing her stories makes me feel less self-conscious about my exhilarations at Berghain, where the dancing circumambulation around the DJ booth felt like a form of worship, with the possibility of finding God among the club's perspiring, half-clothed congregation. Debris is not the only one to equate this dance floor transfiguration to a secular sacrament, of sorts. In his film *Everyone in the Place: An Incomplete History of Britain 1984–1992*, the artist Jeremy Deller speaks of the club as a 'haven, where you can be the person you want to be'. He likens the head-scrambling delirium of an acid house club to the whipped-up frenzy of the early churches. Debris long ago rejected her parents' Mormonism and is agnostic, but her respect for religion remains intact, partly because of these nights out. They are instances when time simply stops and whatever lies beyond it is glimpsed: God, eternity or the euphoric fullness of the present moment.

****

There was a cinema not far from my family home in north London which became famed for its ungoverned all-nighters and hedonistic excess. I was in sixth form when I heard about the Scala, which moved into a rococo-style corner building in King's Cross in 1981 and began screening films through the night, as well as hosting live sets by Boy George and Lily Savage, among others, often while the films were playing, in a magnificent clash of sounds.

The area around King's Cross was still a red-light district, not the shiny, buffed-aluminium hub of gentrification and commerce it has become, and the cinema's increasingly starry clientele mingled with the auditorium's sex workers and strays. A £2.20 ticket allowed all-night entry and, by the late 1980s, it had become London's most infamous cinema. Some came to party, others as a stopgap after a night out, before the first train back home. The lights never went up and there were no ushers, so it remained permanently dark. There were few house rules and management supervised audiences from afar, like the laissez-faire parents of riotous children.

The Scala's lore feeds the notion of the 'social dark' as a place of pleasure and unfettered fun, with the potential for subversion in its depths. Some had sex in the auditorium, while others slept beneath the seats with the resident cats; others got drunk or high in the foyer, dancing to the band.

Many from that time have described it as a meeting place for oddballs, weirdos and misfits, and it sounds like a perfect intersection of hedonism and transgression. Revellers tipped out of the nearby gay bars and into the cinema, some cruising, others extending their drinking session. A neighbourhood, female-run lesbian and gay pub called the Bell began organising women-only all-nighters in the cinema where nothing was off-limits. 'It was much more outrageous than the mixed clubs,' remembers Jane Giles, a former programmer who co-directed *Scala!!!*, a documentary about the cinema's history. 'They had a fisting tent, and there'd be women taking all their clothes off.'

I heard stories about its raucousness from friends at school and although I never went to the overnight shows, I did turn up to a late screening of *The Rocky Horror Picture Show*. I was sixteen, and I remember the cinema's interior as a shabby, cathedral-like space, with uncomfortably hard chairs, no carpets and tube trains thundering directly beneath our seats. Now, I can see it had the same faded glamour as the late-night Punjabi theatre in Lahore. The crowd was dressed in character, and were there to participate with the film rather than to watch it, singing, throwing rice and shooting water pistols from beginning to end.

The all-nighters took place every Saturday, with five consecutive films, Jane tells me. There was an eclectic range on the programme, from sexually explicit fare like Pasolini's *Salò, or the 120 Days of Sodom*, to classics like Fritz Lang's *Metropolis*. You could watch Derek Jarman's homoerotic *Sebastiane* one night, and back-to-back Steve Martin comedies the next, or themed seasons of sexploitation and B-movie horror.

There were screenings of pornographic films too, such as the cult 1975 movie *Thundercrack!*, and explicit rare prints. Where this might have been sordid in another space, it didn't feel like that in the Scala, Jane says. You could just watch without it feeling seamy, and importantly for women, without being propositioned. I think back, once again, to the hostile, hungry gazes of the men watching Vicky Funari's dance at the peep show. Maybe the impact and meaning of pornography is shaped by those with whom you are watching, its effect shifting if it is a prevailingly queer crowd or an auditorium of only women, rather than a darkened room full of straight men. Perhaps its meaning is even created collectively by the many gazing eyes, although of course nowadays pornographic material on film, at least, is most often watched alone, online, rather than en masse.

Still, no one came *only* to watch the films, and Jane remembers the fantastic noise, with laughter and screaming in the auditorium melting into the sound of people singing along to the band outside. If the Scala thrived for years on its dangerous anti-authority spirit, ultimately it became a victim of its own daring after screening Stanley Kubrick's 1971 film, *A Clockwork Orange*, which had been withdrawn from UK distribution in 1974 for the 'copycat' violence it was alleged to have sparked. The Scala defied the ban and lost the subsequent court case, eventually closing in the early 1990s, when its lease ran out.

The uproarious memories of the cinema's all-nighters in Jane Giles's film conjure a wild nocturnal world that has no London equivalent now, but a film critic tells me that there are still films programmed over the course of a night in a few venues. He directs me to the Prince Charles, an indie picture-house tucked around the back of Leicester Square, which appears like a last remaining vestige of a charmingly tatty, bygone Soho. I wonder if some of the self-proclaimed 'weirdos and misfits' from Jane Giles's film have migrated over there to cause Saturday night mayhem. There are all-night screenings of David Cronenberg's and John Waters' movies advertised on the cinema's website, but it offers Disney binges as well. I sign up for the David Lynch night, which features four films, starting at midnight on Saturday and finishing at 9.30 a.m. on Sunday morning. I have seen three of them, long ago, and I wonder how the blurry realities in Lynch's cinematic universe will feel when watched in a seamless single stretch.

As the cinema comes into view, I remember with a jolt that I used to come to late-night screenings here with Fauzia, as a teenager. We would take in buckets of popcorn and watch whatever was on. It was more a way to be up, out and together in the night than a case of coming specifically to see a film. But once here, there was the enveloping dark of the auditorium in which I could switch off and retreat pleasurably into my internal world, snugly ensconced in an anonymous crowd, or get sucked into the world of the film if it gripped me. The foyer looks just the same when I enter, and even the posters highlighting future films are of ones that Fauzia and I once watched together. It is peculiar, being here, with so much time passed, but with the same roster of stories; it is both comforting and unsettling to remember these old celluloid worlds, viewed in darkness decades ago and permanently frozen in youthfulness.

I take a seat in the auditorium and try to take the pulse of the room. The rollicking tales about the Scala's rabble-rousers are fresh in my mind, but this feels like a far more well-mannered crowd. Behind me is a couple with an adult son who open Tupperware boxes and solemnly distribute the food among themselves, as if at a silent, indoor picnic. Another couple whispers politely beside me. I spot bigger groups in the rows at the back; it'll get wilder when the Saturday night drinking gets underway, I think, but it stays respectfully hushed throughout the night. There is no rambunctiousness at all. These people really have come to watch the films together, not for anything more or less subversive.

The seats are cushioned luxury and I am cocooned in their velvet. It is past midnight now and I feel the woozy first signs of sleepiness but also a childish excitement. It is like being at a sleepover with strangers, the physical intimacy of a shared space rubbing up against crowd formality. The first film is *Blue Velvet*, which I watched on television long ago. It is so big and ravishing on a screen this size that it seems to swallow me up. Isabella Rossellini plays a singer who is trapped, manipulated and tortured by a sadist; we see her being subjected to sexual violence, protracted and merciless, but in other scenes she is sultry and glamorous. I try to make sense of this damaged femme fatale and how the aesthetic beauty of the film makes even its violence captivating – I'm not sure I can, although I am in its thrall, uncomfortably so.

There are ten-minute breaks in between films and in the first intermission, I wander out, full of curiosity. People stand sipping coffee in the foyer and buying bags of popcorn, some in David Lynch T-shirts. They are young and all look like serious film fans, not the Scala's drink-soaked bohemians and hobos. I go back in for the road-movie *Wild at Heart*, in which Laura Dern and Nicolas Cage look iridescently cool and full of punkish energy. Again, I am unsure of what Lynch is saying with this story, but I am gripped. By the start of the third film, *Lost Highway*, I am sinking into the seat, my eyes drooping, but it is a very different sleepiness from my experience at the Young Vic, while watching Ruth Wilson play out her single, looping scene on stage, with its painfully forced wakefulness across twenty-four hours. Here, I can doze whenever I like, slip into the film, out again. I enjoy the truancy of being among a crowd of people, all awake together, when we should be sleeping, luxuriating in this dark, velvet, together wakefulness.

The film has taken on a hallucinatory quality, perhaps because I am tired, but also because it has a surreal dream-logic: Patricia Arquette and Bill Pullman play a couple, but a parallel version of them emerges along with a chilling Mephistophelian figure. I lose track of the plot's twists and turns, and find myself slipping into a sleep that is invaded by the film, or maybe its

Mephistopheles has magically sucked me into the realm of the film. It is alluring and alarming; the boundaries between what I have seen on screen, and what I have imagined, bleeding into one another. The blend of sleep and story makes the film's creepiness more perturbing.

By 6 a.m., after drinking a strong cup of coffee just as *Mulholland Drive* is starting up, I am alert again. The film is another hazy story of two female lovers hiding in the Hollywood Hills, and now I see the connective tissue between the films, their characters always plagued by terrifying, abstruse dreams, their swerving sequences mixing desire with dread, their 'midnight movie' schlock and their tacky female nudity. This experience is like an immersion in a vivid, weird, not-quite-real world, filled with forces of the night. And, I realise, there is such glowing celluloid beauty to them all: panoramic horizons of glittering black night, blazing sunsets, gorgeously empty skies. The cinema's darkness tingles as these images unspool and envelop. I am light-headed with tiredness when the movie marathon ends, close to 10 a.m., but I am elated too. As I stutter home my head feels stuffed with a bright and vibrant darkness.

There is a childlike pleasure in hearing stories at night. It seems so visceral that it is not a surprise when I discover it might be an ancient reflex, hard-wired into us. Nicholas Shakespeare, in his eponymous biography of Bruce Chatwin, begins the book with a meeting between the novelist and a palaeontologist in South Africa called Bob Brain, who has written about early human behaviour. He tells Chatwin that storytelling might have evolved from humans wanting to warn each other about the dangers of predators in their midst. 'Language came into being out of a need for a far more precise communication and identification of objects and circumstances, and for more elaborate audible signals,' Brain says.

The advent of firelight led people to sit around the fires they had built, the light from which extended day into night, Shakespeare tells us, and it allowed them to exchange crucial information, as well as to confer and describe what had happened to them in the day. This, it is suggested, gave birth to night-time storytelling and the ancient, oral tradition of tales around a campfire. 'Man is a talking animal, a storytelling animal,' Chatwin wrote in his notebook after meeting Brain. It is a paradox, in a sense, that without firelight there would be no stories, but it is the night that facilitates the storytelling. The two are vital to each other; once critical to human life for the exchange of information and facilitating a more timeless nightly ritual that centres the imagination. It's why theatre is so elemental, I think: the thrill of seeing stories come to life, surrounded by others, in a darkened room – simulated night is part of the magic. And it's *my* night, I realise, after my cinema marathon. I have found my way from my father's stories, and their enchanted darkness, back into that night world. This is where I belong. I was sitting inside it, all along.

Part 7

Crack of dawn

CHAPTER 15
Sacred night

Unlike my father, my mother has never been scared of the dark. I have wondered why that wasn't my inheritance and even whether, on some level, I chose to become my father's fearful daughter over my mother's fearless one. Maybe it was because he was a better storyteller. But she had her own stories, which brought different enchantments to the night.

My mother has always been religious, albeit holding her Muslim faith privately, with no outward displays. She has spoken of visiting Sufi hermits with her mother, in Lahore, as a child, and her faith seems to have been informed by Islamic mysticism. She is also the person in our family who has consistently seen visions in the dark that she believes are from other worlds, both sacred and diabolical: a flea-ridden dog in her family home in Pakistan, disappearing when she followed it into the next room; a pair of stockinged feet hobbling up the stairs of our north London flat; the djinn on the Primrose Hill park bench. She has experienced what she thinks of as sacred darkness too; she speaks about getting up at 4 a.m. as a teenager and hearing the beat of oversized wings, which she believes to have been those of angels, and a moment of transfiguration during a night prayer when the darkness in front of her turned dazzling bright, before fizzling away into blackness again.

I both believed and disbelieved these stories when she told them. Curiously, my father seemed the most doubtful in the family, despite his own superstitions of the dark; it is as if he knew the ghouls he imagined in it were just that – imaginings. I wonder if my mother's faith and her fearlessness are connected.

As much as unseen forces of darkness are believed to be unleashed in the night, in Islamic doctrine, there is also the idea of a divine darkness. Various nights bearing specific spiritual significance are dotted across the Islamic calendar: the Mi'raj sharif, or night journey, in which Prophet Muhammad is believed to have travelled into the sky with Hazrat Jibreel (the archangel Gabriel); particular dates during the month of Ramadan, such as Shab Qadr (translated from its Arabic as the Night of Power), in which a single prayer is worth more than a thousand years of worship. My mother speaks of these as special events, and her descriptions sound wondrous to me. They fill the night with a magical darkness: there is the steadying certainty of 'something' over 'nothing' inside it.

I have wondered whether it is 'nothing' that frightens me, and if it is why I project spectres into the emptiness. But I also see, whenever I stay with her for a few days, that the dark brings fears for her, at the age of eighty, that were not there before. These are practical rather than existential: the fear of tripping up when she goes to the toilet, or bumping into things and breaking a bone. Now, her home is lit up at night, and curtains are left open, the unfeared dark replaced by cautionary light. She is still in the old family flat, which she made her own when we moved out. It is bright, airy, warm and well-furnished. Despite that, I feel a residual discomfort in its few remaining dark corners, particularly as I pass the area outside my old bedroom, where Tariq saw the slumped woman, in childhood. I have noticed over the years how this corner is never empty: there is always something stationed in it – a chair, a hoover, a side table. I wonder if these things have been placed there deliberately, or whether I am finding meanings where there are none.

It is mid-June, the first weekend in Ramadan, and I am cycling over to my mother's flat. I have fasted less and less over the years, partly because I have grown increasingly anxious to go without food for any length of time and certainly not for the long stretch between dawn until dusk of the summer that the religious month has fallen on, this time around, in its yearly lunar revolution. I don't know when I became so afraid of hunger. As children, Fauzia, Tariq and I would wake up in the pre-dawn darkness, keen to be part of the night's rituals before a day's fast. It would be difficult to summon an appetite at that time, but we would eat the warm, wheaty rotis that my mother cooked fresh, well before the crack of dawn. The hallway lights would already be on by the time we got up, and we'd tiptoe down the stairs, whispering so we would not disturb our neighbours. I remember peering at the still, serene road outside, fascinated by its emptiness, on the way back to bed. These are good memories and the hunger then was an adventure, not a sacrifice.

In more recent years, whenever I have steeled myself enough to fast for a few days, I have slept through the ritual pre-dawn meal, because I can't bear the prospect of wrenching myself out of sleep to eat at that time. But for all the notional dread of hunger, I have enjoyed the release it brings from the day's manic productivity: there is a limit to what I can do on such low energy. The day feels richer for its slowness, and I notice its detail: the noise of the traffic, the road's slightest inclines, the burst of colour on the trees along my road, the smell of cherries from a fruit stall.

My mother is too old to fast with me now – she has an assortment of tablets to take with food during the day – so I will be waking up alone. Sunrise is just after 4.30 a.m., and I must try to eat before then. I wake up to an alarm and head downstairs in my mother's flat, but the minute I am out of the bedroom, I feel the old shadows encroaching, despite my mother's dewy night-lights. I do not look to the condemned corner where my brother's spectre sat. I know there is nothing here other than an accumulation of past fears, but those are enough to unsettle me. Just as we return to our old selves when we come back to the family in adulthood, does the house in which we once lived return to its past self when we reconvene in it?

I rush downstairs, to the kitchen, whose window overlooks the building's many little allotments. It is a black mirror, reflecting my face back at me. There are shadows here too. Has the ghost woman pattered down the stairs with me? I eat quickly before racing back upstairs. When I pass the corner, I feel its filled vacancy. I know it is my imagination that gives the darkness its freighted quality, and yet I remain scared. The woman is someone I carry with me now and I place her here every time I pass. It is a story I keep telling myself. A way to fill the darkness with something over nothing.

****

My mother's concept of a *bright* darkness that illuminates and enlightens is not as contradictory as it sounds. Sacred darkness is a spiritual notion, as I am reminded by a priest who visits my father's nursing home. There is a theological tension between light and dark in Christianity. While the liturgical prayer at evening time – Compline – refers to protection against the night's darkness and the sin it hides, the night has the capacity to enlighten and redeem as well. St John of the Cross was, perhaps, the most famous Christian mystic to speak of such sacred darkness. He was mentored by the Spanish Carmelite nun, St Teresa of Ávila, who together with St John reformed the order during Spain's Counter-Reformation of the sixteenth century. In his poetic tract, *The Dark Night of the Soul*, he expounds his theories on spiritual illumination, writing in paradoxes of 'purifying darkness' and contemplation at night as 'a ray of darkness'. The priest at the nursing home explains how this night is not literal but a double-edged metaphor: alongside the lure of the 'evils' that can overtake a soul in darkness, such as sex, lust and violence, there is the potential for a cleansing process by which the soul faces its temptations and overcomes them.

Piqued by the notion of sacred darkness, and maybe wanting to be convinced by it, I make my way to a convent. I am visiting the Poor Clare Colettines in Ellesmere, near the Welsh border, to sit in on the canonical hour of Matins, a service in which psalms are sung at midnight. The Order of St Clare is the second Franciscan order, founded by Clare of Assisi in 1212. They are a contemplative order, with a focus on living basically and in an enclosed way, unseen by the world. On Sundays, and other significant days in the Christian calendar, the liturgy at Ellesmere is heard by a congregation from the other side of the chapel wall, inside their convent. Their Mother Abbess has granted me permission to visit for the night, although Sister Anne Joseph, the only nun among them who liaises with the public, warns me that they have neither mobile phone reception nor Wi-Fi, so I will not be virtually connected while I am there.

The convent is six miles from Gobowen, a postage-stamp-sized village in Shropshire with a pub and a sprinkling of takeaways around its train station. I ask for directions to the convent at the pub but no one inside knows where it is; some are not even aware that there are nuns living nearby. Those who do know tell me it is rare to see them out. I am given a taxi number and I wait on the pub bench outside, hoping I will be delivered to the right place. While I'm there, a man comes out of the pub and offers me a lift to the convent. He doesn't know where it is, exactly, but he'll find it, he says, amicably. Or if not now, he can collect me tomorrow to bring me back to the station.

I ask him if he wants money, but he shakes that suggestion away and says he is simply being friendly. 'That's the way down here.' He would get up before 9 a.m. on a Sunday morning as a kindness to a stranger, I think. We carry on talking, and I discover he spent much of his life as a long-distance truck driver, away from home for months at a time, travelling across Europe, driving through the night as well as the day. I carry on smiling, and answering his questions, but I feel a sudden chill in the presence of this man's warmth. Another long-distance lorry driver comes into my mind, from my Leeds trip, but I push the thought away.

Still, how do you distinguish between quaint village hospitality and a serial killer? Sutcliffe, too, seemed ordinary. The man gives me his phone number but does not ask for mine. Thank god, I think. If I decide to take him up on the offer of a lift, there will be his dog in the car too. She's a terrier who likes to sit in front, so will yap if she sees me take her place, he says. He pulls up his sleeves to show me his arms. There are red gashes from where the dog has scratched him. I feel the guilty prickle of my own distrust, but I am relieved when my taxi arrives.

Sister Anne is standing at the door of Our Lady and St Joseph Convent, which was originally located in nearby Oteley but moved to this site in 1960. It is set within a beautiful, oval front garden, but I am surprised by the main building's modernity: it could be a Travelodge or Barratt home. Sister Anne is a small, warm Filipino woman in a habit and sandals, who shows me around the visitors' living quarters. They have the municipal look of student digs from the 1970s with plain, dorm-like rooms off a long central corridor. But everything is pleasingly in order, and it reminds me of my family home, in Primrose Hill, for its spare, dated neatness. The rooms have single beds and bare walls except for crucifixes above the windows. There are larger crucifixes at various junctures along the corridor, arresting in their size. The accommodation is fully booked over the summer, with visitors coming from all over the world, Sister Anne has told me. It is late June and this is the last weekend these rooms will sit empty, except for my presence. Because the nuns inhabit their own wing of the building, I will be staying here by myself tonight, I realise, with a jitter.

My room has a comfortable simplicity. There are no mirrors, possibly for the same reason as at Berghain: to drive visitors further into themselves. Except the focus here is on meditative silence rather than sound. I leave my door open and strain to hear the sisters in their part of the convent which, Sister Anne has told me, is at least as big as the visitors' space. But there are no footfalls, no distant hum of voices, only birds chirruping outside. Their quarters seem sealed away from mine. But maybe the essence of their monastic contemplation has drifted over to these rooms, because I find my thoughts becoming slower and clearer in the calmness of the space. The pace of time passing feels different too; I remain sitting in my chair for hours without realising. I am lost in thinking – or listening. There is a striking richness to the birdsong outside which reminds me of the pandemic quiet.

It is almost dusk when I get up and go to the garden. The birds are still singing. Up the road is ordinary life: Ellesmere's famed complex of lakes and underground tunnels, a trendy waterside restaurant, an acupuncture centre. I still have time to go exploring but I feel the pull of the convent, with its constant backdrop of birdsong setting off the silence.

Sister Anne collects me after dinner to introduce me to the other sisters in their parlour, a room divided down the middle by a transparent screen. It is the only interface between their enclosed quarters and the world outside it. The sisters are already there when I arrive, sitting in a semicircle. The door on their side of the parlour, which leads into their private area, is slightly ajar. I take fleeting glances to the other side of the divide, but I can't make out anything beyond a blur.

They have such an intense, collective presence that I am initially unnerved by them. There were seven nuns who moved to Ellesmere, and that number went up to fourteen, but now eight remain. This group is composed of five Filipino, two Kenyan and one Irish nun: Sisters Giuseppe, Bonaventure, Mercy, Mary

Clare, Stephanie and Anne. There is Sister Bernadette too, a former abbess, but she is ninety-five and too old to join us. Also, Sister Carmela, who is the 'blood sister' of Sister Giuseppe, and the current Abbess, but she is not here either because she is recovering from a hospital procedure. Sister Bernadette is the eldest and the rest range from their mid-forties to early eighties, but each woman looks younger than her age: fresh-faced, unwrinkled, both guileless and watchful.

I have braced myself for a sombre meeting but the women exude warmth, and a certain nervousness. Other clergy I have met before now have appeared to be well practised at talking to members of the community; they have been smooth, accomplished conversationalists. These women are highly attentive, looking straight at me, but their responses seem entirely unrehearsed. I ask questions about their daily lives and they answer, unruffled. Maybe they are used to this curiosity. They have no newspapers, TV or radio, but they do have a parish priest who visits every day and delivers essential news. It is such a self-elected, small world, I think. I would either go mad or feel freed in it. Their life is not for everyone, they tell me, cheerfully. Some who join the order last two weeks, others two days.

There are prayers seven times a day in the Divine Office of the Liturgy of the Hours, as well as individual prayers and reading in their rooms. They sing hymns at morning and evening prayers, for around forty-five minutes, and chant psalms from the Breviary, standing opposite each other on their side of the chapel wall.

As for midnight worship, it's a Franciscan tradition to first go to bed and then be woken up by a designated 'caller' among them. They wake and move in torchlight, rather than in darkness. Getting up in the middle of the night is part of their penance, they tell me, and they pray for the world as it sleeps, according to the teachings of St Clare. Where the night is the Devil's time, the stroke of midnight is, paradoxically, holy for them too.

'We are united with our Lord who was born at this hour,' says Sister Mary Clare.

The more we talk, the more I find myself wondering who these women are, what brought them to their enclosed lives. Sister Anne has told me she arrived at the convent from the Philippines in 2006. Until then, she was a layperson. I want to ask her, and the rest of the sisters, what they did before joining the Order but I know, instinctively, that the question would constitute a violation. I decide, even if they do not tell me so, that this is a conversational boundary, and that their earlier lives are off-limits.

The tone of our conversation becomes looser and warmer as we talk, until the nuns are delightfully giddy, as curious about me as I am about them. I tell them I am a Muslim and Sister Giuseppe says Muslims in the Philippines, when she lived there, often asked her to pray for them. I wonder if the nuns are scared of the dark, if they argue, if see their families, whether they have rooms of their own. They smile, answer, then begin asking their own questions about my life, my age, if I am scared to sleep in the guest quarters on my own, reassuring me it is a sacred space when I pause, and that any noise I hear will be mice scratching in the walls' hollows.

'Are you married?' asks one sister.

No, I say, and feel compelled to explain. 'There are many ways to be in the world, as a woman, and I feel like this is right for me.'

'We feel the same,' says Sister Mary Clare, the others nodding around her, and I feel a sudden, strong affinity. The glass dividing the room in two is gone and I feel great tenderness towards the sisters by the time I leave the parlour. The meeting, and the quiet, resets me. I am slower and calmer, not twitching to check my phone, and I can still hear birdsong outside, although it is well after dusk. It never seems to stop. Have I begun to imagine it?

I wait for full darkness to fall, and feel a desire to go exploring, not outside but further inside the building, so I can glimpse the nuns in their living space, even from afar, or at least arrive at the partition between my quarters and theirs. But I find that I am scared of the dark corridor outside my room when I open the door, and the sight of all the empty rooms around me, so I retreat back inside. I am in bed by 10.30 p.m., but the serenity of the room is gone, and I feel the unfamiliar darkness close in oppressively. Why am I afraid of it when the nuns have told me this is a safe – blessed! – space? I am exasperated by my irrational night mind, and am still awake when I hear Sister Anne knocking at my door for Matins.

The church seems empty when I enter it, but I see the shadowy figure of Sister Stephanie standing at the far side of the chapel. She waves animatedly. A wooden panel along the wall has been dismantled, and the gap becomes a threshold between this side of the chapel, in which I am standing, and the nuns' quarters on the other side. I peer into the cavity but, again, I can't make out anything solid. I sit on the front pew, and ahead of me, a small window is opened, just above the altar. I see a hand placing a cross in the compartment.

After a silence, the singing begins, accompanied by an instrument that must be an organ but has the amplified pierce of an electric guitar. Their voices do not sound like those of nuns singing hymns either. They have a bluesy quality, edged with folk. It is like a concert in a church, a devotional turn by a cloistered Carole King of the English countryside. The sound is so big it carries the weight of physical exertion, emanating from the belly, boomed up through the chest. And so *modern*; I wonder if the nuns have gone off-piste, not singing psalms but songs they have composed themselves.

Their voices sound like a body of sound, filled with what? – yearning? joy? submission? love? – splitting into individual voices and then unifying again as one. They transmit the same guileless honesty as in our conversation in the parlour. The effect is psychedelic in the pin-drop silence of the night, the darkness pushing at the windows of the chapel, the voices pushing back with life, soul, bared emotions that channel a magnificent clarity, an intangible truth. It does not seem far removed from the transcendence that Debris Stevenson spoke of finding through clubbing.

There are such long silences between the songs that I think they must have finished their service, and have rustled away. I am surprised by how disappointed I feel that it is over so abruptly, but suddenly they start up again, and every song until the end leaves me stunned. After the singing comes the chanting of prayers, which brings a more meditative tone. A calm, after the passion of the songs. I catch some sentences: 'God makes no distinction between man and man.' I can't quite piece their meaning together, but I feel their profound, epic quality all the same. The full liturgy lasts around forty-five minutes, after which a hand opens the door to the compartment above the altar and takes the cross back inside. The service is over.

I sit unmoving, imagining the nuns on the other side of the wall. I want to speak to them about the emotion their ceremony has evoked in me, and share my thrill at hearing their glorious voices. I hope they might come out to chat afterwards, but the panel is back on the wall, and the night is silent again. I feel more strongly now the pronounced sense of another chapel *over there*, in the hollow of their altar, and an invisible world as big and possibly more capacious than mine. I tiptoe out of the chapel, back to bed, my head full of their seductive song.

The sound is very different at 6.30 a.m., at Lauds, or early morning prayers. I have told Sister Anne that I will make my own way to the chapel, but they are already chanting when I arrive. I can't make out the words at all this time, but the sound is sombre and distant, so I move from the pew to the bench behind the dismantled wood panel. The singing is more traditionally liturgical, the organ recognisable in its ecclesiastical sound. The light from outside slants in from the skylights, and the birdsong is back in force. My eyes feel gritty from the lack of sleep, but I am listening carefully. The choir seems to turn into solos, and then back into a chorus. Is it just one sister singing now or all of them? I try to guess which voice belongs to which woman, attempting to unpick the timbre of one from the next.

Separated by just a few hours, the difference between Matins and Lauds is startling. The morning song is not as immediately arresting as that of midnight, but the sisters' softer volume and plainer sound gradually well into a testimony or confession, with a sense of unfolding that reminds me of watching the sun rise, in a beautiful spot, on holiday. It is so quietly, joyfully infectious that I have to suppress the urge to hum or sing along. It sounds like a cleansing. There is release in it.

The songs gather a note of whimsy, as if the nuns are singing out their dreams, some lines filled with tears, others with longing. Sister Carmela sings with them, from her wheelchair, I am told afterwards, and their morning chorus carries such a clear sense of their closeness to each other that I remember how much like a family of sisters they seemed when I spoke to them in the parlour.

I am fully awake, and refreshed, by the time they finish the liturgy, even though I barely slept overnight. Sister Stephanie's figure appears in the gap in the wall and she puts the panelling back into place. I strain to hear the sisters on the other side again, but there is nothing. It is as if they live in a separate universe and have returned to it after their service.

My mind keeps returning to their part of the convent, and the garden they described to me yesterday, which sounded rich with hidden abundance. It was bigger than the grounds at the front of the convent, they said. All keen gardeners, the sisters had come to life as they described what they grew: cabbages, tomatoes, cucumbers, onions, kale, squash, spinach, lettuce, pears, apples, grapes, strawberries, blackberries, blackcurrants, gooseberries, a cherry tree. They also had roses, lilies, hydrangeas – and so on. The garden seemed to expand in their descriptions of it, and I wondered if it was an effect of their magical thinking, or mine.

When I meet them in the parlour to say goodbye some hours after Lauds, they give me cabbages from the garden, along with homemade marmalade and damson jam. I carry this produce home with me like preserved pieces of Eden. The next night, back in my flat, I am up at midnight, as usual, but suddenly struck by the quiet outside; I think of the nuns' song, resounding in the empty chapel at this moment, their voices baring their souls. It is not a performance, there is no congregation, no one hears the music they create but them. For a while, I feel sad that the beauty of their prayers, sung for the world as it sleeps, is hidden by the night. But, I think, these prayers are sung in the dark, *for* the dark, and it is this that makes the darkness sacred. I sit and listen as their voices fill my head.

Chapter 16
Dark Edens

I am on another night-bus, much slower than the last one, balancing a crate of cherries on my lap, with a rucksack filled with premium-grade avocados slung on my back. I have been sitting, swaying under the weight of the fruit, for well over an hour as the bus putters from east London into town. The sky, in constant flux throughout the day, is a still, sleeping grey at the window. It is 3 a.m. and I am frustrated by the bus's slow pace. The effort of clutching the cherries, and holding up the weight on my back, leaves me dripping with sweat. Some passengers cast a cursory glance at me as they board the bus, but most seem too tired, or drunk, to pay attention to a woman carrying fresh fruit in the middle of the night.

I need to get home and put these goods into the fridge, before they start to ripen and bruise with the heat. The fruit feels like plunder even though I have paid for it: it was a fraction of its usual price, bought wholesale. New Spitalfields Market is where grocers and restaurateurs go to buy their fresh produce, and it is where I am returning from. A vast warehouse just off a dual carriageway in east London, opening at midnight and closing at 9 a.m., six nights a week, it is a fruit and veg stall of gigantic proportions. Servicing fresh food businesses within the M25 area, it is its own hermetically sealed, lit-up night world.

A thrum of trucks is lined up and waiting for entry when I arrive, shortly after midnight. From the road, the complex looks like a gated community or a remote, industrial island, with giant barn-like buildings, floodlights, turnstiles and semaphores that are raised by invisible operators in roadside Portakabins to let the juggernauts in. Because it is a marketplace primarily for wholesalers, very few ordinary shoppers come here by foot. The pavement is empty and I can't find an entrance for pedestrians. I approach two passing guards, so I can try to get some bearing. One of them, the woman, is a site controller who oversees the running of the market. There are 115 merchant businesses in the market hall with produce from around the world, she says. The market's busiest times are between 1 a.m. and 3 a.m., with a second wave starting around 6 a.m., so I have arrived just before the rush.

The market itself is ancient, with records stretching back to 1638, and it takes place at night because it would bring London's traffic to a standstill by day, with two hundred HGVs and a total of four thousand vehicles in transit. It used to be part of the original Spitalfields Market, more centrally located in Liverpool Street, where vendors now sell high-end crafts and trendy street food, but it moved to this dedicated site in 1991. Both these guards have worked in London's other two main fresh food markets: Smithfield, which sells meat, and Billingsgate, specialising in fish. Of the three, New Spitalfields is the biggest. Its tenants are their own breed, the guards say, sturdy in the face of a lifetime's night work, the market a core part of who they are. 'It's in their blood,' says the controller.

It seems as if the guards have the market in their blood too. They reel off facts, names, statistics. There are butchers in Smithfield whose families have traded at the market for generations, they say. The controller has seen a rent-book from 1918 which lists the grandfather of a current tenant, while a woman at Billingsgate who sells mixed eels has family connections that go way back too.

I ask about the demographic of the workforce, and she tells me that the porters who do the lifting and shifting are largely men. There are not as many women here as in the other two

London markets, and the staff has a large immigrant population. It has a helter-skelter speed and energy to it, she adds, 'as you'll see for yourself'.

They point me towards the white pedestrian crossings that lead the way inside and melt back into their night circuit of the site. I enter the hubbub and it is overwhelming at first. The hall is massive, bare-boned, with girders exposed, and it has an exoskeletal beauty to it. Crates are piled high around stalls, company banners brandished above them. There is continuous movement with electric buggies zooming up and down, wholesalers arranging their boxes, and the first of the customers threading their way between them. There is the smell of vegetation, cabbage-like, and an organised chaos to the buggies as they zip across the gangways, loading or unloading their crates.

The stacked boxes in the stalls make it look like a giant packing factory, with mezzanine floors containing more boxes and sacks, but when I stop at individual stalls, the vivid colours and variety of the produce spring to life: there really is every fruit and vegetable imaginable here, with some stalls specialising in South Asian and Caribbean groceries, among other specialities. I see swollen watermelons, shiny red chillis, okra, mooli, dainty-leaved coriander with stems so delicate that they would make my mother's eyes light up, and a box of spiky round karelas that look like cartoon grenades.

One column of crates is crammed with rhubarb, another with a lilac vegetable that I don't recognise, but it is as glossy, as shapely, as a still-life composition. One end of the warehouse is entirely filled with potatoes. There are sacks of onions, and deep purple cabbages, so smoothly flawless that they look good enough to pick up and bite into, like an apple.

This is how big and fecund I had imagined the hidden garden to be in the convent at Ellesmere. The nuns would love it here, I think. There is no sleepiness in this world; I feel slightly dizzy at the movement in the room. It is wide awake. It reminds me of a Peshawar street bazaar, with its solely male hawkers and the rising smell of petrol fumes. A Babel of languages is being spoken: cockney English, Punjabi, Arabic, Polish, Portuguese. Some men turn to look at me but most are too busy to be curious. It *is* male-dominated, as the controller said. I can't spot a single woman working on the stalls; although, when I stop to buy the cherries and avocados, a smiling woman takes my payment.

There are five cafés in the complex but although I wander around for two hours, I find only one. It is brightly lit and as busy as any daytime café in London. Men are smoking, chatting, drinking coffee, as if they are on a mid-morning break. Two women, glamorously made-up, serve at the counter, and the menu is that of a greasy spoon café, but with a global edge: köfte and Polish patisserie alongside toasties, omelettes and jacket potatoes. It is 2 a.m. now and I would like to carry on looking, buying, maybe order an omelette and a cup of builder's tea at the first sign of light, but I am keen to get my fruit home so I reluctantly leave this invigorating, mercantile Eden of the night.

The following day I wake up and go straight to the stack of fruit in my kitchen. It fills me with delight, but also a slow dawning awareness of just how much I have bought, and how quickly it may rot. I offer some to my mother, some to a neighbour. I bag up the cherries and cram them into my fridge, beside the avocados, but they leave room for little else. I eat a pile of the cherries for breakfast, followed by two avocados. They are the finest quality, and the cherries are plump, juicy, luscious. I want to keep eating. I return to them throughout the day, eating so many cherries that my stomach begins to hurt. The contrast between the hectic buying and selling of the market and the sense of a lush, vegetative oasis within the city stays with me. How could I have not known of it, after a lifetime of living in London? Maybe these earthbound Edens are not only to be found in cloistered spaces but are right there, under our noses.

****

I stumble across other night Edens after my visit to the fruit market. Or maybe I just become aware of a parallel world of animals and vegetables that has always lived and breathed while we sleep. My walk around Suffolk with Melissa Harrison takes place at dusk when the landscape is in a grand state of winding down, with tired flutters and caws rising from the long grass. I can feel and hear another world rousing itself awake beneath these sights and sounds. Melissa takes me to a disused barn where a white owl has taken up residence, and we wait to see if it flutters out for the night. It doesn't, but I remember her trailcam video snippets of field animals, gambolling in the dead of night.

A friend, Katherine, tells me of a trek she took with her uncle into the Australian outback, more than a decade ago, and describes a night that reared up with dramatic life. She was in Woonoongoora, or Lamington National Park, which lies along the Great Dividing Range, between Queensland and New South Wales, and she took a guided night walk into the ancient rainforest of Gondwana. It was autumn, and because darkness descends so quickly in the southern hemisphere, sunset was fast, the forest dark by 7 p.m., but the lulled life of the forest sparked awake in that darkness: under a rock the earth teemed with insects; a nest in a tree trunk crawled with funnel web spiders, more active by night – and so lethal their bite can kill a human in minutes. What struck Katherine most of all was the sound of this night. The volume was immense, with layers to it, the orchestral clash of bat-calls and nocturnal birdsong piercing the sub-tropical forest, but underneath that the vibrating hum and scratch of insects and reptiles in the foliage, and behind that the swooshing wind, exhaling through the 5,000-year-old Antarctic beech trees.

Katherine, in her story, spoke of the uncle who took her to Australia as a kind of father figure. He had been a vital presence in her life ever since her dad died in her childhood, in Ireland. The uncle had lived in Australia in the 1960s, posted as a young priest to a remote part of the country, when much of the outback was classed as 'hostile territory' by the non-Indigenous, white settler population, who seemed to view it as dark, spiky and unpredictable in its foreignness. He saw the bush very differently, as a wonderland, to be appreciated and experienced. The way Katherine talked of it made me think of how the night had seemed to me – in my insomnia – to be 'hostile territory', with all the sounds around me turned to polluting noise. Over the years, that noise has started to revert to sound again. It is no longer as hostile. I don't mind hearing the muffled conversations, the hum of neighbours' TV sets, or the birds singing outside if I am still awake for the dawn chorus. I have found some peace within the waking world of the night.

As I begin tuning into the night Edens around me, I meander past a Mayfair art gallery one evening and see a large canvas inside with a lush night-time landscape painted on it. I go in to find other canvases bursting with night fauna and flora. They are by the Lebanese artist Omar El Lahib, and they look like different versions of a perfumed, nocturnal paradise, where the night is decorative and the darkness is spot lit to appear glittery and fabular. There are figures in these paintings with translucent white skin that remind me of Edvard Munch's gothic figures, touched by death, but they are surrounded by a beautiful abundance of multicoloured foliage. Exotic flowers in vivid oranges, luminous greens and purples. Wisteria creeping up the sides of canvases, fronds of elms draping down, and the sky sequinned with stars. I can almost hear the piercing whistles and caws of the birds that Katherine described in the Antipodean forest.

The nocturnal birdsong she described stays with me: the torrent of different whistles mixed with the imitating sounds of the lyrebird. I make a plan to hear the night's birdsong closer to home and sign up for a nightingale walk in Kent, where there is a known community of these West African migratory birds. But nightingales, to my surprise, also sing throughout the day during breeding season, which is between April and June, and the walks advertised take place in the morning.

So I find myself at the entrance of the RSPB Cliffe Pools bird reserve at 9 a.m. It is in Rochester, close to the Thames Estuary, and it was a dump before being turned into a reservation area, which includes an estimated thirty male nightingales. The local Medway RSPB birders collecting around me are genial and full of facts once they find out I am interested in the nightingale's song. Its sound is instantly distinguishable, full-bodied and able to hit a large scale of chords and pitches, which are made through the syrinx, an internal organ of all songbirds with two bronchial tubes and bellows that are manipulated with great complexity and symphonic effect by nightingales. This is situated at the base of the windpipe, closer to the heart than the larynx, giving their song a certain romance: a serenade from the heart, most ardent earlier on in the mating season. But it is a secretive bird, small, relatively drab and prone to hunkering down in the trees, so it is far easier to hear than to see.

The walk sets off, and the group's hushed concentration forces me to tread softer and listen harder. There, I'm told, is the blackcap, whose jiving call swings from high to low, as if it is dancing, and there goes the Cetti's warbler, with its mechanical, machine-gun bursts of sound. A black-headed gull is spotted above us, then a buzzard with wings that look like the wide white sails of a ship.

Adrian, an RSPB volunteer in our group, says that at 7 a.m. the nightingales of this reserve are thunderous, but they become quieter and more cautious by late morning. It is a two-and-a-half-hour walk, and I sense the group losing heart as we head into its final stretch, but then a man ahead of us comes to a sudden standstill, and Adrian puts a finger to his lips. The group creeps forward. For a while, there is nothing. Then, the song flies out, streaming above all the others, like a bright kite rising from between smaller, plainer ones in the sky. Two nightingales are serenading. The sound is full-throated, effortlessly exquisite, with melodies that are long and lustrous, but then followed by eccentrically jagged harmonies. One man jokes that if this were classical music, it would be a symphony by an experimental modernist like Béla Bartók.

After that first encounter, there are more and more. Each time the sound is a surprise, brimming with romance, as if the birds are lyricising. I stand listening and feel a well of emotion in my chest, and then in my throat. I see Saint Francis of Assisi, talking to the birds, with the night twinkling around him, in the medieval panel at the Courtauld Gallery. And I see my father walking across the gallery space to stand in front of it, taking in the patterned down of the birds, which are all turned towards Saint Francis, in worshipful song. Perhaps my father's world is one long night now, I think, all his days swallowed up by darkness. Or maybe there are pieces of illuminated day in the night, as beautiful and surprising as the sound of nightingales singing mid-morning.

CHAPTER 17
Day, again

I go home full of the sound of these nocturnal songbirds. It really is a piece of the night in the day, and a reminder that there is communion between the two. I might have passed the lone, wandering woman on Waterloo Bridge in daylight and simply not have noticed her, or sat next to the night-workers from the Hertfordshire nursing home on a morning tube ride.

Of course, I understood instinctively that night overlapped with day, however imperceptibly, but what would it be like if night were banished, and its irrational forces vanquished with it? If my father could have his days back again, clear as the rising sun. Svalbard is the place to find out. The Norwegian archipelago floats in the Arctic Ocean and has the world's longest period of polar nights. There are twenty-four hours of darkness for four months, followed by polar day, when the sun does not set between 20 April and 22 August. I am going to experience the latter: the obliteration of all darkness, leaving a continuum of total, unadulterated day.

As one of the world's northernmost communities, its population floats at the edge of the inhabitable world, just five hundred miles from the icy wastes of the North Pole. It takes me over six hours to get there from London, flying first to Oslo and a further three hours to Spitsbergen, the largest of the islands. Beyond it, there are multicultural 'settlements' scattered across the archipelago, I learn, such as Pyramiden and Barentsburg, which has a population of largely Russian heritage, and a significant Ukrainian community too. The largest town, Longyearbyen, on the west coast, is a Norwegian settlement, with a thousand people living there, though tourists boost that number in both the summer and winter months, visiting for the novelty of the midnight sun, and its opposite. Beyond the settlements is Ny-Ålesund, a station lying further north, where only scientists are permitted to stay overnight. It sounds like a curious, isolated society: there is little tarmacked road on the archipelago, so it is not always easy to explore.

It is almost 7 p.m. when I land at Svalbard airport, and there is a shift of atmosphere inside the aircraft as it gets closer to the ground. The air inside, and the light outside, acquire a different weight and hue. I have a window seat and am taken aback by the primeval terrain coming into view below: brown undulating mounds with bright light falling dramatically across it. We have landed on an outer stretch of the planet, but it feels like a place far beyond this world, as I imagine the moon might look when I step out into this new, clear light and air.

The temperature is a mild twelve degrees, because of the moderating influence of the northern Atlantic gulf stream. It is July, the warmest month here, but in winter it is not uncommon for temperatures to drop to minus thirty degrees. It is a shock to feel the sun in my eyes. It is evening, but the light has the quality of high noon, a brighter and sharper edge to it than summer evenings in London.

I am told to get on any of the coaches outside the airport, which take all incoming tourists to their respective hotels: the town is small enough to make this circuit well inside an hour. I have read about Spitsbergen's coal-mining history and the landscape is dotted with industrial drums, heaps of soil, tractors, warehouses and smallholdings, starkly visible from the bus and then from the fourth-floor view of my hotel room. I don't go out to explore immediately but keep returning to the window to look at the sun, high and static above the peaks, not quite believing it will stay this way. But by ten o'clock, there is the same noon-blue sky and low clouds that greeted my plane's arrival. I head out after 11 p.m., before it gets too late, I think.

The high street is opposite the hotel and the town is so concentrated that it takes under an hour to circumnavigate its boundary. I spot a supermarket, chocolatier, café, gift shop and a centre organising adventure trips. This seems like a weirder version of Sark – a 1960s Scandinavian new town nestling in ancient hills. The houses are low, multicoloured and modernist in their minimalism, painted in pastels to offset the bleak winter months with their visual cheeriness. Some have covered their windows with tin foil to stop the light getting in, and later, I see this thick, rolled foil for sale in the supermarket. Instead of the relentless sunlight of the summer months, and relentless dark of the winter, these residents choose to live with artificial light, and dark, at home, their body clocks not regulated by nature but by the foil at their windows.

Svalbard has no native population; it was discovered in 1596 by explorers seeking to conquer the North Pole, and it falls under Norwegian sovereignty. The terrain's industrialised look, with heaps of rubble or stone across it, is framed by a halo of white glaciers in the distance. The island is in fact 60 per cent glacier and has no trees because the permafrost does not allow them to take root. American industrialist John Munro Longyear initiated coal mining here in 1906 and so the town of Longyearbyen is named after him. Initially regarded as a 'company town' – a place to work, dominated by men, and most of them miners, with only managers permitted to bring their wives with them – most of the mines have shut down. There were once seven, but only one is still operating, and even that is due for closure. It is a muscular and unpretty sight, I think, taking in the vista of pylons and chimneys, the heavy machinery and the Lego-like corrugated iron blocks that give the town centre the look of a building site. It makes it seem as if Svalbard is either in the process of being developed or in a state of disrepair, with all this rubble lying around. There are not many people out at this time, other than the odd tourist holding a map and looking as wide-eyed at these surroundings as I am.

Longyearbyen was deemed inhospitable to women for a long time. Pioneers led the way into public life: Léonie d'Aunet, a French nineteen-year-old, was the first woman to set foot on Svalbard, in 1839. She travelled on an expedition ship with her fiancé, François-Auguste Biard, and wrote of its rugged beauty but also feared she would perish here. Hanna Resvoll-Holmsen took part in another expedition, in 1907, and returned the following year to become Svalbard's first female research botanist; Wanny Woldstad became a trapper in the 1930s, then seen as an entirely male preserve; Dagrun Bakketun Hansen was the first female miner, in 1985. When I go on a walk the following day, the guide, a man in his sixties whose parents came here from the mainland and put down roots before he was born, says there are as many prominent women as men now.

People come to the archipelago for the low tax rates, he adds, and again this motivation reminds me of the resident population of Sark. But the archipelago's terrain seems to resist the rise of any potential nativism: Norwegians need to have a listed address on the mainland to qualify to live here, the guide says, and even those who have spent a lifetime on Svalbard are not permitted to be buried here: because of the permafrost, bodies would eventually bob back up. The idea of 'home' must sit awkwardly for people who consider themselves local alongside this requirement to be simultaneously located elsewhere.

I have walked for nearly an hour when I stop to take a breath, looking out to the empty road in front, the snowy mountains to the west, and above them a sky which is gargantuan, dwarfing the size of the mountains, and as roiling as one of Turner's stormy seascapes. The sun looks like it is about to set, colour flaring around it, violets and blues that blend and bleach the mountains with a pink watercolour wash. With its ultraviolet shadow, the sun resembles a glinting white moon. The sky around it constantly changes from purple to blue, the colours surging and ebbing, like a daylight version of the Northern Lights. Or the night sky, battling to be seen in the day.

The light show lasts about twenty minutes, and after it is over, the colours fade from the horizon and the sun dips slightly but refuses to sink any lower. I walk on, confused by what I have seen – was it a stalled sunset leading to yet more day? I arrive at a church whose doors are still open, with a notice for visitors to remove their shoes. I shuffle up the stairs in galoshes and find a mint green nave and altar. It is now close to midnight and the sun is streaming through a central stained-glass window, drawing patterns across the church's wooden floor. It is so bright, it looks celestial. I take in its beauty, but also the weirdness of light pouring in from the daylit night outside.

It leaves everything gleaming, from the baby piano to a baptismal brass basin and pewter beaker. Teacups are laid out on tables at the back of the church, with a notice: 'Please take a biscuit.' Its cheery welcome has an uncanny edge, like an unpeopled coffee morning that has been abandoned in an emergency, in this bright dead of night.

After the church, the road curves towards town and as I make my way back to the hotel, I see a woman striding down the road with her dog. She is alone and so much in her thoughts that she does not see me as I pass. Soon after, two more women, who might be tourists or locals, amble along, carefree. More women come crunching along the path. I realise, almost with a start, that they are out at night, on their own. How does this permanent state of visibility change their relationship to the night? Are there no longer any dangers to navigate? Does the midnight sun afford them a freedom and safety that no other landscape confers upon women?

I have been told, by the hotel receptionist, that the biggest predatory threat here is from polar bears, which are deadly. She has strongly advised me not to stray beyond the warning signs on the inner circumference of the town. Venturing past these points requires a firearm: every local or guide carries a flare-gun or pistol. I later hear stories of violent maulings in the mountains, and of one instance in the 1980s when, to widespread terror, a polar bear was seen padding through the centre of town and had to be shot down.

I come to one such warning sign on my walk and stand under it, scouring the landscape, wondering where this leaves the online Man Versus Bear debate. Here, the bear is the more dangerous predator, both for women *and* men. Statistics indicate that there is very little crime or violence in Svalbard, sexual or otherwise. What does that say about the men who prey on women elsewhere? That it is not men themselves but the cover of darkness that unleashes predatory, animal behaviour?

After I have circled back to my hotel, I do not go to sleep straight away because I am not sure if I am tired. I can't be, if it is still day – and surely this can't be night – so I busy myself, reading, watching a film, wandering to the terrace downstairs to stare out at the mountains. I wonder if, because I have never had a regular sleep routine, I would adapt well to the artificial night that needs to be created here, or if I would become addicted to daytime, doing more and more and more, without the framework of diurnal light and dark to steady me, and would eventually find myself unravelling with exhaustion.

By 2 a.m., the continuous day begins to look maddening, with what seems like an artificial brightness at my window, discernible behind the blinds, thick as they are. The sun leaks in regardless and it has the piercing glare of a spotlight. Yet, when I finally nod off, I sleep better than I do in most unfamiliar places. I don't feel the creeping fear or superstition that I sense in most new spaces, because of the absence of any and all darkness, both around me and outside. All the things that lurk in the night have lost their power here.

The following evening, I find another dark Eden in Svalbard. I am at the Seed Vault, a metal safe tunnelled deep inside a mountain which functions as a seed and crops gene-bank. Created in 2008, it holds more than 7.4 million original seed and crop samples from across the world, in case of climate or manmade catastrophe. This scenario is not as far-fetched as it might sound: some plants would have been wiped out by the Syrian civil conflict had it not been for the vault ensuring their continued existence. It is a frozen garden inside a mountain, and standing outside its fortified iron doors I think of the nuns, in their own protected enclave, in Ellesmere.

It is close to midnight and, again, the sun looks like it might set; it sinks in the sky and my shadow grows longer, but then it just hovers, as cool as a daytime moon. The hotel receptionist has told me that the sun does not travel from east to west, but follows another trajectory, and that its journey can look erratic, like a pinball spinning in a machine. It is an apt image for the head-spinning confusion I begin to feel on my second night in Spitsbergen. Because of the light, I have begun to lose track of time. The continuum of day confounds my inner sense of time. It seems to be eternally at the same wakeful hour, at a standstill. I am as alert and energetic at midnight as I was in the morning, then at one, and two . . .

Day pours into my window. It is more agitating tonight. I go to the bigger window in the corridor outside my room to take in the sky from this broader angle. I do this several times, almost disbelieving what I see in front of me: the deranged, insomniac orb of the sun. My brain seems increasingly confounded by the lack of night; it may have been accepted as a novelty at first, but now it has become a source of biological confusion. This is the opposite of the sedative dark at my window in Sark, which made me feel instantly sleepy. I feel like I am experiencing a psychic jet lag here.

The Austrian artist Christiane Ritter, who travelled to north Svalbard to join her husband there for the winter of 1934, was first shocked by the starkness of the archipelago, and then fell in love with it, writing a book about this changing relationship. *A Woman in the Polar Night* (1938) became a bestseller and is full of unsentimental and profound insights. She mainly writes of the non-stop night of the winter months, and the terrible bleakness of days growing shorter until they are 'nothing more than dawn and twilight'. But her descriptions resonate with my experience of Svalbard's non-stop summer. 'The sun rolls like a fiery ball across the mountains,' she notes, reminding me of the spectacle of streaking colour across the sky on my first night here. In polar winter, when it is only ever dark, she is too confused at night to be tired or wakeful, and she wonders: 'Perhaps the sun will never come back again. Perhaps it is dark all over the world.' This sounds like a landscape that, for her, has become overwhelming and apocalyptic, with nothing beyond it but darkness.

Ritter feels a similar discombobulation in summer: 'My eyes are smarting from unending daylight.' Her responses to the continuous day and night and its scrambling of time articulate mine so neatly. I have only been here for three days but I am craving the change of mood and pace and texture of light that the night brings. We need the darkness as a border, to feel the day beginning again. There is no boundary here, no stop and start. When all the darkness is banished, there is only this unending day, with its lunatic light, its plastic sameness. The day, devoid of night, is no solution to anything, other than to remind me of the pleasure of darkness.

This is an extreme way to live. I remember what the nuns said about those who came to join their enclosed convent but couldn't hack it. The same is said by several locals I speak to here. Many people apparently intend to stay but can't take the darkness in the winter, so they flee – or worse. I read about 'rar', the Norwegian term for the malaise that the polar nights provoke in some, so intense that they unravel completely, sometimes throwing themselves into icy waters. Ritter herself, when she first encounters the archipelago, says there is nothing more than water, fog and rain here, and that 'it bemuses people until they go out of their minds'.

But long after her travels, she is also known to have said that a year in the Arctic should be compulsory for everyone, so that they could realise what was important in life, and what wasn't. If there is a lesson in my own journey to Svalbard, it is my new-found appreciation for light and shade. Day and night. Action and rest. Sunrise and sunset represent pivotal moments of transition. They are required for St John's transfiguration, and maybe for a secular one too. They stand at the threshold between yesterday and tomorrow, and all the hope that it might bring. The midnight sun takes that hope away.

****

I am standing on my roof terrace on an August morning at 4.41 a.m., the exact moment for the break of dawn today, which is the beginning of twilight, when indirect sunlight is scattered on the earth's atmosphere. I am preparing myself for sunrise. I have seen the evening turn to night, walked into the thick of it, and the transition, from night back to day, is what I want to catch now: when darkness turns to light again. The terrace is west facing, overlooking a green grid of neighbourhood gardens and opening up to an enormous bowl of sky, but from here it looks as if dawn has already happened. I rub my eyes, caught out. When did this strange, hazy, blue-grey light start brightening the night? How have I missed dawn if this is the official moment it emerges? But when I look out of the kitchen window at the other side of the building, it is still night outside. Daylight is inching in on the dark, in patches.

I hurry out because I have planned to watch the sun come up from Kite Hill, whose summit offers a magnificent panorama of the city. Sunrise – when the sun breaks the horizon and the day is bathed in *direct* light – is at 5.30 a.m. and I'll get a handsome view of it, if I make it in time. I see scudding red clouds at the horizon as I charge up to the park. The street lamps are still switched on, and there is the same soupy grey-blue haze that I saw on my terrace. It is neither morning nor night, the day is awake and asleep at once, like the simultaneously opposing duality of the human brain that Dr Leschziner mentioned in *The Nocturnal Brain.*

The dawn chorus has begun and the birds seem to be flying somewhere with purpose; I wonder if they have their own ritual gathering at sunrise. The streets are empty of traffic except for the odd motorbike and there are no pedestrians ahead or behind me. The growing light gives me a false sense of safety. Surely, I think, nothing untoward can happen at this time, when the darkness is almost gone, though of course I know different. And when a car abruptly slows and pulls up near me, I instinctively start strategising. A man gets out and peers into his boot. I walk into the middle of the road. After some time, he moves off, and I watch the car until it has disappeared out of sight.

The park, at the bottom of the hill, is flat, open grassland, so other people can be seen from a distance. It looks like there is no one else here; not even the dog walkers have arrived yet. But as I start climbing, I spot a few lone figures. A man in a white hooded top who has walked out of a shadowy, tree-lined corner; a jogger, whose footfalls and heavy breathing I hear behind me long before I see her; a man walking on the path near the running track that my father would take us to as children.

When I stop, halfway up the hill, to look at the sky behind me, I see that a burning red light has spread further above the horizon and is cracking the sky open. I walk faster to get to the top. There is a couple already sitting on the grass when I arrive, holding hands as if on a date, and the man with the hooded top is on a bench, his head in his hands, as if poised between wonder and despair. We keep our distance but it is clear we have all come to watch the sunrise. The moment feels private and yet communal; I am less nervous of being out alone now.

London looks even more modern with the ancient sun emerging from its steel and concrete skyline. Sound is magnified and it is as if I can hear the whole city stirring awake. The nearby railway line screeching, a distant car engine, squawking gulls, aeroplanes, crows, wood pigeons. The gravel crunches as more joggers make their way up the hill. Their panting sounds up-close and intimate.

'You can hear the dew falling, and the hushed town breathing,' writes Dylan Thomas, as night descends on his fishing town in *Under Milk Wood*. It is the same in this north London morning. And when the day begins to climb out of the night in his poem, Thomas speaks of the lightening of the sky, 'over our green hill, into spring morning larked and crowed and belling'. The only thing that distinguishes his Llareggub hill of the 1950s from my hill here, three quarters of a century later, is the morning bell, which tolls his townsfolk awake. I can hear all the other sounds of nature. They're eternal, always present for the sunrise, it seems.

A dog walker talks to his over-excited terrier. Joggers ignore the rising sun. I am envious of these morning people, larks, for whom this glorious sight is a daily backdrop, just wallpaper. I look to the sky. The sun has turned from a thin yellow curve to a semicircle, to a bright white orb. It launches quickly, just after 5.30 a.m., but with none of the manic, pinball energy of Svalbard. It doesn't seem like the same sun. It is steady and graceful in this declaration of itself to the world. I think of all the sunrises I have seen, against ancient or natural surroundings, beaches or mountains, and this flaring city sun is just as majestic. No sunrise can fail to be so. It is the most important part of any day, and yet, as soon as it has happened, the least important. Another day happening, momentous and quotidian.

The soupy haze from earlier has grown whiter and more transparent until all trace of midnight blue has vanished. Then, just as I am thinking of leaving the hilltop, the light blazes yellow and dazzles across the ground, as if the sun is throwing golden confetti at us. It is a brief instance, gone two minutes later. I remember my mother's description of the transformational flash of light during night worship which offers miraculous possibilities. Is this what she means? Should I have made a wish, said a prayer?

I get up and walk around to the other end of the park, which has a path shaded by trees and rows of benches sloping down the hill. A dedication written on a plaque across one bench catches my eye: it is to a woman 'for all the days she spent here'. I pause for a while, and consider the days I have spent here, in this park.

Smart Georgian houses look onto this side of the hill, with grand bay windows that Fauzia and I, on our way back from school, would stare into, in awe and resentment, asking ourselves 'who could afford to live there?' I spot all the other old haunts below: my school, its side entrance almost hidden by the park's foliage; the lido where we'd go for swimming classes in the shivering summer; the running track that my father took the three of us to, which felt like it went on for so long that I'd give up on running halfway through a lap and watch my sister and brother straggling behind him. The paddling pool beside it and the playground where we spent endless days.

I feel the peculiar sense now, that while I have got on with life, these cherished people from my past still roam here. Tariq, a boy, adventuring around the bracken-filled canopy of trees on the other side of Kite Hill, lighting fires with his friends. Me, sitting self-consciously on the grass as a sixth-former. Fauzia, rakish, with long blue eyeshadow and a streak of pink blusher, bunking off school on a bench, listening to Boy George on her Walkman. My father, ambling up the hill at his typically wandering pace, with us ambling behind him, so we felt no sense of exertion. My father, again, telling us stories on the dusky walk home, light giving way to darkness.

Of course, we had always been here. As Linda Cracknell retraces her steps in *Doubling Back*, she is able to see 'a clear pathway' between her seventeen-year-old self and the woman she has become, decades later. 'We are not so different,' she writes. For so many years, I hadn't been able to see this 'past' me, or maybe I had refused to recognise her. But here she is, walking towards the school gate, quiet as a mouse and swallowed up by an oversized purple blazer. This is not only an encounter with my past self, or my father's 'well' self, but with our eternal selves, who will roam the park we know so well, long after we have gone. He, my father, is down at the bottom, jogging leisurely around the track. She, another me, is standing on the other side of the hill, serene and sure of herself, a woman much older than me now, watching the sun rise. It is a reassuring feeling, not frightening. She is not a haunting from the past or a vision from the future, but an indelible part of the park, standing beside the woman to whom the bench is dedicated.

By the time I have come around the other side of the hill, it is a hive of activity. Park keepers are mowing the grass, the path is lined with joggers, dog walkers, cyclists. On the road: buses, cars, bustle. I think of the night that has come before this, and the desperation brought on for some by its darkness. If only they could hold on, count the minutes from 4 a.m. to the first sign of light. Would it make a difference? Daybreak, even with its eternal repetition, seems to contain a moment of undiminishable joy: that first golden blaze of sunlight I felt at the top of the hill. I can't help but feel its hope. If it has been a long night, there is always this, another day, again.

Epilogue
Into the light

On my second, and last, night on Sark, it rains heavily and I recoil at the prospect of leaving the guesthouse for another night walk, but this is what I have come for, after all. I am here to experience natural dark and figure out what, exactly, I am so afraid of.

I force myself out and, initially, the night seems just as thick and hostile as it was yesterday, yet different. More slanting rain, but today it is light and spritzy, the wind still blustering, but no longer a dangerous wave that could sweep me under, just as dark but my eyes adjust faster to it. I look up and the sky is filled with a mess of starry splotches. There is a sliver of moon but its light is so laser sharp that it leaves cut-glass shadows across my path. The more I look into the darkness around me, the more it melts into lighter shades of grey and milky white, so that it is soon impossible to distinguish light from dark. The clouds are so vividly outlined, so close and clear that I feel like I could reach out and touch them.

This morning, when I had spoken to the guesthouse manager, Jacqui, she had talked of the freedom she had found in Sark's nights. 'It's a different world here. All of us go out on our own,' she had said, and then she had pointed to the various homes of elderly women who lived unaccompanied on the island, around this guesthouse. There were so many more she mentioned that I wondered if they had been drawn here, to Sark's safe night, to form an alternative community, free to roam outside anytime they wished.

Maybe it is Jacqui's words that give me succour, but the night does not charge into me tonight. Rather, this darkness feels like it is opening something up inside. It is as serene as a sunset or sunrise. I want more of it. It is ornamental, dilating, full of sparkle. I have to tear myself away to come back inside. This beautiful, unknown darkness, inside and out, is no less frightening. But I am as exhilarated as I am scared. It is an enchanted inheritance, as big as my imagination.

Bibliography

Non-fiction

Abbs, Annabel: *Windswept: Why Women Walk* (Two Roads, 2022)

Andrews, Kerri: *Wanderers: A History of Women Walking* (Reaktion Books Ltd, 2021)

Aubenas, Florence; translated by Brown, Andrew: *The Night Cleaner* (Polity, 2011)

Beaumont, Matthew: *Night Walking* (Verso, 2016)

Bettelheim, Bruno: *The Uses of Enchantment: The Meaning and Importance of Fairy Tales* (Penguin, 1991)

Bhairav, J. Furcifer and Khanna, Rakesh: *Ghosts, Monsters and Demons of India* (Watkins, 2023)

Brown, Louise: *The Dancing Girls of Lahore: Selling Love and Saving Dreams in Pakistan's Pleasure District* (Harper Perennial, 2006)

Cracknell, Linda: *Doubling Back: Paths Trodden in Memory* (Saraband, 2024)

Dickens, Charles: *The Uncommercial Traveller* (Oxford University Press, 2021)

Night Walks (Penguin Books, 2010)

Frayling, Christopher: 'Fuseli's The Nightmare: Somewhere Between the Sublime and the Ridiculous', in *Gothic Nightmares: Fuseli, Blake and the Romantic Imagination* (Tate Publishing, 2006)

Greenhalgh, Hugo: *The Diaries of Mr Lucas: Notes From a Lost Gay Life* (Atlantic, 2024)

Gillett, Ed: *Party Lines* (Picador, 2023)

Harrison, Melissa: *Rain: Four Walks in English Weather* (Faber & Faber, 2016)

Hartley, Jenny: *Charles Dickens and the House of Fallen Women* (Methuen, 2009)

Hofstede, Bregje; translated by Tetley-Paul, Alice: *In Search of Sleep: An Insomniac's Quest to Understand the Science, Psychology and Culture of Sleeplessness* (Greystone Books, 2023)

Kelkar, Govind and Nathan, Dev: *Witch Hunts: Culture, Patriarchy, and Structural Transformation* (Cambridge University Press, 2020)

Kryger, Meir: *The Mystery of Sleep* (Yale University Press, 2017)

Leschziner, Guy: *The Nocturnal Brain: Nightmares, Neuroscience and the Secret World of Sleep* (St Martin's Griffin, 2020)

Mackay, Finn: *Radical Feminism: Feminist Activism in Movement* (Palgrave Macmillan, 2015)

Miller, Kenneth: *Mapping the Darkness: The Visionary Scientists Who Unlocked the Mysteries of Sleep* (Oneworld, 2023)

Nagle, Jill, ed: *Whores and Other Feminists* (Routledge, 1997)

O'Sullivan, Suzanne: *The Sleeping Beauties: And Other Stories of Mystery Illness* (Picador, 2021)

Rietveld, Hillegonda C.: *This Is Our House: House Music, Cultural Spaces and Technologies* (Routledge, 2019)

Ritter, Christiane, translated by Degras, Jane: *A Woman in the Polar Night* (Puskhin Press Classics, 2024)

Rubenhold, Hallie: *The Five: The Untold Lives of the Women Killed by Jack the Ripper* (Doubleday, 2019)

Saeed, Fouzia: *Taboo! The Hidden Culture of a Red Light Area* (Oxford University Press, 2002)

Shakespeare, Nicholas: *Bruce Chatwin* (The Harvill Press, 1999)

Shane, Charlotte: *Prostitute Laundry* (Serpent's Tail, 2023)

Smith, Joan: *Misogynies* (The Westbourne Press, 2013)

Solnit, Rebecca: *A History of Walking* (Granta, 2014)

St John of the Cross: *The Dark Night of the Soul* (Crossreach Publications, 2019)

Woolf, Virginia: *Street Haunting: A London Adventure* (Read & Co., 2021)

Fiction

Farooqi, Musharraf Ali, trans: *The Adventures of a Trickster Woman* (Getz Pharma Library of Urdu Classics, 2021)

James, M.R.: *Oh, Whistle and I'll Come to You, My Lad (Firestone Books, 2013)*

Kipling, Rudyard: *The City of Dreadful Night* (Echo Library, 2020)

Le Fanu, Sheridan: *Carmilla* (Pushkin Press, 2020)

Moshfegh, Ottessa: *My Year of Rest and Relaxation* (Jonathan Cape, 2018)

Murakami, Haruki; translated by Rubin, Jay: *After Dark* (Vintage, 2008)

Pain, Barry: *The Moon Slave* (Grant Richards, 1901)

Poe, Edgar Allan: *The Murders in the Rue Morgue & Other Stories* (Independently Published, 2019)

Rhys, Jean: *Good Morning, Midnight* (Penguin Classics, 2020)

Selvon, Sam: *The Lonely Londoners* (Penguin Books, 2006)

Sleeping Beauty and Other Tales of Slumbering Princesses (Pook Press, 2015)

Tales of the Brothers Grimm. Drawings by Natalie Frank (Damiani, 2015)

Taylor, Elizabeth: *The Sleeping Beauty* (Virago, 2011)

Thomas, Dylan: *Under Milk Wood (Penguin Modern Classics, 2000)*

Plays

Alabanza, Travis and Hannan, Debbie: *Sound of the Underground* (Royal Court, London, 2023)

Kane, Sarah: *4.48 Psychosis* (Bloomsbury, 2022)

Randall, Nat and Breckon, Anna: *The Second Woman* (Young Vic Theatre, London, 2023)

Shakespeare, William: *Macbeth*, 1606

Stevenson, Debris: *Poet in Da Corner* (Royal Court, London, 2018)

Van Hove, Ivo: *Opening Night* (Gielgud Theatre, London, 2024)

Zeldin, Alexander: *Beyond Caring* (Methuen Drama, 2015)

Films

Amirpour, Ana Lily: *A Girls Walks Home Alone at Night* (2014)
Baker, Roy Ward: *The Vampire Lovers* (1970)
Cassavetes, John: *Opening Night* (1977)
Coen, Joel: *The Tragedy of Macbeth* (2021)
Deller, Jeremy: *Everybody in the Place: An Incomplete History of Britain 1984–1992* (2018)
Frears, Stephen: *Dirty Pretty Things* (2002)
Gammon, Lottie: *Sarah Everard: The Search for Justice* (2024)
Lynch, David: *Blue Velvet* (1986)
Wild at Heart (1990)
Lost Highway (1997)
Mulholland Drive (2001)
Murnau, F.W.: *Nosferatu: A Symphony of Horror* (1922)
Nakata, Hideo: *Ring* (1998)
Rodney, Ascher: *The Nightmare* (2015)
Sadiq, Saim: *Joyland* (2022)
Scott, Tony: *The Hunger* (1983)
Varda, Agnès: *Vagabond* (1985)

Visual art

Botticelli, Sandro: *The Trinity with Saints* (1491–94)
Bourgeois, Louise: *The Insomnia Drawings* (1994–95)
Breitz, Candice: *TLDR* (2017)
Cézanne, Paul: *The Card Players* (1890–92)
Crucifixion Triptych (1375–99)
El Lahib, Omar (solo exhibition): Saachi Yates, London, (January–March 2024)
Fuseli, Henry: *The Nightmare* (1781)
Goya, Francisco: *The Black Paintings* (1820–23)
Grøndal, Herta Lampert and Grøndal, Leif Archie: Layers of Time – Everyday Life in Svalbard, Nordnorsk Kunstmuseum, Spitsbergen (April–November 2024)

Hopper, Edward: *Night Windows* (1928)
Hussain, Iqbal and Mandi, Heera series, Lahore Art Gallery
Krasner, Lee: *Night Creatures* (1965)
Manet, Édouard: *A Bar at the Folies-Bergère* (1882)
Manchot, Melanie: *Dance (All Night, Leeds)* (April 2024)
Monet, Claude: *Vase of Flowers* (1882)
Renoir, Pierre-Auguste: *Spring, Chatou* (1873)
Rubens, Peter Paul: *Landscape by Moonlight* (1635–40)
Sickert, Walter (solo exhibition): Tate Britain, London (April–September 2022)
Van Gogh, Vincent: *Van Gogh: The Immersive Experience,* Commercial Street, London
Van Gogh, Vincent: *The Starry Night* (1889)
Warhol, Andy: *Sleep* (1964)

Acknowledgements

Beginning this book felt like wandering into the dark. Thank god for Clare Alexander, a friend as well as my agent, who helped to formulate it and for Sceptre editor Charlotte Humphery, without whose hard work and pragmatism I might still be walking in circles. Thanks also to Juliet Brooke, who commissioned the book.

A subject this vast felt initially daunting and I was encouraged and inspired by conversations with dear friends Faiza Khan, Katherine Butler, Aysha Rafaele and Claire Armistead. Thanks also to the ever trusty Andrew Wilson for his many leads.

I'm immensely grateful to Melissa Harrison for her recommendations as well as for inviting me into her home, and to Joanna and Brian Casson for allowing me into theirs; Simon Raw, who made my behind-the-scenes West End theatre trip possible, along with Emily, Ben, Max and Sarah from Wessex Grove, Forest Healthcare's CEO Amanda Scott, for her generosity and insights. Ryan Gilbey for his suggestions and solidarity, and Maria Garbutt-Lucero for leading me to New Spitalfields Market (and for sending me Chappell Roan's 'After Midnight', a song that kept me on track).

Several others are owed sincere gratitude: Lynn Greenwood, Beverley Edwards, Tim Bano, Barbara Behrendt, Quddus Mirza, Rafay Alam, Musharraf Ali Farooqi, Annie Zaidi, Michelle Hedger, Sos Eltis, Alex Needham, Kate Abbey and Chris Wiegand for their help and guidance along the way. Same for Professors Christopher French and Derk-Jan Dijk, for their time and expertise, along with Muneer Ahmad, the former Press Secretary at the Pakistani High Commission in London, for his Lahore contacts. Thank you as well to Nico Parfitt, for his meticulous work on the manuscript.

Thanks to the *Guardian* for entrusting me with the dream 'night job', which has been pivotal for the writing of this book. My work as the paper's theatre critic informed several sections, including the second chapter, which is a longer version of an article.

Thanks to my dear father Muhammad Akbar for the old ghost stories and for his big imagination, my brother Tariq for his boyhood tales and reflections about the night, and my mother Bela for her dedicated and eternal interest in my interests. Lastly, the Wellcome Collection Library, an amazing resource and sanctuary, all free of charge.